Introducing Qualitative Research in Psychology

Second edition

Introducing Qualitative Research in Psychology

ADVENTURES IN THEORY AND METHOD

Second edition

Carla Willig

Open University Press

Open University Press
McGraw-Hill Education
McGraw-Hill House
Shoppenhangers Road
Maidenhead
Berkshire
England
SL6 2QL

email: enquiries@openup.co.uk
world wide web: www.openup.co.uk

and Two Penn Plaza, New York, NY 10121–2289, USA

First published 2008
Reprinted 2009

A catalogue record of this book is available from the British Library

ISBN10: 0 335 22115 7 (pb)
ISBN13: 978 0 335 22115 8 (pb)

Library of Congress Cataloging-in-Publication Data
CIP data applied for

Typeset by RefineCatch Limited, Bungay, Suffolk
Printed in Finland by WS Bookwell, Ltd

The **McGraw·Hill** Companies

To my students

Contents

List of boxes

Acknowledgements

I would like to thank Pete Green, Maria Iglesias, Katherine Johnson, Lynne Segal, Frances Stanton and Catherine Marie Sykes for their thoughts on the meaning of 'adventure'. Thanks also to Jonathan Smith for his helpful comments on Chapter 4. I would also like to acknowledge my debt to those students who took part in my Qualitative Research Methods in Psychology module at Middlesex University, which ran from 1994 to 1999 and which provided the inspiration for this book. Most particularly, I would like to thank Goran Petronic, Kris dew Valour and Karolina Mörnsjö for making available their undergraduate research reports for inclusion in this book. Thanks also to Goran for helping me put together the original book proposal.

Since the publication of the first edition of this book in 2001, I have gained further knowledge and experience in the use of phenomenological methods thanks to undertaking training in existential counselling psychology at Regent's College, London. I would like to thank staff at the School of Psychotherapy and Counselling at Regent's College and in particular Ernesto Spinelli and Harriet Goldenberg for providing guidance and inspiration.

Finally, I am aware that supervising numerous postgraduate students' qualitative research projects over the years has helped me to question, clarify and refine my own ideas about qualitative research. I would, therefore, like to acknowledge my M.Sc. and Ph.D. students' indirect contribution to this second edition.

1
From recipes to adventures

How, and what, can we know? • Positivism • Empiricism • Hypothetico-deductivism • Critique of the 'scientific method' • Feminist critique of established epistemologies • Social constructionism • Epistemology and methodology • Qualitative research • Overview of the book • Three epistemological questions • Further reading

'It involves opening up to new and possibly unsettling experiences.'

'It means venturing into new territory.'

'It's discovering something new and exciting; there's a little bit of danger.'

'It is exciting and unusual, out-of-the-ordinary. There's a big element of enjoyment and there may be an element of challenge. It's something that will develop me as a person.'

'Enid Blyton stories . . . [laughs] . . . It's exciting, possibly involving a degree of risk to oneself; scary on occasion but it comes out alright at the end. You're glad you've had them.'

'An exploration involving new places, meeting new people and having new experiences outside of the norm. These could be both positive and negative in nature.'

'Adventures are sudden, surprise events which are pleasurable, because they are unexpected.'

Talk of an 'adventure' captures the imagination. We want to know what it was like, how it felt, what happened next. We look upon the adventurer as someone who has been changed by the experience, someone who will never be quite the same again.

The definitions above were provided in response to my question 'What does the term "adventure" mean to you?' Most of them include references to something 'new' and as yet unknown, something we have not experienced before. At the same time, the 'adventure' is perceived as a positive, if somewhat risky, enterprise. I suggest that we should think about the research process as a form of adventure. When I was an undergraduate student, I thought of 'research methods' as recipes. Research appeared to involve choosing the right ingredients (a representative sample, a standardized measurement instrument, the appropriate statistical test) and administering them in the right order (the 'procedure'). Having done our best to 'get it right', we would hold our breath, hoping that the experiment had 'worked' – much like hovering about the kitchen, waiting for the perfect roast to emerge from the oven. Now I look upon research in a different light. 'Research methods' have become ways of approaching a question. They are also ways of justifying an answer (this is where research methods meet *epistemology*, to be discussed below). Either way, my understanding of research has moved from a mechanical (how-to-apply-appropriate-techniques-to-the-subject-matter) to a creative (how-can-I-find-out?) mode. In the process, I have replaced the metaphor of research-methods-as-recipes with a view of the research-process-as-adventure.

In this chapter, I want to explore in some detail what 'research' is all about and how qualitative research methods in psychology fit into this picture. To do this, I need to introduce some key concepts from the philosophy of science, such as 'epistemology', 'positivism', 'empiricism' and 'hypothetico-deductivism'. In the process, I shall problematize familiar concepts such as 'science' and 'knowledge'. The aim of the chapter is to provide a context within which to place qualitative research methods in psychology and to identify the defining features of such research.

How, and what, can we know?

Epistemology is a branch of philosophy concerned with the theory of knowledge. It attempts to provide answers to the question, 'How, and what, can we know?' This involves thinking about the nature of knowledge itself, about its scope and about the validity and reliability of claims to knowledge. Research methods provide ways of approaching, and hopefully answering, our research questions. Research methods can be described as 'the way to the goal' (Kvale 1996a: 278). However, first we need to identify our goal and be able to justify our choice. We need to be clear about the objectives of our research and we need to have a sense of what kinds of things it is possible for us to find out. In other words, we need to adopt an epistemological position.

Positivism

One epistemological position is *positivism*. Positivism suggests that there is a straightforward relationship between the world (objects, events, phenomena) and our perception, and understanding, of it. Positivists believe that it is possible to describe what is 'out there' and to get it right. Such a position is also referred to as the 'correspondence theory of truth' because it suggests that phenomena directly determine our perception of them and that there is, therefore, a direct correspondence between things and their representation. Kirk and Miller's (1986: 14) definition of positivism emphasizes positivism's assumption that 'the external world itself determines absolutely the one and only correct view that can be taken of it, independent of the process or circumstances of viewing'. A positivist epistemology implies that the goal of research is to produce objective knowledge; that is, understanding that is impartial and unbiased, based on a view from 'the outside', without personal involvement or vested interests on the part of the researcher.

Positivism has a long history and few, if any, scientists and researchers today claim to be unreconstructed positivists. In fact, when the label is used in contemporary epistemological debates, it usually constitutes an insult. This is because it is now generally accepted that observation and description are necessarily selective, and that our perception and understanding of the world is therefore partial at best (for a clear discussion of the nature and limitations of scientific knowledge, see Chalmers 1999). What people disagree about is the extent to which our understanding of the world can *approach* objective knowledge, or even some kind of truth, about the world. The different responses to this question range from naïve realism, which is akin to positivism, to extreme relativism, which rejects concepts such as 'truth' or 'knowledge' altogether. In between, we find positions such as critical realism and the different versions of social constructionism (see Parker 1998).

Empiricism

Empiricism is closely related to positivism. It is based on the assumption that our knowledge of the world must be derived from 'the facts of experience' (see Chalmers 1999: chapter 1). In other words, sense perception provides the basis for knowledge acquisition, which proceeds through the systematic collection and classification of observations. These include experiments. According to this view, simple observations are combined to give rise to more complex ideas, and theory follows from observations. That is to say, theory is constructed to make sense of the data collected through observation. Again, few, if any, scientists and researchers subscribe to a pure form of empiricism nowadays. It is generally accepted that sense perception does not provide direct and uncontaminated access to 'the facts'. The more we know about a phenomenon, the more detail we perceive when we observe it. Perception is inevitably selective and people can be trained to observe the same phenomenon in different ways, depending on the purpose of the observation. However, modern-day empiricists would argue that knowledge acquisition depends on the collection and analysis of data. They do not believe that purely theoretical work can move us closer to the truth, and they propose that all knowledge claims must be grounded in data. At this point, it is important to differentiate between the terms 'empiricist' and 'empirical'. While 'empiricist' refers to the attitude that all knowledge claims must be grounded in data, 'empirical' is a descriptive term referring to research involving the collection and analysis of data.

Hypothetico-deductivism

A number of serious practical as well as logical limitations of positivism and empiricism led to the development of alternative theories of knowledge. Karl Popper's critique of *inductivism* and subsequent formulation of *hypothetico-deductivism* constitutes the most influential alternative. It now forms the basis of mainstream experimental psychology. Popper was aware of the fact that a collection of observations could never give rise to a categorical statement such as 'a follows b'. However many times we observe that a follows b, we can never be sure that our next observation will be the same again. There is always the possibility that the next occurrence will be an exception. This is the problem of *induction*. Popper was also unhappy about the fact that many influential theories appeared to be able to accommodate a wide range of observations, interpreting them as confirmation of the theory's claims. It seemed that no scientific theory could ever be conclusively verified. This is the problem of *verification*. To circumvent these problems, Popper proposed that instead of induction and verification, scientific research ought to rely upon *deduction* and *falsification*. Popper's *hypothetico-deductive method* does just that. Here, theories are tested by deriving *hypotheses* from them that can then be tested in practice, by experiment or observation. The aim of the research is to put a theory's claims to the test to either reject the theory or retain it for the time being. Thus, rather than looking for evidence that *confirms* a theory's claims, hypothetico-deductivism works by looking for disconfirmation, or *falsification*. In this way, we can find out which claims are *not* true and, by a process of elimination of claims, we move closer to the truth.

Critique of the 'scientific method'

Popper provided science with a method that avoided the problems associated with induction and verification. However, Popper's hypothetico-deductivism, in turn, was challenged in the 1960s and 1970s for failing to acknowledge the role of historical, social and cultural factors in knowledge formation. The critique of hypothetico-deductivism includes the following charges:

1 *Hypothetico-deductivism does not provide sufficient space for theory development*
Here, it is argued that the method's reliance on hypotheses generated by existing theories forecloses the possibility of generating completely new theories. If all we can do is test existing theories to either reject or retain them, we are unlikely to come across entirely new and unexpected insights in our research practice. To be fair, Popper (1969: 231) did propose that researchers should be adventurous and test 'bold conjecture(s)', since most is learned from mistakes; however, even the boldest hypotheses are based upon existing knowledge and expectations. What hypothetico-deductivism does not allow for is that the evidence overturns received wisdom and makes us see things in a completely different light.

2 *Hypothetico-deductivism is elitist*
Since hypothetico-deductivism works with existing theories and relies upon deduction from existing systems of thought, it excludes those people who are not familiar

with such theories and systems from its practice. The hypothetico-deductive method encourages the formation of communities of scientists and researchers who test their own and each other's theories. For the outsider or novice, it is difficult, if not impossible, to contribute to knowledge generation, if knowledge is defined as the rejection or retention of existing theories.

3 Hypothetico-deductivism is a myth

Popper proposed that knowledge generation should be a piecemeal process. Through the rejection of false hypotheses, knowledge would grow, slowly but continuously. Individual scientists contribute to this process by testing their hypotheses to identify those theories that could be discarded. Thomas Kuhn ([1962] 1970) fundamentally disagreed. He argued that, in reality, theories are not really put to the test in this way. While scientists were attached to a particular theory, they did not reject it on the basis of experimental evidence. Instead, if the evidence did not support the theory, they assumed that the experiment had gone wrong in some way. Thus, failure was attributed to the scientist and the design of the experiment rather than to the inadequacy of the theory. Kuhn argued that science did not progress in an evolutionary, piecemeal fashion, as Popper had suggested, but that it developed in leaps, through scientific revolutions leading to paradigm shifts. Here, a paradigm – a particular conceptual framework – is stretched to accommodate all kinds of evidence. Anomalies and inconsistencies accumulate until wider socioeconomic and historical processes allow a new paradigm to emerge and to provide a legitimate alternative to the previous one. Once the new paradigm has gained the upper hand, it in turn will resist change for some time to come.

Feminist critique of established epistemologies

Many of the problems and limitations associated with the established epistemological perspectives outlined above were identified by feminist scholars. In the 1960s and 1970s, they drew attention to the fact that women had been largely invisible in social scientific work and that where women had been 'studied', they had been found to be inferior to men in terms of attributes such as moral development, intelligence and conversational style. Such 'findings', feminists argued, were then used to justify and perpetuate existing inequalities between men and women in society. To challenge these inequalities and to end the oppression of women, feminist scholars questioned the epistemological (and methodological) foundations upon which sexist knowledge claims rested. This gave rise to an extensive critique of 'male science'. This critique includes the following key arguments:

1 The male as the norm

The vast majority of studies using human participants were carried out with male subjects. This was partly due to opportunity (most researchers used university undergraduates as easy-access subjects and most of these were men) and partly due to the assumption that men constitute the prototypical 'human subject'. As a result, findings based upon studies with (young, white, middle-class) male subjects were generalized to the population as a whole. In other words (young, white, middle-class), men set the standard against which other members of society were then measured. This meant that when women were later used as participants, their performance and behaviour were assessed against the male norm and found to be wanting. One of the most well-known critiques of the 'male as norm' approach in relation to moral development was formulated by Carol Gilligan (1982). Gilligan challenged Kohlberg's (1976) claim that, on average, women's moral development was less advanced than that of men. Kohlberg's claim was supported by many studies that had used his moral development scale. This scale places individuals somewhere between Level 1 (lowest) and Level 3 (highest) of moral development. The levels, and stages in between, represent a transition from basic moral considerations (e.g. in terms of the outcome for the individual) through those based on external approval to those involving personal conscience. The scale had been developed by presenting male subjects with a series of hypothetical moral dilemmas and by categorizing their responses. Gilligan argued that men and women were socialized to develop different moral orientations, whereby girls were encouraged to develop a care orientation and boys were encouraged to develop a justice orientation. Kohlberg's scale was based upon a justice orientation and was therefore bound to favour male participants. Gilligan conducted research that identified alternative patterns of moral reasoning used by female participants who faced a real-life moral dilemma (abortion). She argued that the women's moral considerations based around non-violence within a care orientation were just as advanced as Kohlberg's Level 3 (personal conscience). They were merely different.

2 *The God trick*

'Male science' claimed to be, or at least aimed to be, 'objective'. This meant that researchers had to remain detached from and impartial towards their subject matter. Various procedures were developed to ensure that data collection and analysis were not 'contaminated' by the researcher. These included standardized instructions for subjects, minimization of contact between researcher and participants, blind or double-blind procedures for data collection and analysis, as well as various attempts to 'neutralize' the research environment (e.g. by removing any personal items from the laboratory or by having the researchers wear white coats). Feminist critics argued that the attempt to be 'objective' and the strategies adopted towards this aim did, in fact, serve to obscure the fact that the researcher's identity and standpoint do fundamentally shape the research process and the findings. They argued that it is impossible for a researcher to position themselves 'outside of' the subject matter because the researcher will inevitably have a relationship with, or be implicated in, the phenomenon that he or she is studying. Donna Haraway (1988) refers to attempts to pretend otherwise as the 'God's eye view'. The alternative to the 'God's eye view' is for researchers to reflect upon their own standpoint in relation to the phenomenon that they are studying and to attempt to identify the ways in which such a standpoint has shaped the research process and findings. This notion of *reflexivity* will be discussed in more detail later in this chapter and will be returned to throughout this book.

Even though there can be said to be a general feminist critique of established epistemologies and 'male science', there is no one feminist epistemology or even methodology. Feminist scholars have responded in different ways to the problems and limitations associated with positivism, empiricism and hypothetico-deductivism.

Among the various alternative approaches developed by feminist social scientists and philosophers are standpoint epistemology (e.g. Harding 1991), ethnomethodology (e.g. Stanley and Wise 1983) and various versions of feminist post-structuralism (e.g. Henriques et al. 1984; Haraway 1991).

Social constructionism

In recent years, *social constructionism* has become an increasingly influential approach (see Burr 2003). Social constructionism draws attention to the fact that human experience, including perception, is mediated historically, culturally and linguistically. That is, what we perceive and experience is never a direct reflection of environmental conditions but must be understood as a specific reading of these conditions. This does not mean that we can never really know anything; rather, it suggests that there are 'knowledges' rather than 'knowledge'. Language is an important aspect of socially constructed knowledge. The same phenomenon or event can be described in different ways, giving rise to different ways of perceiving and understanding it, yet neither way of describing it is necessarily wrong. An obvious example of this is the choice between describing a glass of water as 'half-full' or 'half-empty'; both descriptions are equally accurate, yet one of them provides a positive, optimistic gloss on the situation ('half-full'), whereas the other emphasizes absence and a lack ('half-empty').

Research from a social constructionist perspective is concerned with identifying the various ways of constructing social reality that are available in a culture, to explore the conditions of their use and to trace their implications for human experience and social practice. Social constructionist researchers in psychology, for instance, have critically examined psychological categories such as 'emotion' (e.g. Harré 1986), 'prejudice' (e.g. Potter and Wetherell 1987) and 'psychopathology' (e.g. Parker et al. 1995) to show how they provide a way of constructing reality rather than simply reflecting it.

Epistemology and methodology

What is the relationship between epistemology and methodology? To what extent does the epistemological position we adopt prescribe which research methods we ought to use? To address these questions, we first need to differentiate between 'method' and 'methodology'. Although often used interchangeably, the two terms do, in fact, refer to different aspects of doing research. Silverman (1993: 1) suggests that 'methodology' identifies 'a general approach to studying research topics', whereas 'method' refers to 'a specific research technique'. (A further distinction can then be made between methods of data collection and methods of data analysis; see Chapter 2.) It is helpful to differentiate between 'a general approach to studying research topics' and 'specific research techniques' because the former is much more directly informed by the researcher's epistemological position than the latter. For example, a researcher who takes a predominantly empiricist view of knowledge acquisition will approach research topics through the collection of data rather than through theoretical formulations. However, exactly *how* such data are collected (e.g. through observation, questionnaires, interviews) is another question, and it is not something that the researcher's empiricist epistemological position prescribes. Hypothetico-deductivism constitutes an exception here, since it offers the researcher both an epistemological position *and* a research method, namely hypothesis-testing through experimentation (but see Chapter 5 for the use of hypothetico-deductivism in case study research).

However, not *all* research methods are compatible with *all* methodologies. Even though there is some flexibility in relation to our choice of methods, a researcher's epistemological and methodological commitments do constrain which methods can be used. For example, a social constructionist methodology is not compatible with methods that are designed to measure variables in a population. This is because social constructionism problematizes given constructs such as 'psychological variables'; it questions their validity and it is concerned with exploring the various ways in which they are 'made real'. This cannot be achieved through an attempt to 'measure' such constructs. According to a social constructionist viewpoint, the measurement of psychological variables is itself one more way of making them real, of constructing them.

Qualitative research

This book is about qualitative research in psychology. Having introduced the concept of epistemology and having considered, briefly, some major epistemological positions, it is now time to explore how qualitative methodology fits into this picture.

First, it is important to acknowledge that qualitative research methods can be, and are, used by researchers with quite different epistemological positions. For example, there are empiricist as well as social constructionist qualitative researchers. This means that, strictly speaking, there are 'qualitative methodologies' rather than 'qualitative methodology'. However, qualitative researchers also share a number of concerns, and it is these that are commonly referred to as 'qualitative methodology'. In this section, I shall: (1) identify these shared concerns and provide a general characterization of 'qualitative methodology'; (2) introduce the 'small q/big Q' dichotomy; and (3) draw attention to epistemological differences between approaches to qualitative research.

Shared concerns: 'qualitative methodology'

Qualitative researchers tend to be concerned with meaning. That is, they are interested in how people make sense of the world and how they experience events. They aim to understand 'what it is like' to experience particular conditions (e.g. what it means and how it feels to live with chronic illness or to be unemployed) and how people manage certain situations (e.g. how people negotiate family life or relations with work colleagues). Qualitative researchers tend, therefore, to be concerned with the quality and texture of experience, rather than with the identification of cause–effect relationships. They do not tend to work with 'variables' that are defined by the researcher before the research process begins. This is because qualitative researchers tend to be interested in the meanings attributed to events by the research participants themselves. Using preconceived 'variables' would lead to the imposition of the researcher's meanings and it would preclude the identification of respondents' own ways of making sense of the phenomenon under investigation. The objective of qualitative research is to describe and possibly explain events and experiences, but never to predict. Qualitative researchers study people in their own territory, within naturally occurring settings (such as the home, schools, hospitals, the street). These are 'open systems' where conditions continuously develop and interact with one another to give rise to a process of ongoing change. Participants' (and researchers') interpretation of events itself contributes to this process. Therefore, 'prediction of outcomes' is not a meaningful goal for qualitative researchers. Instead, they ask questions about processes, such as 'What do people do when they form groups?', 'How do people manage change in the workplace?' or 'How do people live with chronic pain?'

'Small q' and 'big Q'

Kidder and Fine (1987) distinguish between two meanings of 'qualitative research'; 'big Q' refers to open-ended, inductive research methodologies that are concerned with theory generation and the exploration of meanings, whereas 'little q' refers to the incorporation of non-numerical data collection techniques into hypothetico-deductive research designs. For example, researchers may include an open-ended question in an otherwise forced-choice questionnaire and then use content analysis to 'score' the qualitative material. 'Little q' does not work from the bottom up. That is, 'little q' methods of data collection and analysis do not seek to engage with the data to gain new insights into the ways in which participants construct meaning and/or experience their world; instead, they start with a hypothesis and researcher-defined categories against which the qualitative data are then checked.

   This book is about 'big Q' methodology. The six approaches to qualitative research introduced here are all concerned with the exploration of lived experience and participant-defined meanings. They do take different positions in relation to *epistemology, reflexivity* and *critical language awareness* (see next section), but they can all be classified as 'big Q'. I have decided to exclude 'little q' methods because, although non-numerical in nature, they are characterized by the imposition of the researcher's meanings during data collection and analysis, and strict control over what can emerge from the analysis through the application of predetermined categories for coding. This is, in my view, not compatible with the spirit of 'qualitative methodology'.

Epistemological differences: 'qualitative methodologies'

Silverman (1993: 1) argues that 'without theory there is nothing to research'. This statement draws attention to the role of theory in the interpretation of data (see Anfara and Mertz 2006 for a detailed discussion of the role of theory in qualitative research). For example, if our data consist of several pages of interview transcript, we need to decide what this transcript represents before we can analyse it (see Kvale 1996a: 278). It could represent a factual account of what happened to the interviewee. On the other hand, it could represent the interviewee's attempt to disclaim responsibility for what happened. Alternatively, it could be read as an expression of the interviewee's unconscious desires. Or it could provide insight into the interviewee's view of the world. Which view we take of what the transcript represents – that is, how we define the 'status of the text' (see Flick 1998) – will depend on the theoretical framework from within which we approach the text. And this framework, in turn, is informed by our epistemological stance. For example, if our epistemological position is a social constructionist one, we may approach the text using a discourse analytic framework. This means that the text is seen as a manifestation of available discursive resources that the interviewee is drawing upon to construct a particular version of events. If, however, our epistemological position is an empiricist one, we might use a version of the grounded theory method or interpretative phenomenological analysis to identify the categories of meaning used by the interviewee to make sense of events. In this case, the text is seen as a verbal expression of the interviewee's mental processes. In both cases, the analysis of the interview transcript would be qualitative. In a recent exhibition, French artist Sophie Calle provided a fascinating illustration of how a text (in this case, an email message ending a romantic relationship) can be read in innumerable ways, each one based upon the attribution of a different 'status' to the text. Calle invited 107 women of different backgrounds and professions (including a psychoanalyst, a forensic psychiatrist, a Talmudic scholar, a judge, an etiquette consultant, a social worker and a copy editor) to read and interpret the message that had been sent to her by her (then) boyfriend. The exhibition and companion text (Calle 2007) displays these readings alongside one another, demonstrating how what appears to be a simple message can be decoded in as many ways as there are professional (and personal) perspectives.

'Qualitative methodologies' can also be differentiated according to the extent to which they emphasize reflexivity and by the importance they place on the role of language. These two features are related. *Reflexivity* requires an awareness of the researcher's contribution to the construction of meanings throughout the research process, and an acknowledgement of the impossibility of remaining 'outside of' one's subject matter while conducting research. Reflexivity, then, urges us 'to explore the ways in which a researcher's involvement with a particular study influences, acts upon and informs such research' (Nightingale and Cromby 1999: 228).

There are two types of reflexivity: personal reflexivity and epistemological reflexivity. *Personal reflexivity* involves reflecting upon the ways in which our own values, experiences, interests, beliefs, political commitments, wider aims in life and social identities have shaped the research. It also involves thinking about how the research may have affected and possibly changed us, as people and as researchers. *Epistemological reflexivity* requires us to engage with questions such as: How has the research question defined and limited what can be 'found'? How has the design of the study and the method of analysis 'constructed' the data and the findings? How could the research question have been investigated differently? To what extent would this have given rise to a different understanding of the phenomenon under investigation? Thus, epistemological reflexivity encourages us to reflect upon the assumptions (about the world, about knowledge) that we have made in the course of the research, and it helps us to think about the implications of such assumptions for the research and its findings. Qualitative researchers differ in the emphasis they place upon reflexivity in their research. For some, both personal and epistemological reflexivity are central to the research process and form an integral part of the research report.

Others acknowledge the importance of reflexivity but do not include an in-depth discussion of it in their research reports.

Critical language awareness (Fairclough 1995) forms part of reflexivity. The words we use to describe our experiences play a part in the construction of the meanings that we attribute to such experiences. Language has a constructive dimension; it does not simply mirror reality. This means that the categories and labels researchers use during the research process will shape their 'findings'. For example, certain answers are made impossible by certain kinds of question. If the researcher asks a respondent 'how she felt' during, say, a medical procedure, the researcher is invoking the category 'emotion'. This means that whatever the respondent chooses to say in response to the question, 'emotion' will have to be oriented to. It has been made salient and the respondent's answer will position her in relation to this construct, even when she denies its importance. Qualitative researchers take different views of the extent to which language constructs versions of reality. At one end of the continuum, researchers argue that language plays a central role in the construction of meaning and that it is the task of researchers to study the ways in which such constructions are produced, how they change across cultures and history, and how they shape people's experiences. At the other end of the continuum, we find qualitative researchers who believe that it is possible to describe, more or less accurately, 'what is going on' in a particular setting; here, language is simply a means to an end or a tool. In between, there are many degrees of critical language awareness.

There are various ways in which we may classify qualitative approaches in order to highlight their epistemological differences. Readers will come across a number of different classifactory systems and terminologies in the literature, and this may be confusing at times. The important thing to remember is that in order to understand differences between approaches, we need to ask a series of questions of them. These will be discussed in the final section of this chapter.

Overview of the book

This book aims to introduce people unfamiliar with qualitative research methods to some of those methods that are most appropriate for qualitative research in psychology. Chapter 2 discusses key aspects of qualitative research design. These include the formulation of a research question, the selection of suitable data collection techniques, as well as ethical considerations and reflexivity. Chapters 3–8 introduce six approaches to qualitative research in psychology: grounded theory, phenomenology, case studies, discursive psychology, Foucauldian discourse analysis and working with memories. Each chapter introduces the approach and its procedures and techniques for gathering and analysing data. It identifies its advantages and disadvantages, and it discusses ways of writing up the research. To facilitate comparison between the six methods, I shall raise three epistemological questions in relation to each approach. These questions are identified in the next section. The concluding chapter (Chapter 9) addresses the question of evaluation of qualitative research. The book also reproduces three research reports written by third-year psychology undergraduates (see Appendices 1–3). These reports illustrate how qualitative research methods can be applied in practice, within the real-world constraints of an undergraduate course. All three reports are of a high quality. For the reader's benefit, I have inserted explanatory comments into the reports. These are italicized and preceded by the initials C.W. for easy identification.

Three epistemological questions

To be able to evaluate research in a meaningful way, we need to know what its objectives were and what kind of knowledge it aimed to produce. For example, there is no sense in criticizing a study for not identifying the cognitive precursors of a particular behaviour, when the aim of the study was to find out what it felt like to engage in the behaviour. On the other hand, a study concerned with the subjective quality of a particular experience *can* be criticized for using methods that constrain participants' ability to express their feelings openly and in sufficient detail. To be able to compare methodological approaches with one another and to be able to evaluate the extent to which studies using these approaches have met their own objectives, we need to have a clear understanding of their epistemological basis and their methodological requirements. The following questions can help us identify a methodology's epistemological roots:

1 *What kind of knowledge does the methodology aim to produce?*
Qualitative research can produce descriptions or explanations. It can aim to 'give voice' to those whose accounts tend to be marginalized or discounted. It can aim to interpret what people have said in order to explain why they may have said it. It can aim to make links between micro-processes, such as doctor–patient communication, and macro-structures, such as economic and social relations. It may be designed to capture the subjective 'feel' of a particular experience or condition, or it may wish to identify recurring patterns of experience among a group of people. What kind of knowledge a methodology aims to produce depends on its epistemological position (i.e. its view of what can be known and how). Epistemological positions commonly adopted within qualitative psychology range from radical relativist to naïve realist (Madill et al. 2000). A realist position entails the belief that the data we collect ought to provide us with information about the world, about how things really are. This means that the methods we use ought to be designed (and implemented) in such a way as to facilitate true and undistorted representations. For example, a study of the quality of life of the elderly in inner cities from a realist perspective would need to find ways of accessing the true feelings and experiences of a relevant group of participants. A key challenge for the researcher in this situation would be to find data collection methods that encourage participants to express themselves as freely and openly as possible. By contrast, a relativist position subscribes to the view that there is no such thing as 'pure experience' and that the aim of research ought to be an exploration of the ways in which cultural and discursive resources are used in order to construct different versions of the experience of ageing within different contexts. This type of research requires the use of methods that can identify and unpack such resources. Methods of data collection and analysis, in this case, would need to be sensitive to tensions, contradictions and variations in accounts. There is a range of positions in-between the 'realist' and 'relativist' endpoints of the continuum. These include a

perspective that combines the realist ambition to gain a better understanding of what is 'really' going on in the world with the acknowledgement that the data the researcher gathers may not provide direct access to this reality. Such a position may be described as critical realist. Another 'in-between' position is one that argues that while experience is always the product of interpretation and, therefore, constructed (and flexible) rather than determined (and fixed), it is nevertheless 'real' to the person who is having the experience. This position could be described as phenomenological. While classification of methods along the realism–relativism continuum can be helpful, it is also clear that the terminology used raises as many questions as it answers (e.g. What does it mean for something to be 'real'? What is the relationship between truth and reality?). As a result, it is important that we do not get too hung up about the use of the correct labels; rather, what matters is that we identify, clearly and correctly, what type of knowledge we aim to produce and that we select a research methodology that is designed to generate that type of knowledge.

2 What kinds of assumptions does the methodology make about the world?
This question takes us into the realm of *ontology*. Ontology is concerned with the nature of the world. While epistemology asks 'How can we know?', the question driving ontology is 'What is there to know?' It can be argued that ontological concerns are fundamental and that it is impossible not to make at least some assumptions about the nature of the world. For example, our starting point may be the assumption that events are generated by underlying structures such as socioeconomic relations. This would constitute a materialist ontology. Alternatively, we may assume that psychological phenomena are independent from such structures. This would be an idealist position. Ontological positions can be described as 'realist' and 'relativist'. A realist ontology maintains that the world is made up of structures and objects that have cause–effect relationships with one another. Materialism, for instance, subscribes to a realist ontology. A relativist ontology, by contrast, rejects such a view of the world and maintains instead that the world is not the orderly, law-bound place that realists believe it to be. A relativist ontology questions the 'out-there-ness' of the world and it emphasizes the diversity of interpretations that can be applied to it. Idealism is an example of a relativist ontology.

3 How does the methodology conceptualize the role of the researcher in the research process?
All qualitative methodologies recognize that the researcher is, in one way or another, implicated in the research process. However, there are differences in the extent to which qualitative methodologies see the researcher as being the author, as opposed to the witness, of their research findings. Some methodologies (usually those with relativist leanings) see the researcher as the central figure in the research process because it is the researcher who constructs the findings. A helpful metaphor here would be to describe the researcher as a builder who constructs a house. The same bricks (the data) could be used to build a number of very different buildings. Other (usually more realist) methodologies, while acknowledging the importance of the researcher, do not perceive the researcher as the author of the findings. Instead, they see the researcher as someone who uses their skills to unearth the evidence. Here, the research process is perceived as a treasure hunt rather than a construction process.

These three epistemological questions will be raised again in relation to each of the six qualitative method(ologie)s introduced in this book. They will provide a framework for discussion, evaluation and comparison of the six approaches in the final chapter.

Further reading

Anfara, V.A. and Mertz, N.T. (2006) *Theoretical Frameworks in Qualitative Research*. London: Sage.

Burr, V. (2003) *An Introduction to Social Constructionism*. London: Routledge.

Chalmers, A.F. (1999) *What is this Thing Called Science?*, 3rd edn. Buckingham: Open University Press.

Harding, S. (1991) *Whose Science? Whose Knowledge? Thinking from Women's Lives*. Buckingham: Open University Press.

Hollway, W. (1989) *Subjectivity and Method in Psychology: Gender, Meaning and Science*. London: Sage.

Kirk, J. and Miller, M. (1986) *Reliability and Validity in Qualitative Research*. London: Sage.

Kvale, S. (1995) The social construction of validity, *Qualitative Inquiry*, 1(1): 19–40.

Willig, C. and Stainton Rogers, W. (eds) (2008) *The Sage Handbook of Qualitative Research in Psychology*. London: Sage.

2

Qualitative research design

General principles of qualitative research design • *The research question* •
Choosing the 'right' method • *Semi-structured interviewing* • *Participant
observation* • *Diaries* • *Focus groups* • *Further reading*

In Chapter 1, I identified a set of concerns shared by qualitative researchers (see
pp. 8–9). These centred around the construction and negotiation of meaning, and the
quality and texture of experience. These concerns have implications for research
design. Qualitative data collection techniques need to be participant-led, or bottom-
up, in the sense that they allow participant-generated meanings to be heard. They
need to be open-ended and flexible enough to facilitate the emergence of new, and
unanticipated, categories of meaning and experience. Pre-coding and the use of
researcher-generated categories are not compatible with 'big Q' methodology (see
p. 9). There are, therefore, a number of general principles associated with qualitative research design, and these are outlined in the next section. This is followed by a
discussion of the formulation of research questions and the selection of appropriate
data collection techniques. In the remainder of the chapter, four major data collection
methods are introduced (semi-structured interviews, participant observation, diaries,
focus groups). Ethical and reflexivity issues are also addressed in this chapter.

General principles of qualitative research design

These concern the type of data we should aim to collect, and the role of participants in
the research process. The *type of data* we collect for a qualitative study need to be
naturalistic. This is to say, the data must not be coded, summarized, categorized or
otherwise 'reduced' at the point of collection. Strictly speaking, this is impossible
because any process of collecting data requires some form of translation from one
medium to another. For example, a verbatim transcript of what a participant says is
not the same as the participant's performance of their speech in real time. Even a
video-recording of that performance constitutes a transformation of the real-life act.

Nevertheless, qualitative data collection methods are designed to minimize data reduction. In qualitative research, the objective of data collection is to create a comprehensive record of participants' words and actions. This means making sure that as little as possible is lost 'in translation'. As a result, qualitative data tend to be voluminous and hard to manage. Qualitative researchers have to wait for the data analysis phase of the research before they can begin to 'reduce' the data, and even then they need to be very careful about what they 'leave out' (for a detailed discussion of this process, see Chapters 3–8).

Such considerations raise the issue of *validity*. To what extent can we ensure that our data collection (and analysis) really addresses the question we want to answer? That is, how can we be sure that we are, in fact, researching what we think we are researching? Validity can be defined as the extent to which our research describes, measures or explains what it aims to describe, measure or explain. As a result of their flexibility and open-endedness, qualitative research methods provide the space for validity issues to be addressed. Unlike quantitative research, which relies on pre-coded data collection techniques such as multiple-choice questionnaires or structured interviews, qualitative data collection allows participants to challenge the researcher's assumptions about the meaning and relevance of concepts and categories. For example, throughout the 1950s and 1960s, experimental social psychological research had demonstrated that women were more conformist than men. However, it later transpired that a validity error had been made: the studies had, in fact, measured familiarity rather than conformity (see Kirk and Miller 1986: 27–8). When Sistrunk and McDavid (1971) repeated the experiment, this time using a wide range of statements with which participants could agree or disagree, they found that women were more conformist when it came to statements about specialist tools, whereas men were more conformist in relation to statements about needlework. There was no difference between men and women in relation to gender-neutral statements. In the earlier studies, gender-related lack of familiarity with stimuli had been taken for female conformity.

Even though validity can be a problematic concept for qualitative researchers, qualitative methodologies engage with concerns about validity in a number of ways. First, qualitative data collection techniques aim to ensure that participants are free to challenge and, if necessary, correct the researcher's assumptions about the meanings investigated by the research. Some qualitative researchers also obtain feedback on their study's findings from participants (participant validation). If the study and its findings make sense to participants, the argument goes, it must at least have some validity. Second, much qualitative data collection (and in some cases also analysis) takes place in real-life settings, such as workplaces or youth clubs. As a result, there is no need to extrapolate from an artificial setting, such as the laboratory, to the real world, which means that such studies have higher ecological validity. Third, reflexivity (see p. 10) ensures that the research process as a whole is scrutinized throughout and that the researcher continuously reviews his or her own role in the research. This discourages impositions of meaning by the researcher and thus promotes validity.

An important aspect of quantitative data collection is *reliability*. A measurement is reliable if it yields the same answer on different occasions. Qualitative researchers are less concerned with reliability. This is because qualitative research explores a particular, possibly unique, phenomenon or experience in great detail. It does not aim to measure a particular attribute in large numbers of people. However, there are qualitative researchers (e.g. Silverman 1993) who emphasize that qualitative research methods, if applied appropriately and rigorously, ought to generate reliable results. That is, the same data, when collected and analysed by different researchers using the same method, ought to generate the same findings, irrespective of who carried out the research. It has to be acknowledged that there is disagreement among qualitative researchers about the extent to which reliability ought to be a concern for qualitative research.

Finally, data collection needs to confront the issue of *representativeness*. Quantitative research relies upon representative samples. To be able to generalize their findings to the general population, quantitative researchers need to ensure that participants in their study are representative of this population. Qualitative research tends to work with relatively small numbers of participants. This is due to the time-consuming and labour-intensive nature of qualitative data collection and analysis (for more detail, see Chapters 3–8). As a result, qualitative studies do not work with representative samples. Is this a problem?

The answer to this question depends at least in part on the research question the study is designed to answer (see next section). If the study is a case study (of an individual, a group or an organization), representativeness is not an issue. Here, the aim of the study is to understand the internal dynamics of the case. However, if the study aims to explore a phenomenon that is relevant to more people than are actually involved in the study, representativeness can be an issue. This is because, in such circumstances, we are likely to want to be able to generalize from our study. For instance, if we study six women's experiences of childbirth, it is likely that we would want to move beyond our data and say something about its implications for women's experience of childbirth in general. Even though, strictly speaking, we cannot generalize from small-scale qualitative research of this type, it could be argued that, if 'a given experience is possible, it is also subject to universalisation' (Haug 1987: 44). Thus, even though we do not know who or how many people share a particular experience, once we have identified it through qualitative research, we do know that it is available within a culture or society. If we assume that our participants' experiences are at least partially socially constituted, we can agree with Kippax and co-workers' (1988: 25) claim that 'each individual mode of appropriation of the social . . . is potentially generalisable'.

Another way of attempting to solve the problem of generalizability is through accumulative techniques. These can be applied within and across studies. Within a study, accumulative techniques ensure that a particular observation made in one context is checked against related observations in other contexts, in case a more generalized, or overarching, category may be identified. Across studies, accumulative techniques allow us to review different studies' findings in relation to one another. Here, rather than relying on one isolated qualitative study, we aim to integrate the findings from a number of comparable studies to draw wider conclusions.

The *role of participants* in qualitative research can differ dramatically from that of the 'subjects' of quantitative studies. There are, however, also big differences between qualitative methodologies in this regard. At one end of the continuum, there are qualitative methodologies, such as feminist approaches, participatory action research or memory work (see Chapter 8), where the distinction between 'researcher' and 'participant' is blurred. Here, the researcher becomes a participant in the research, and the participants contribute to the analysis of the data they generate. In some cases, there is no distinction between researchers and participants because the researchers actually study themselves (e.g. in memory work). At the other end of the continuum, there are qualitative methodologies, such as conversation analysis or discursive psychology (see Chapter 6), where the participants generate the type of data required by the researcher without any further involvement in the research. This is particularly the case where the data are recordings of everyday interactions that would have occurred anyway and in the absence of any data collection.

Reflexivity

As indicated in Chapter 1, qualitative research acknowledges that the researcher influences and shapes the research process, both as a person (*personal reflexivity*) and as a theorist/thinker (*epistemological reflexivity*) (see p. 10). Reflexivity is important in qualitative research because it encourages us to foreground, and reflect upon, the ways in which the person of the researcher is implicated in the research and its findings. It is not easy to focus attention on our own role within the research process, especially if we have been trained to think of 'the researcher' as (ideally) detached, neutral and unbiased – more of an instrument than a person. Reflexivity, however, means more than acknowledging personal 'biases'; reflexivity invites us to think about how our own reactions to the research context and the data actually make possible certain insights and understandings. In this sense, reflexivity in qualitative research has much in common with how psychoanalytic psychotherapists use 'countertransference' – the therapist's emotional response to the client's behaviour – in order to gain a better understanding of the client (see also Frosh and Saville Young 2008: 111–15).

Reflexive considerations can be discussed under a separate heading (e.g. 'reflexivity'); for example, at the end of a research report the researcher may reflect on how the research has changed her and her way of thinking about the subject matter of the research. Alternatively, they can be integrated into the report and raised in context, whenever they are relevant. For example, in the methods section there may be a discussion of the researcher's person (e.g. gender, ethnicity, age, personal experience of the subject matter of the research, etc.) and the ways in which this may affect data collection and/or analysis. Reflexivity can be revisited many times within the same report. There are ways of highlighting and differentiating reflexivity considerations from the rest of the report, for example, by introducing a different font or colour, or by positioning reflexive comments as a series of footnotes throughout the report. However, there is no set format for addressing reflexivity. The important thing is to include reflections on the researcher's role in the research in a way that is clear, honest and informative.

Ethics

The same basic *ethical considerations* apply to the treatment of participants in both qualitative and quantitative research. These include (see Elmes et al. 1995):

1 *Informed consent.* The researcher should ensure that participants are fully informed about the research procedure and give their consent to participate in the research *before* data collection takes place.
2 *No deception.* Deception of participants should be avoided altogether. The *only* justification for deception is when there is no other way to answer the research question *and* the potential benefit of the research far exceeds any risk to the participants.
3 *Right to withdraw.* The researcher should ensure that participants feel free to withdraw from participation in the study without fear of being penalized.
4 *Debriefing.* The researcher should ensure that, after data collection, participants are informed about the full aims of the research. Ideally, they should also have access to any publications arising from the study they took part in.
5 *Confidentiality.* The researcher should maintain complete confidentiality regarding any information about participants acquired during the research process.

To summarize, researchers should protect their participants from any harm or loss, and they should aim to preserve their psychological well-being and dignity at all times. However, many qualitative researchers go beyond these basic ethical guidelines. Brinkmann and Kvale (2008: 263) argue that qualitative research is saturated with ethical issues because '[T]he human interaction in qualitative inquiries affects researchers and participants, and the knowledge produced through qualitative research affects our understanding of the human condition'. From this point of view, ethical issues arise from the very beginning of the research (e.g. regarding the formulation of the research question), they stay with us throughout our interactions with our research participants, and they continue to be relevant throughout the process of dissemination of the research findings. For example, instead of merely protecting participants from any harm or loss, some qualitative researchers aim to deliver positive benefits for participants. Action research is designed to generate knowledge about a process or system through changing it for the better. Here, any action taken has to be 'in the best possible interests of the people involved' (see Hart and Bond 1995). Similarly, critical discourse analysis aims to challenge social inequality, injustice and relations of power. Van Dijk (1987: 4) identifies the following aims for critical science:

> Beyond description or superficial application, critical science in each domain asks further questions, such as those of responsibility, interests and ideology. Instead of focussing on purely academic or theoretical problems, it starts from prevailing social problems, and thereby chooses the perspectives of those who suffer most and critically analyses those in power, those who are responsible and those who have the means and the opportunity to solve such problems.

Brinkmann and Kvale (2008) caution against the practice of ethics as rule-following. They suggest that ethical issues and concerns cannot be addressed and 'solved' once and for all during the planning stages of the research. Rather, ethical dilemmas will surface throughout the research process, requiring the researcher to remain ethically attuned throughout. This may mean, for instance, that the issue of consent is revisited throughout the study, something known as 'processual consent' (Rosenblatt 1995). Instead of simply learning the ethical rules for the treatment of participants in psychological research (see list 1–5 above), Brinkmann and Kvale (2008: 276–8) recommend that researchers learn 'ethical research behaviour' and develop 'the ability to sense, judge and act in an ethically committed fashion' (ibid.: 278).

This is particularly useful in qualitative research because the open-ended, exploratory nature of such research means that apparently straightforward requirements such as informed consent and confidentiality can become an ethical challenge (e.g. How can we obtain informed consent for a study whose direction and remit is likely to change during the research process? How can we guarantee confidentiality in a case study of one exceptional individual? What happens if criminal behaviour comes to light during a confidential interview?). Furthermore, qualitative in-depth interviews can lead to quasi-therapeutic relationships between researcher and participant, potentially giving rise to feelings and expectations on the part of the participant that the researcher may not be equipped to deal with. In addition, interviewees may feel betrayed when reading research reports offering interpretations of their accounts that do not tally with their own understanding of their experience (see also Willig 2004). Power relations between researchers and participants are perhaps more subtle and more covert in qualitative research; however, this does not mean that they should be ignored or denied by qualitative researchers. To the contrary, it could be argued that the close personal relationship between researcher and participants in qualitative research carries a particular risk for the abuse of trust, for example, when the researcher 'fakes friendship' in order to obtain information (see Duncombe and Jessop 2002).

The research question

Most qualitative research projects are guided by one or more research questions. Research questions are different from hypotheses. A hypothesis is a claim, derived from existing theory, which can be tested against empirical evidence. It can be either rejected or retained. A research question, by contrast, is open-ended. That is, it cannot be answered with a simple 'yes' or 'no'. A research question calls for an answer that provides detailed descriptions and, where possible, also explanations of a phenomenon.

Qualitative research questions identify the phenomenon (i.e. the process, object or entity) that the researcher wants to investigate. It points us in a direction without predicting what we may find. Good qualitative research questions tend to be process-oriented. They ask *how* something happens. For example, we may ask 'How do women with chronic illness manage a pregnancy?' or 'How do married couples negotiate child-care arrangements?' Qualitative research questions are always provisional because the researcher may find that the very concepts and terminology used in the research question are, in fact, not appropriate or relevant to the participants' experiences. Asking the wrong question undermines the validity of the findings; qualitative research is open to the possibility that the research question may have to change during the research process. It could be argued that one of the outcomes of qualitative research should be an understanding of what would have been an appropriate research question to ask in the first place!

The research question does, however, play a slightly different role in different qualitative method(ologie)s. In some methodologies, such as Discursive Psychology or discourse analysis, the research question is directly shaped by the methodology itself. That is, the methodology, through its epistemological assumptions, dictates what we can and cannot ask. For example, a methodology informed by a social constructionist epistemology can (only) address research questions about the social and/or discursive construction of phenomena. Appropriate research questions within this context might be 'How is "failure" constructed in contemporary academic institutions?' or 'How do clinical psychologists construct "mental health" in their interactions with clients and colleagues?'

Other methodologies can address a wider range of research questions. For example, a realist version of the grounded theory method (see Chapter 3) assumes that the data themselves generate categories that emerge during the research process and which capture the reality of the phenomenon under investigation. As a result, research questions for Grounded Theory research can be about processes, experiences, structures or even cognitions. Examples of appropriate research questions within this context are: 'How do students make decisions about their future careers?'; 'How does a telephone helpline train its volunteers?'; 'What is it like to undergo a gender reassignment process?'

When formulating our research question, we also need to think about its ethical and political dimensions. We need to think about in whose interest it may be to ask the question in the first place, and how the answer to it may be used by individuals and organizations in society. We need to reflect on the value of the knowledge that our research question aims to produce and for whom we are producing this knowledge. If our research is funded, we should consider the motives of the funding body in supporting the research, and the extent to which we share these motives. *Reflexivity* also demands that we examine very carefully our own personal and professional reasons for asking our research question. The formulation of research questions is discussed in more detail in relation to each of the six qualitative method(ologie)s (see Chapters 3–8).

I conclude this section by citing Lorion (1990: 321–2), whose 'street lamp' metaphor reminds us that our research question should always precede our choice of methodology:

> I am frequently reminded of the old joke about the individual who explained that he was looking for his missing keys under the street lamp because 'the light is better there' ... The 'street lamp' draws us to it by its apparent capacity to facilitate our search.

Lorion makes the point that we should not look for answers in certain places simply because they are familiar or easily accessible; rather, we need to look in places where the answer is likely to be, no matter how inhospitable these places may be. This insight can be applied to research methods. Methods are a means to an end. They are 'the way to the goal' (Kvale 1996a: 278). This means that our research question (the 'goal') should inform our choice of methods, not the other way around. It may be tempting to choose a research question that can be answered by the method we know best. For example, we may have learned how to do t-tests and then decide to carry out research that addresses a question about differences in performance between two groups of people. But is this really what we want to know about the two groups? If it is, we can go ahead with our between-subjects design. If it is not, however, we ought to formulate our research question first and then choose the most appropriate research method to answer our question. It is within this context that research can take on the characteristics of an adventure (see pp. 1–2).

Choosing the 'right' method

Strictly speaking, there are no 'right' or 'wrong' methods. Rather, methods of data collection and analysis can be more or less appropriate to our research question. Having formulated a research question, the researcher needs to make a decision about how to collect the sort of data that can answer that question. That is to say, he or she needs to choose a method of data collection. The researcher also needs to think about how the answer to the research question may be extracted from the data. That is, he or she needs to select a method of data analysis. It is important to understand that the research question, data collection technique and method of data analysis are dependent on one another. They cannot be considered separately and they should not be chosen independently from one another. A good qualitative research design is one in which the method of data analysis is appropriate to the research question, and where the method of data collection generates data that are appropriate to the method of analysis. Researchers should never collect data without having decided how to analyse it. It could be argued that both qualitative and quantitative researchers share a common purpose, and that, ideally, they 'share a belief in the fallibility of knowledge, the need to link theory and empirical observation, the obligation to carry out research rigorously and conscientiously, and the necessity of critique and dissemination of research' (Yardley and Bishop 2008: 363).

From a pragmatic point of view, the aim of research is not to gain access to an abstract truth independent from human experience but rather to generate understanding that will be useful to us. It is designed to answer our questions, and as such, research designs and methods of data collection and analysis cannot be in themselves 'wrong' but they can be more or less appropriate (to the question put). Sometimes, the most appropriate way to answer a research question requires the use of two or more research methods (mixed methods design). We can combine qualitative and quantitative methods within the same study in order to answer related questions. For example, we can use a questionnaire to establish whether there are significant differences between two groups of people in terms of a particular behaviour or preference, and then use semi-structured interviews and/or focus groups to find out why there may be such differences by obtaining more information about what the behaviour or preference means to the two groups of people. Similarly, we can use more than one qualitative method within one study if our research question requires it. For example, we may want to gain a better understanding of a particular community (e.g. singles' clubs, football clubs, reading groups, etc.) and the participants' experience of it. To achieve our research aim, we may choose to conduct some participant observation in order to identify the implicit and explicit rules of behaviour associated with it. This could be followed by semi-structured interviews with a selection of participants (perhaps representing different social categories (e.g. women and men, regulars and newcomers, etc.) that would provide us with information about how participants feel about their role within the community. Again, the important thing is to select methods that are able to generate data which will help us to answer our research question(s).

There is a wide range of qualitative data collection techniques that generate quite different kinds of data. Even though one technique (e.g. audio-recording of semi-structured interviews) may generate data that can be analysed in a number of different ways (including Interpretative Phenomenological Analysis and discourse analysis), there are other techniques that are simply not compatible with some methods of data analysis. For example, notes written by the interviewer during the course of a semi-structured interview cannot be subjected to conversation analysis. In the remainder of this chapter, four major data collection methods are introduced: semi-structured interviews, participant observation, diaries and focus groups. Their relationship with various forms of qualitative data analysis are highlighted.

Semi-structured interviewing

Semi-structured interviewing is the most widely used method of data collection in qualitative research in psychology. This is partly because interview data can be analysed in a variety of ways, which means that semi-structured interviewing is a method of data collection that is compatible with several methods of data analysis (e.g. discourse analysis, grounded theory, interpretative phenomenology). Another reason for the popularity of semi-structured interviews is that they are somewhat easier to arrange than other forms of qualitative data collection. This is not to say that the actual process of semi-structured interviewing is 'easy'; rather, I am suggesting that there may be fewer logistical difficulties in arranging a series of semi-structured interviews with a small number of volunteers than to design a longitudinal study that may involve the negotiation of access to organizations or groups for the purpose of participant observation or gaining participants' commitment to keeping diaries over a period of time. The popularity of semi-structured interviews as a method of data collection has given rise to a debate about the role of interviews in qualitative research (see *Qualitative Research in Psychology* 2005). Potter and Hepburn (2005) have drawn attention to the fact that much qualitative analysis of interview-generated data does not pay attention to the many contextual features of the interview material (e.g. interactional features, its status as a conversation between two people, the stake that both participants inevitably have in the interview, etc.) and instead takes such data at 'face-value'. It is important to reflect on the meaning and experience of the interview for both interviewer and interviewee, and to take care not to assume that the interviewee's words are simple and direct reflections of their thoughts and feelings.

Semi-structured interviewing requires careful preparation and planning. The researcher needs to think about who to interview (and why), how to recruit participants, how to record and transcribe the interview, what style of interviewing to use, and what to ask participants. In this section, I discuss (1) the general characteristics of semi-structured interviewing, (2) the interview agenda and (3) recording and transcription of the interview.

General characteristics of semi-structured interviewing

The semi-structured interview provides an opportunity for the researcher to hear the participant talk about a particular aspect of their life or experience. The questions asked by the researcher function as triggers that encourage the participant to talk. This style of interviewing is sometimes described as non-directive; however, it is important to acknowledge that it is the researcher whose *research question* drives the interview. Through his or her questions and comments, the interviewer steers the interview to obtain the kind of data that will answer the research question. The interviewer needs to find the right balance between maintaining control of the interview and where it is going, and allowing the interviewee the space to redefine the topic under investigation and thus to generate novel insights for the researcher. This can be difficult. A carefully constructed *interview agenda* can go some way towards ensuring that the interviewer does not lose sight of the original research question (see below).

To encourage the participant to speak freely and openly, and to maximize their own understanding of what is being communicated in the interview, researchers are advised to consider the possible effects of their own social identities (i.e. gender, social class, ethnicity, nationality, age, etc.) on the interviewee. They should also familiarize themselves with the participant's cultural milieu, and the status of 'the interview' within this milieu. For example, a middle-aged professional may be more comfortable with a formal interview than an unemployed youth because, in the latter's experience, such interviews may be associated with administrative distrust and judgemental assessments. The researcher needs to know what the interview means to the interviewee to fully understand the interviewee's contribution.

The researcher also needs to be aware of linguistic variability. The same term may not mean the same thing to all interviewees. In semi-structured interviewing, the emphasis is upon meaning rather than lexical comparability. This means that the researcher needs to try to understand what the interviewee *meant* by what he or she said, irrespective of *how* they chose to say it (discourse analysis constitutes an exception to this; see Chapters 6 and 7). It is also worth bearing in mind that language is indexical; that is, the meanings of words depend on the context within which they are spoken. For example, waiting for 'a long while' probably refers to something like 20 minutes within the context of waiting for a bus, whereas the same expression used when talking about buying a house may mean months or even years.

Semi-structured interviewing, perhaps more than other types of interviewing, depends on the rapport established between interviewer and interviewee. The semi-structured interview is, however, somewhat ambiguous. This is because it combines features of the formal interview (e.g. fixed time limit; fixed roles of 'interviewer' and 'interviewee'; the existence of an interview agenda) with features of an informal conversation such as the open-endedness of the questions and the emphasis on narrative and experience. This means that although rapport can be established quickly between interviewer and interviewee, it can also be disrupted suddenly when the interviewer's role as researcher becomes salient. This can happen during the interview; for example, when the interviewer needs to turn over the audiotape, thus reminding the interviewee that they are 'being interviewed'. It can also happen after the interview; for example, when the interviewee reads the transcript of the interview and realizes how much they revealed about themselves in comparison with the interviewer who revealed very little in what appeared, at the time, to be a 'normal' conversation. The semi-structured interview requires sensitive and ethical negotiation of rapport between the interviewer and the interviewee. Interviewers should not abuse the informal ambience of the interview to encourage the interviewee to reveal more than they may feel comfortable with after the event.

The interview agenda

The interview agenda for a semi-structured interview consists of a relatively small number of open-ended questions. It is a good idea to start with more public questions and move on to more personal matters when rapport has been established. Some researchers prefer to identify topic headings instead of questions, around which they then formulate questions during the course of the interview. This allows the researcher to incorporate the interviewee's own terms and concepts into the questions, and thus to make the questions more appropriate or relevant to the interviewee. However, the problem with using topic headings is that, as a result of their intense involvement in the interview process, researchers may formulate questions that are less open and more directive than necessary. Better formulations of questions may emerge from careful reflection and consideration of alternative versions before the interview, especially where the interviewer is a novice. However, it is a good idea to restate interviewees' comments and to incorporate them into further questions throughout the interview. This demonstrates to the interviewee that the interviewer is indeed listening, and it allows the interviewer an opportunity to check with the interviewee that they have understood correctly. It also serves to maintain coherence and continuity throughout the interview.

A good way to obtain detailed and comprehensive accounts from interviewees is to express ignorance. A naïve interviewer encourages the interviewee to 'state the obvious' and thus to give voice to otherwise implicit assumptions and expectations. This can be extremely enlightening. Another way to encourage interviewees to elaborate is to ask for illustrations of events or experiences. This is particularly helpful when abstract concepts or general opinions are being referred to. For instance, having heard the interviewee say that people do not take him or her seriously, the interviewer can ask the interviewee for a concrete example of when he or she felt this way and how he or she dealt with it.

Spradley (1979) has produced a useful guide to formulate four different types of question: descriptive, structural, contrast and evaluative:

- *Descriptive* questions prompt the interviewee to provide a general account of

'what happened' or 'what is the case'. Such questions ask for biographical information (e.g. 'What do you do for a living?'), anecdotes (e.g. 'What happened that
day?'), life histories (e.g. 'How did you come to live in London?'), and so on.

- *Structural* questions are about how the interviewee organizes his or her knowledge. They prompt interviewees to identify the categories and frameworks of
meaning that they use to make sense of the world. Here we may ask questions
such as 'What does it mean to be an innocent victim of a crime?' or 'How did you
decide to have an HIV antibody test?'

- *Contrast* questions allow the interviewee to make comparisons between events
and experiences. For example, we may ask 'Would you rather report a crime and
run the risk of revenge, or keep quiet and be safe from harassment?' or 'Did you
prefer working in the public or the private sector?'

- *Evaluative* questions are about the interviewee's feelings towards someone or
something. We can be vague in our formulation and ask 'How do/did you feel
about this?', or we can be more specific and ask about a particular emotion (e.g.
'Did you feel afraid when you took the blood test?').

Finally, it is important to ensure that the questions asked are actually meaningful
to the participants. Cross-cultural researchers have drawn attention to the fact that
not all questions make sense in all cultures. For example, Deutscher (1978) reminds
us of Lerner's observation that hypothetical questions ('What would you do if
. . .?') may be considered unworthy of attention by some (e.g. the French) but be
unproblematic for others (e.g. North Americans).

Recording and transcription of the interview

To be able to carry out a full analysis of the data, it is necessary to audio- or video-
record and transcribe the interview. Most qualitative methods of analysis require that
the material is transcribed verbatim, or near verbatim. Taking notes during the interview is no substitute for a full recording. Note-taking also distracts both the interviewee and interviewer. It interferes with eye contact and non-verbal communication
and does not encourage the development of rapport between interviewee and interviewer. However, taping the interview may also affect what is being said. Participants
may not be entirely comfortable and relaxed in the presence of a tape-, or worse, a
video-recorder. It is important that the researcher explains why the recording is being
made and how it is going to be used. It is also a good idea to offer the interviewee a
copy of the transcript of the interview, if at all possible. The researcher may ask the
interviewee to comment on the transcript. Such feedback constitutes additional data.

If the interview is being tape-recorded, the researcher needs to make sure that
the recorder is placed in a position where it will record clearly. This could be on a
table between the interviewer and the interviewee. Such positioning also allows the
researcher to keep an eye on the recorder to make sure that it is taping the interview. It
also allows the researcher to change the tape if necessary. It is vital that the researcher
checks that the tape-recorder is working before the interview. It is a good idea to use
a new set of batteries for each interview. It is extremely frustrating to find that an

hour-long interview has not been recorded or has been recorded so badly as to be inaudible. Badly recorded interviews also take much longer to transcribe.

There are different ways in which an interview can be transcribed. If we are interested in the subtleties of communicative interaction between interviewer and interviewee, we need to transcribe the words as well as the way in which they are spoken. This means including pauses, interruptions, intonation, volume of speech, and so on. These various features of speech are represented by the signs of the *transcription notation*. A commonly used form of notation for such detailed transcription was developed by Gail Jefferson. Guidance to using this type of notation can be found in Potter and Wetherell (1987) and in Atkinson and Heritage (1984). Detailed transcription is required for conversation analysis and some types of discursive analysis. If we are interested only in the content of the interview, we do not need to transcribe non-linguistic features of speech. In this case, it is sufficient to transcribe what is being said (the words). This would be appropriate for grounded theory analysis. However, even here we need to make a decision about what we wish to include. For example, we may wish to include incomplete sentences, false starts, laughter and repetition of words. Alternatively, we may wish to 'tidy up' the transcript. It all depends on what we aim to do with the transcript. That is, our decision about what type of transcription to use depends on our research question and the method of analysis we have chosen. It is important to bear in mind, however, that *all* types of transcription constitute a form of translation of the spoken word into something else. An interview transcript can never be the mirror image of the interview.

Participant observation

'Observation' is part of a wide range of research activities. It could be argued that without engaging in some type of observation, a researcher would not be able to carry out any kind of research. In this section, however, we are concerned with 'observation' as a method of data collection. Flick (1998: 137) identifies five features that define types of observation. They include the extent to which the observation is covert, the extent to which it is systematic (or standardized), whether or not it takes place in a natural setting, whether or not the observer takes part in the activity that is being observed, and how much of it involves self-observation (or reflexivity). The type of observational method we are concerned with here is *participant observation*. This tends to take place in natural settings (e.g. a school or hospital; a bar or a club), where the observer can be either incognito (covert) or known as a researcher (overt). It tends to involve at least some self-observation (see *reflexivity*, p. 10), and the observations made tend not to be standardized (i.e. not systematic), at least in the early stages of the research. Participant observation requires the researcher to engage in a variety of activities including participation, documentation, (informal) interviewing and reflection. The researcher needs to maintain a balance between participation and observation. In other words, the researcher needs to be involved enough to understand what is going on, yet remain detached enough to be able to reflect on the phenomenon under investigation. This can be extremely difficult, particularly when the research is concerned with emotionally charged subject matter. For example, it may be easier to maintain reflective distance when we are observing visitors to an art gallery (see

Appendix 2) than when we are engaged in participant observation in an intensive care unit. In their book about soccer fans, Marsh et al. (1978: 119) remind us of the importance of emotional involvement in participant observation:

> A point should be made here concerning participant observation. Many people seem to equate this kind of methodology with going along to events and simply looking at what goes on – they seem to leave out the participation bit. But an involvement, albeit a rather restrained one, in the action is a basic requirement. One needs not only to observe what is happening but also to *feel* what it is like to be in a particular social situation. This experiential aspect does not come about by being a totally disinterested onlooker. It comes about through an attempt to share in the excitement and emotions which, for soccer fans, constitute the 'electric' atmosphere which is seen as being the most important aspect of Saturday afternoons. (emphasis in original)

The participant observer needs to keep detailed notes of any observations made. In some settings, it is a good idea to phase observation and writing. This is particularly the case where participation in the activities under investigation requires the researcher's full attention. Note-taking will then have to wait. However, it is important that the researcher records his or her observations as soon as possible after they have been made. This is partly to counteract forgetting but also because we may see things differently after a period of reflection. First impressions cannot be recaptured. Observational notes should feature as much detail as possible, including verbatim, or near verbatim, quotes of what people said, concrete descriptions of the setting, people and events involved. In the early stages of the research, in particular, the researcher should take care not to exclude observations that appear trivial at the time. This is because apparent trivia may well turn out to contain crucial information, the value of which may only emerge in later stages of the research. Some researchers find it helpful to think about observational notes in terms of their focus.

Most of what is recorded will be concerned with the actual observations made. Such notes will include descriptions of settings, events and people, as well as quotations and/or summaries of what people said. These may be referred to as *substantive notes*. Another set of notes will be concerned with the process of observation itself. Such notes will reflect on the researcher's role in the research, his or her relationship with the other participants, and problems encountered in the field, such as any difficulties associated with the negotiation of roles. These are *methodological notes*. Finally, the researcher will wish to record emerging themes, connections, patterns, and so on. These constitute the beginnings of data analysis and theory-building; they may be referred to as *analytical notes*.

Some approaches to participant observation *combine* data collection and analysis. This is how participant observation is used in ethogenic research. In this case, the analytical notes will be extensive and progressively complex. Others *phase* data collection and analysis whereby a period of data collection is followed by a period of analysis of the observational notes. Preliminary data analysis then gives rise to another, this time more focused, phase of data collection, and so on. This is how grounded theory researchers use participant observation. A third approach to participant observation involves a period of data collection followed by analysis of the data. This is suitable when the researcher has little time or is unable to return to the field for whatever reason.

The first two approaches (*combining* and *phasing* of data collection and analysis) require focused observation. Focused observation involves the identification of a particular aspect of the phenomenon as the focus for intensive observation. Focused observation constitutes a move beyond a purely descriptive approach to observation. It is based upon emergent theoretical formulations and it is designed to 'test' the researcher's hunches against reality. For example, if we think that we may have identified a recurrent pattern in our observational data (e.g. that nurses take cigarette breaks after particularly stressful or distressing encounters with patients), we may wish to focus our observations around relevant situations or events (e.g. stressful or distressing encounters with patients) to further explore the pattern. It is important, however, to maintain an open mind and to observe widely enough to allow disconfirming observations to occur. Emerging theory should not constrain the researcher's ability to consider alternative explanations. A shift from a descriptive to an explanatory level needs to be managed carefully.

Diaries

Diaries are not widely used as a method of data collection in psychological research. This is because the diary method constitutes a challenge for both researcher and participant. Participants make a commitment to maintain a record (of their experiences, of their activities, of their feelings) over an extended period. Keeping the diary will inevitably have an effect upon their daily routines and most probably also on their experiences. The diary becomes the participant's companion, and yet it has to be handed over to the researcher at the end of the data collection phase. The researcher in turn has to face the challenge of recruiting participants who are willing to keep a diary. Some sections of the population will be more likely to agree to take part in such a study than others. Literacy, however, should not have to be a pre-condition for taking part in a diary study. Tape-recorders can take the place of journals. The researcher has to formulate a set of instructions that will guide participants in their diary-keeping without constraining them unnecessarily. Participants are likely to differ in their expectations of what is involved in keeping a diary for research purposes. Some of them will have kept diaries for themselves; others will find the idea of writing about themselves strange and possibly uncomfortable. The researcher needs to identify the appropriate medium of communication for their participants. Recruitment and initiation of participants, therefore, require a lot of thought.

As with interviews, diaries can be more or less structured. Here, we are concerned with unstructured diaries. That is, participants are asked to keep a record of their experiences, activities and feelings in relation to a particular issue or topic (e.g. their pregnancy, their spouse, their work, their chronic illness), *in their own words*. They are not provided with a set of questions or rating scales to complete each time they make an entry in their diary. However, even with unstructured diaries, the researcher needs to provide participants with some guidance as to:

- how frequently they are expected to make entries (e.g. every hour, day, week, month, etc.);
- which medium of reporting is to be used (e.g. audio-taping, written, photographic, video, etc.);
- what to write about (i.e. the focus of the study);
- the time period covered (e.g. one day, week, month, year, etc.).

Depending on the research question, there may be more or less flexibility in relation to any one, or all, of these. In addition, the researcher may need to indicate to participants in how much detail they are expected to write about their experiences. However, it is important not to be too prescriptive, as this may undermine participants' motivation to take part in the study. It is a good idea for the researcher to collect diary entries regularly (e.g. daily or weekly) to maintain contact with participants, answer any questions they may have and to motivate them to continue keeping the diary.

When used successfully, the diary method of data collection can provide access to information that is otherwise very hard to obtain. The diaries generate data that are temporally ordered; that is, they reveal how events unfold prospectively, in real time. They avoid problems associated with retrospective reporting, which can easily be coloured by the participant's present circumstances, retrospective interpretation of events or simply forgetting of details. Diaries can also facilitate access to very personal or intimate information that may not emerge in a face-to-face interview. However, the diary method does suffer from poor recruitment and high drop-out rates, due to the high demands it places upon participants. Its success depends very much on the participants' motivation and commitment to the study. There are also ethical concerns. Keeping the diary may sensitize participants to certain experiences. For example, keeping a pain diary may increase some participants' pain. Keeping a diary may also prompt the respondent to reflect upon aspects of their lives that they feel unhappy about. The commitment to keep the diary may increase pressure on participants, particularly during stressful episodes. Researchers need to monitor any harmful effects of keeping the diary on participants and offer support where needed.

Focus groups

Focus groups have only recently emerged as a standard data collection technique for qualitative researchers in psychology. However, focus groups are rapidly gaining in popularity, particularly in qualitative health psychology (e.g. Wilkinson 1998). Focus groups provide an alternative to semi-structured interviewing. The focus group is really a group interview that uses the interaction among participants as a source of data. Here, the researcher takes on the role of moderator whose task it is to introduce the group members to one another, to introduce the focus of the group (e.g. a question or a stimulus such as an advert or a photo) and to gently 'steer' the discussion. Such 'steering' may involve periodically recalling the original focus of the group, prompting group members to respond to issues raised by others, or identifying agreements and disagreements among group members. The moderator also sets certain limits to the discussion, such as its beginning and its end.

The strength of the focus group as a method of data collection lies in its ability to mobilize participants to respond to and comment on one another's contributions. In this way, statements are challenged, extended, developed, undermined or qualified in ways that generate rich data for the researcher. Such data allow the researcher to address questions about the ways in which attitudes may be formed and changed, and about how participants jointly construct meanings. It provides evidence of the ways in which participants may justify their positions, and how they may be persuaded by others to change their views. In addition, the focus group provides a setting that is less artificial than the one-to-one interview, which means that the data generated by it are likely to have high(er) ecological validity.

Ideally, focus group participants should interact with one another in the same way that they would interact with peers outside of the research context. This is more likely to be the case if participants are already acquainted with one another before they take part in the focus group. Focus groups should consist of no more than six participants. This is to ensure that all participants remain actively involved in the group discussion throughout the data collection phase. Also, it is extremely difficult to transcribe a group discussion of more than six participants accurately.

Depending on the research question, focus groups can be: (1) homogenous (where participants share key features) or heterogeneous (where participants are different), (2) pre-existing (e.g. a group of friends or work colleagues) or new, and (3) concerned (where participants have a stake in the subject matter) or naïve (where participants do not have any particular commitment in relation to the subject matter). For example, we may be interested in the experience of pregnancy in women whose partners have died shortly after conception. Our research question may be 'How do women whose partners have died shortly after conception manage their pregnancies?' To address this research question, we need to recruit a homogeneous focus group (i.e. women whose partners have died shortly after conception). The group could be either pre-existing (e.g. a support group for women in this situation) or new (brought together through the researcher). The group would probably be concerned rather than naïve, since the subject matter of the focus group discussion concerns their personal circumstances.

Even though focus groups may appear to be more productive than the one-to-one interview, they are not appropriate to all research questions. If the subject matter is sensitive and the participants are expected to talk about intimate aspects of their experience, semi-structured interviews may be more appropriate. Disclosure is not necessarily enhanced through the presence of other participants, although mutual questioning within a group may have this effect. The researcher needs to think carefully about the extent to which the focus group setting would, or would not, facilitate disclosure in relation to the research question. It is also important to be clear about one's aims in analysing focus group-generated data. If our aim is to obtain valid and reliable information about the participants' views and/or experiences in relation to a particular concern (i.e. a *realist* research aim), then we need to employ analytic techniques that will allow us to detect, and remove from our analysis, distorting influences such as the contributions of domineering group members or overly acquiescent comments. On the other hand, if the aim of the research is to trace the ways in which meanings are collectively constructed within a group and how consensus may be achieved through discussion (i.e. a *social constructionist* research aim), then all contributions are equally useful to our analysis. In both cases, however, the researcher needs to pay careful attention to the group dynamics within the group. A focus group with six participants is never the equivalent of six individual interviews because, as Kidd and Parshall (2000: 294) point out '(. . .) individuals in groups do not speak or answer questions in the same way as they do in other settings'.

Semi-structured interviewing, participant observation, diaries and focus groups are not the only qualitative methods of data collection available. New ways of collecting data for qualitative analysis are being developed by researchers as they attempt to answer new research questions. For example, in recent years qualitative researchers have begun to use the Internet as a source of data (see Evans et al. 2008; Mann and Stewart 2000). The Internet can provide access to a range of data sources, including unsolicited data (e.g. web pages, blogs, newsgroups, bulletin boards and chat rooms) (see Robinson 2001), as well as Internet-mediated interviews and discussions. It is important to consider ethical issues when planning to use unsolicited data in particular; after all, those who expressed their thoughts and feelings within the context of an Internet-based support group or discussion group may not wish their words to be used for research purposes. The Association of Internet Researchers provides a set of guidelines for ethical decision-making in Internet research (see Ess and the AoIR Ethics Working Committee 2002). The British Psychological Society has also produced guidelines for ethical practice in psychological research online (www.bps.org.uk/webethic).

The four methods introduced in this chapter can generate a wide range of qualitative data. In addition, methods of data collection can also be used in combination (e.g. participant observation and semi-structured interviewing) to view the same phenomenon from different angles. This constitutes a form of *triangulation*.

Finally, there are qualitative approaches for which methods of data collection and methods of data analysis are inseparable. Here, the gathering of data and the process of analysing the data do not take place at different, and consecutive, points in time. Instead, the researcher collects and analyses data in a cyclical fashion so that initial attempts at data analysis inform strategies for further data collection, and so on. Such studies' findings emerge, in cumulative and piecemeal fashion, from the research process as a whole. Grounded theory (see Chapter 3), phenomenology (Chapter 4) and memory work (Chapter 8) are examples of such qualitative approaches.

Further reading

Flick, U. (2006) *An Introduction to Qualitative Research*, 3rd edn. London: Sage.

Brinkmann, S. and Kvale, S. (2008) Ethics in qualitative research, in C. Willig and W. Stainton Rogers (eds) *The Sage Handbook of Qualitative Research in Psychology*. London: Sage.

Qualitative Research in Psychology (2005) Special Section on Interviewing, 2: 281–325.

Kidd, P.S. and Parshall, M.B. (2000) Getting the focus and the group: enhancing analytical rigor in focus group research, *Qualitative Health Research*, 10(3): 293–308.

Kvale, S. (1996) *Interviews: An Introduction to Qualitative Research Interviewing*. London: Sage.

O'Connell, D.C. and Kowal, S. (1995) Basic principles of transcription, in J.A. Smith, R. Harré and L. Van Langenhove (eds) *Rethinking Methods in Psychology*. London: Sage.

Smith, J.A. (1995) Semi-structured interviewing and qualitative analysis, in J.A. Smith, R. Harré and L. Van Langenhove (eds) *Rethinking Methods in Psychology*. London: Sage.

Wilkinson, S. (1998) Focus groups in health research: exploring the meanings of health and illness, *Journal of Health Psychology*, 3(3): 329–48.

3
Grounded theory

There are two good reasons for dedicating the first of the six methods chapters to
Grounded Theory. First, grounded theory is designed to facilitate the process of 'discovery', or *theory generation*, and therefore embodies one of the key concerns of
qualitative methodology (see Chapter 1). Second, grounded theory works with *categories*, which makes it more accessible to those trained in quantitative methods than
are method(ologie)s that problematize categorization itself (e.g. discursive approaches,
see Chapters 6 and 7).

Grounded theory was originally developed by two sociologists, Barney Glaser
and Anselm Strauss. They were unhappy about the way in which existing theories
dominated sociological research. They argued that researchers needed a method that
would allow them to move from data to theory so that new theories could emerge.
Such theories would be specific to the context in which they had been developed.
They would be 'grounded' in the data from which they had emerged rather than rely
on analytical constructs, categories or variables from pre-existing theories. Grounded
theory, therefore, was designed to open up a space for the development of new,
contextualized theories.

Since the publication of *The Discovery of Grounded Theory* by Glaser and Strauss
in 1967, the grounded theory method has undergone a number of revisions. Most
significantly, Glaser and Strauss themselves parted company and proposed different
ways in which grounded theory ought to be practised (see Box 1 at the end of this
chapter). In this chapter, I introduce the basic principles of grounded theory. This
is followed by an illustration of the application of the method to the study of nurse–
patient interaction. Having thus outlined the basic process of grounded theory,
I identify some of the differences between the various versions of the grounded theory

method. I then go on to draw attention to the limitations of grounded theory as a qualitative method for psychological research. The chapter concludes by examining what grounded theory may have to say in response to the three epistemological questions identified at the end of Chapter 1.

Basic principles of grounded theory

Building blocks

Grounded theory involves the progressive identification and integration of *categories of meaning* from data. Grounded theory is both the process of category identification and integration (as *method*) and its product (as *theory*). Grounded theory *as method* provides us with guidelines on how to identify categories, how to makes links between categories and how to establish relationships between them. Grounded theory *as theory* is the end-product of this process; it provides us with an explanatory framework with which to understand the phenomenon under investigation. To identify, refine and integrate categories, and ultimately to develop theory, grounded theory researchers use a number of key strategies, including *constant comparative analysis, theoretical sampling* and *theoretical coding*. Let us take a closer look at the major analytical constructs, or *building blocks*, of the grounded theory method.

Categories

These designate the grouping together of instances (events, processes, occurrences) that share central features or characteristics with one another. Categories can be at a low level of abstraction, in which case they function as *descriptive labels* (or *concepts*; see Strauss and Corbin 1990: 61). For example, references to 'anxiety', 'anger' and 'pity' can be grouped together under the category heading of 'emotions'. As grounded theory analysis progresses, the researcher is able to identify categories at a higher level of abstraction. These categories are *analytic* rather than descriptive. They interpret, rather than simply label, instances of phenomena. For example, references to diverse activities such as getting drunk, jogging and writing poetry could be categorized as 'escape' if they appear to share the objective of distracting the individual from thinking about a problem. Both descriptive and analytic categories are based upon the identification of 'relations of similarity and difference' (see Dey 1999: 63); however, they function at different levels of abstraction. Category identification in grounded theory is very different from content analysis, with which it should never be confused. Content analysis makes use of categories that are defined *before* data analysis commences and which are designed to be mutually exclusive. This is to say, the same data cannot be allocated to more than one category. By contrast, categories in grounded theory *emerge from the data*, they are not mutually exclusive and they evolve throughout the research process.

Coding

This is the process by which categories are identified. In the early stages of analysis, coding is largely descriptive. Here, descriptive labels are attached to discrete instances of phenomena. New, low-level categories emerge frequently as a result. As coding progresses, the researcher is able to identify higher-level categories that systematically integrate low-level categories into meaningful units. In other words, analytical categories are introduced. Because grounded theory aims to develop *new, context-specific* theories, category labels should not be derived from existing theoretical formulations but should be grounded in the data instead. Ideally, category labels should be *in vivo* – that is, they should utilize words or phrases used by the participants in the study. This helps the researcher to avoid importing existing theory into the analysis. *Theoretical coding* involves the application of a *coding paradigm* to the data. A coding paradigm sensitizes the researcher to particular ways in which categories may be linked with one another. Different versions of grounded theory subscribe to different coding paradigms. These will be discussed in more detail below (see also Box 1).

Constant comparative analysis

This ensures that the coding process maintains its momentum by moving back and forth between the identification of similarities among and differences between emerging categories. Having identified a common feature that unites instances of a phenomenon, the researcher needs to refocus on differences *within* a category in order to be able to identify any emerging *subcategories*. The earlier example of 'emotion' as a category may be expanded to illustrate this process. I suggested that references to 'anxiety', 'anger' and 'pity' could give rise to the category 'emotion'. Further instances of this category could be 'joy', 'jealousy' and 'hate'. Comparing the various instances of emotion allows us to construct subcategories of emotion, such as emotions that require an object (e.g. hate and jealousy) and those that do not (e.g. joy and anxiety). Constant comparative analysis ensures that the researcher does not merely build up categories but also breaks them down again into smaller units of meaning. In this way, the full complexity and diversity of the data can be recognized, and any homogenizing impulse can be counteracted. The ultimate objective of constant comparative analysis is to link and integrate categories in such a way that all instances of variation are captured by the emerging theory.

Negative case analysis

This ensures that the researcher continues to develop the emerging theory in the light of the evidence. Having identified a category, or a linkage between categories, grounded theory researchers need to look for 'negative cases' – that is, instances that do not fit. The identification of such instances allows the researcher to qualify and elaborate the emerging theory, adding depth and density to it, so that it is able to capture the full complexity of the data on which it is based.

Theoretical sensitivity

This is what moves the researcher from a descriptive to an analytic level. In grounded theory, the researcher *interacts* with the data. That is, he or she asks questions of the data, which are in turn modified by the emerging answers. Each emerging category, idea, concept or linkage informs a new look at the data to elaborate or modify the original construct. The researcher engages with the data by asking questions, making comparisons and looking for opposites. This may involve going back to source to collect further data. Data collection and coding are both part of the process of grounded theory analysis.

Theoretical sampling

This involves collecting further data in the light of categories that have emerged from earlier stages of data analysis. Theoretical sampling means checking emerging theory against reality by sampling incidents that may challenge or elaborate its developing claims. While the earlier stages of grounded theory require maximum openness and flexibility to identify a wide range of predominantly descriptive categories, theoretical sampling is concerned with the refinement and, ultimately, *saturation* (see below) of existing, and increasingly analytic, categories.

Theoretical saturation

Ideally, the process of data collection and data analysis in grounded theory continues until theoretical saturation has been achieved. In other words, the researcher continues to sample and code data until no new categories can be identified, and until new instances of variation for exisiting categories have ceased to emerge. At this point, a set of categories and subcategories captures the bulk of the available data. However, theoretical saturation functions as a goal rather than a reality. This is because even though we may (and ought to) strive for saturation of our categories, modification of categories or changes in perspective are always possible. Glaser and Strauss (1967: 40) draw attention to the way in which grounded theory is always provisional:

> When generation of theory is the aim, however, one is constantly alert to emergent perspectives, what will change and help develop his theory. These perspectives can easily occur on the final day of study or when the manuscript is reviewed in page proof: so the published word is not the final one, but only a pause in the never-ending process of generating theory.
>
> (cited in Dey 1999: 117)

Memo-writing

This is an important part of the grounded theory method. Throughout the process of data collection and analysis, the researcher maintains a written record of theory development. This means writing definitions of categories and justifying labels chosen for them, tracing their emergent relationships with one another, and keeping a record of the progressive integration of higher- and lower-level categories. Memos will also show up changes of direction in the analytic process and emerging perspectives, as well as provide reflections on the adequacy of the *research question* (see below). As a result, memos provide information about the research process itself as well as about the substantive findings of the study. Memos can be long or short, abstract or concrete, integrative (of earlier memos or ideas) or original, use words or diagrams (e.g. flowcharts). All memos, however, should be dated, contain a heading and state which sections of the data they were inspired by.

Research process

Grounded theory is unlike most other research methods in that it merges the processes of data collection and analysis. The researcher moves back and forth between the two in an attempt to 'ground' the analysis in the data. The aim of this movement is *theoretical saturation* (see above). As a result, grounded theory does not provide the researcher with a series of steps, which, if followed correctly, will take him or her from the formulation of the research question through data collection to analysis and, finally, to the production of a research report. Instead, grounded theory encourages the researcher to continuously review earlier stages of the research and, if necessary, to change direction. Even the research question is no permanent fixture in grounded theory. Simply serving to identify the phenomenon we wish to study at the outset, the research question becomes progressively focused throughout the research process. Alternatively, it can change altogether in the light of emerging categories (see Morse's study of nurse–patient interaction below). Having drawn attention to the integrated and cyclical nature of the grounded theory method, I shall nevertheless attempt to provide an outline of what is involved in a typical grounded theory study. This outline is not meant to serve as a blueprint; however, without any such guidelines, it may be difficult to get started on grounded theory research.

The research question
Grounded theory researchers need an initial research question to focus their attention upon the particular phenomenon they wish to investigate (see Strauss and Corbin 1990: 37–40). The initial research question should serve to identify, but not make assumptions about, the phenomenon of interest. This is difficult, if not impossible, to achieve. The process of labelling itself imports assumptions about a phenomenon (see Chapters 6 and 7 for an in-depth discussion of this process); for example, if we ask 'How do women manage a pregnancy complicted by chronic illness?' (see Strauss and Corbin 1990: 38), we assume that women 'manage' their pregnancies (as opposed to being 'subjected' to them, for example) and that chronic illness constitutes a 'complication' in relation to pregnancy. We cannot ask questions without making assumptions. However, we can attempt to remain at a descriptive level and use our question simply to identify the phenomenon (e.g. 'How do women with chronic illness experience pregnancy?') rather than to offer an explanatory account that requires testing against reality (e.g. 'To what extent does social support improve the ability of women with chronic illness to cope with a pregnancy?').

The initial research question in grounded theory should be open-ended and should not be compatible with simple 'yes/no' answers. It should identify the phenomenon of interest without making (too many) assumptions about it. It should never employ constructs derived from existing theories. It is also recommended that the question orientates the researcher towards action and process (e.g. '*How* do people do *x*?') rather than states and conditions (e.g. '*What* do people want?' or '*Why* do people do *x*?') (see Strauss and Corbin 1990: 38). As the research progresses, the researcher is able to focus the research question more narrowly. This process is facilitated by *theoretical sampling* and *theoretical sensitivity* (see above). By the time *theoretical saturation* has been achieved, the initial research question can have changed almost beyond recognition.

Data collection
Grounded theory is compatible with a wide range of data collection techniques. Semi-structured interviewing, participant observation, focus groups, even diaries can generate data for grounded theory. In addition, existing texts and documents can also

be subjected to grounded theory analysis. However, it is important to differentiate between the full implementation of the method, which requires the researcher to move back and forth between data collection and analysis, and an abbreviated version that involves the coding of data only.

In the *full version*, the researcher collects some data, explores the data through initial open coding, establishes tentative linkages between categories, and then returns to the field to collect further data. Data collection is progressively focused and informed by the emerging theory (see 'Theoretical sampling' above). In this version, the researcher is able to *triangulate*; that is, he or she can draw on different data sources and use different methods of data collection. For example, in a study of eating habits, initial coding of a transcript of a group discussion among office workers may lead to the identification of the category 'context' with the subcategories 'work' and 'leisure'. This may lead the researcher to carry out a semi-structured interview with a professional cook to further explore the relevance of context to the experience of eating. The full version of grounded theory allows the researcher to push outwards, to seek out manifestations of categories, negative cases and opposites, until category development is dense, detailed and differentiated. This gives the researcher confidence that theoretical saturation is being approached.

The *abbreviated version* of grounded theory, by contrast, works with the original data only. Here, interview transcripts or other documents are analysed following the principles of grounded theory (i.e. the processes of *coding* and *constant comparative analysis*); however, *theoretical sensitivity, theoretical saturation* and *negative case analysis* can only be implemented *within* the texts that are being analysed. The researcher does not have the opportunity to leave the confines of the original data set to broaden and refine the analysis. Consequently, the abbreviated version of grounded theory should never be our first choice; it should only be used where time or resource constraints prevent the implementation of the full version of grounded theory (see also Henwood and Pidgeon 1995, and Pidgeon and Henwood 2004, for a discussion of smaller-scale grounded theory studies).

Data analysis
Coding constitutes the most basic as well as the most fundamental process in grounded theory. Coding can be carried out line-by-line, sentence-by-sentence, paragraph-by-paragraph, page-by-page, section-by-section, and so on. The smaller the unit of analysis (e.g. one line of text), the more numerous the descriptive categories that emerge initially. Later stages of analysis will integrate a lot of these into higher-level analytic categories. Line-by-line analysis ensures that our analysis is truly grounded and that higher-level categories, and later on theoretical formulations, actually emerge from the data, rather than being imposed upon it. If we code larger chunks of text, such as a whole page, our attention may be captured by one particularly striking occurrence. As a result, less obvious but perhaps equally important instances of categories, whose true significance has yet to emerge, can be missed. If there is sufficient time available, line-by-line coding should always be carried out. This is particularly important when the *abbreviated version* of grounded theory is used; here, the depth of analysis generated by line-by-line coding is needed to compensate for the loss of breadth that accompanies the researcher's dependence on the original data set.

There are differences in the ways in which grounded theory researchers approach the coding process. For most grounded theorists, initial open coding involves the generation of largely descriptive labels for occurrences or phenomena. Such labels give rise to low-level categories. To establish linkages between such categories and to integrate them into higher-order analytic categories, we can use a *coding paradigm*. A coding paradigm sensitizes the researcher to particular ways in which categories may be linked with one another. It helps us to arrange our categories in a meaningful and hierarchical way, with some categories constituting the 'core' and others the 'periphery'. It is here that grounded theory researchers disagree with one another. Some (e.g. Strauss 1987; Strauss and Corbin 1990) propose the use of a coding paradigm that explicitly focuses upon, and thus alerts the researcher to, manifestations of 'process' and 'change' in the data. This is done by asking certain questions of the data. These include questions about the context within which a category is embedded, the interactional strategies used by participants to manage the category, and the consequences of such interactional strategies. Strauss and Corbin (1990) refer to this process as 'axial coding'. Others (e.g. Glaser 1978, 1992) caution against the use of a coding paradigm that presupposes the relevance of particular constructs (such as 'process' or 'change') to the data. Instead, they argue that any kind of coding paradigm should only be used when it is indicated by the data. Glaser (1978) identifies a wide range of *theoretical codes* that could potentially come into play when low-level categories are integrated. However, according to this view, the data themselves are the best source of relevant theoretical codes.

The research report

Qualitative research can be written up in a variety of ways; qualitative researchers are much less constrained by convention than quantitative researchers when it comes to the presentation of their work. A qualitative research report should contain information about the rationale of the study (including references to relevant literature), about how it was carried out (including both data collection and analysis), what was found and what these findings may mean (including their implications for theory and practice). As long as the report contains this information, it does not matter precisely how, and in what format, it is presented. The author of a qualitative research report should strive for clarity first and foremost. For those who are new to qualitative research, however, it may feel safer to stick to the conventional research report format. In the remainder of this section, I present some guidelines for writing up grounded theory research using the standard sub-headings of 'Introduction', 'Method', 'Results' and 'Discussion'.

Introduction The introductory chapter (or section) of the report should present a rationale for the study to be reported. Such a rationale can be informed by theoretical or practical concerns. For example, the author may argue that a particular phenomenon has not been explained convincingly in the literature, and that his or her study was designed to fill this gap. Alternatively, the author may identify a recent social phenomenon that has not been investigated. Or there may be a large research literature about the phenomenon but none of the studies reported asked the type of question that the author wants to ask about it. This is often the case when most of the studies reported have used quantitative methods, which meant that certain questions (e.g. about the quality of experience, about the negotiation of meanings) could not be addressed satisfactorily by the research. Since grounded theory research aims to develop new, contextualized theories, a review of existing research has to be undertaken with caution. It is important that the researcher maintains a certain distance from such literature; the grounded theory study reported must not be seen as an extension of, or a test or, an existing theory. Some grounded theorists even recommend that the researcher does not review relevant literature until *after* the research has been completed. However, it could be argued that this is impossible, since most researchers are already working within a discipline (e.g. psychology, nursing studies, social work) and that they are already familiar with the major theories in the field. A systematic review of the literature is unlikely to 'contaminate' their grounded theory study within such a context. It may, however, help them to formulate a useful research question that has not been asked before in quite the same way.

Method   In this section, the researcher describes exactly what they did and why. This means including information about data collection techniques, choice of contexts and participants, and about how data were coded and how categories were integrated. If the researcher chose the *full version* of the grounded theory method, he or she needs to provide an account of how the cyclical process of data collection and analysis progressed throughout the research. If the *abbreviated version* was used, the researcher needs to explain why this was done. The method section should also contain ethical considerations and, where appropriate, a discussion of *reflexivity*.

Results   This is likely to be the longest section of the report. Within the context of a thesis, the results of the study can be presented in a number of consecutive chapters. The presentation of the findings of a grounded theory study are best organized around the key categories identified. If there is a core category at the centre of the phenomenon under investigation and with which all other categories have some kind of relationship, this should be discussed first. If there is no one core category, the major categories should be discussed in sequence. It is also a good idea to include a visual representation of the major categories and their relationships with one another. This can take the form of a flowchart or a table (for helpful illustrations of how categories can be presented diagrammatically, see Morse 1992a).

   The results section of the report can be divided by sub-headings that refer to the major categories identified. Under each heading, the relevant category and its sub-categories are introduced and defined. This is where data can be used to support analytical points made. For example, quotations from participants can illustrate the use of a particular category in a particular context. It is important, however, to use data only to illustrate, but never to substitute for, analysis. Following the introduction and discussion of each category, a further section (or chapter) can be devoted to a detailed examination of the relationships between categories. This is also where emerging theoretical formulations are spelled out and explored. Alternatively, the introduction of categories and a discussion of their relationships with one another can be merged; however, this is a more challenging way to write up grounded theory clearly and systematically.

Discussion   Here, the author addresses the theoretical and practical implications of the study. What has the study contributed to our understanding of the phenomenon under investigation? What may be the practical applications of our findings? We may also want to reflect upon the focus of our study. Was our initial research question the right question to ask? Why may we have got it wrong? What does this tell us about our assumptions about the phenomenon? At this point, we can raise further issues in relation to both *personal* and *epistemological reflexivity* (see p. 10). This section is also the place where we discuss our findings in relation to the existing literature. To what extent does our research challenge or support existing theories? What can our work contribute to theoretical developments in the field? What kind of research ought to be done in the future to build upon our study? And how may our participants benefit from the research to which they have contributed?

References and appendices   All research reports should include a list of references, including all authors referred to in the report. There may also be appendices containing additional data supporting the analysis presented in the report. These should be clearly labelled and identified at relevant points in the report itself. However, there should be nothing in the appendices that is essential to the reader's comprehension of the report. Authors cannot assume that appendices will necessarily be read.

An example of grounded theory
'Negotiating commitment and involvement in the nurse–patient relationship' by Janice Morse (1992b)

Morse's initial research question was 'What is the role of gift-giving in the patient–nurse relationship?' Morse had noticed that patients frequently offered nurses gifts in response to the care that they had received. She was interested in exploring the role gift-giving played in the development of the relationship between patient and nurse. Morse and her research assistants conducted semi-structured interviews with nurses. During the initial stages of data analysis, it became clear that gift-giving was a way of negotiating a certain type of relationship. It played a symbolic role that could potentially be played by other actions. This led Morse to broaden the focus of the study and to ask 'How does the nurse–patient/patient–nurse relationship develop?' Theoretical sampling allowed Morse and her research assistants to obtain data that shed light on the development of nurse–patient relationships in more general terms. They conducted further interviews, this time with nurses who had themselves been patients. All interviews were transcribed and coded.

Morse used a version of Strauss and Corbin's *coding paradigm*, which meant that she explored the categories she had identified in terms of 'process' (i.e. experiences of nurses and patients over the course of the relationship) and 'change' (i.e. factors and circumstances that impact upon the nurse–patient interaction). 'Negotiating the relationship' emerged as the core category. Other categories included 'types of relationship', which were subdivided into 'mutual' and 'unilateral'. 'Mutual relationships' were characterized by mutual interest and investment in the relationship between nurse and patient, whereas 'unilateral relationships' involved a degree of mismatch between the participants' willingness to develop the relationship. 'Mutual relationships' in turn contained four subcategories: 'clinical', 'therapeutic', 'con-nected' and 'over-involved'. Morse identified six dimensions according to which the four types of 'mutual relationships' could be differentiated. These included time spent together (e.g. long-term vs. transitory), the purpose of the interaction (e.g. perfunc-tory *vs* supportive), the patient's needs (e.g. minor vs. extensive), the patient's trust (e.g. basic vs. complete), the patient's role (e.g. patient vs. person) and nursing com-mitment (e.g. professional vs. personal). Morse presents the types of relationship and their six dimensions in table format.

Morse's study develops an 'explanatory model for describing the various types of relationship that occur' between nurses and their patients (Morse 1992b: 334). Gift-giving, which had originally been the focus (and the inspiration) of the study, ended up being just one among a number of strategies used by patients for increasing involvement in the nurse–patient relationship. It was part of the process of negotiating a mutual relationship that had moved beyond its clinical remit and into a realm of connectedness between nurse and patient. Grounded theory as a method was able to accommodate a shift in the focus of the study. It allowed Morse to identify different types of nurse–patient relationship, their characteristics, and the strategies participants use to negotiate these relationships.

Versions of grounded theory

There are three major issues around which debates have evolved in grounded theory research. They concern the role of induction in grounded theory, discovery versus construction, and objectivist versus subjectivist perspectives. When *The Discovery of Grounded Theory* was published in 1967 (Glaser and Strauss), it introduced qualita-tive researchers in the social sciences to a new methodology. Once researchers adopted it for their own purposes and grounded theory studies began to be published, it became clear that the new methodology could be interpreted and applied in a number of different ways. As time went by, even the creators of grounded theory, Barney Glaser and Anselm Strauss, began to disagree about the nature of the method and how it ought to be practised (see Box 1). As a result, a number of versions of the grounded theory method have emerged. Although all of these are still referred to as 'grounded theory', some (e.g. Glaser 1992) have suggested that this label should be reserved for the original formulation by Glaser and Strauss (1967) and that more recent versions and developments ought to find new, and more appropriate, names for themselves. However, others (e.g. Dey 1999: 44) argue that 'later difficulties and disagreements over grounded theory can be traced to ambiguities in the original presentation'. This suggests that there is, in fact, no *one* original and unambiguous version of the methodology that alone is entitled to the label 'grounded theory'.

In the remainder of this section, I aim to identify the major debates in grounded theory research and to differentiate between the various versions of the grounded theory method that have emerged around them.

The role of induction in grounded theory

The grounded theory method was developed to allow new, contextualized theories to emerge directly from data. It was a reaction against the pervasiveness of hypothesis-testing and the application of existing theories to new data. Grounded theory was designed to minimize the imposition of the researcher's own categories of meaning upon the data during the research process. However, with the production of detailed, step-by-step guides to the method (e.g. Strauss and Corbin 1990, 1998), grounded theory was becoming more prescriptive. The inclusion of a specific coding paradigm, for instance, ensures that the researcher will be looking for the manifestation of particular patterns in the data. This adds a deductive element to grounded theory; instead of taking the data themselves as our starting point to determine which categories may emerge, a coding paradigm identifies a set of dimensions of interest and explores the data in the light of these. Here, through the use of the coding paradigm, the researcher is sensitized to those aspects of the data that are considered to be essential to our understanding of social phenomena. For example, Strauss and Corbin's (1990) axial coding paradigm is designed to sensitize the researcher to the role of 'process': 'unless the analyst is made keenly aware of the need to identify process, to build it into the analysis, it is often omitted or done in a very narrow or limited fashion' (p. 143). Similarly, Strauss and Corbin recommend the use of a 'conditional matrix' to introduce higher-level constructs such as class, gender, race and power into the analysis.

Those who subscribe to the earlier, less prescriptive version of grounded theory are concerned that such a deductive element undermines the original purpose of grounded theory (i.e. the *emergence* of theory from data) by imposing researcher-defined categories, or 'pet codes' (Glaser 1992). As Melia (1996: 376) puts it: 'I always have a nagging doubt that the procedures are getting in the way; the technical tail is beginning to wag the theoretical dog'. These researchers argue that, to maintain its creative potential, grounded theory must retain the openness of its original formulation. According to this view, the grounded theory method needs to be flexible enough to respond to the data. Highly prescriptive procedures and coding frames encourage analytic rigidity and are not compatible with such flexibility.

Discovery versus construction

In 1967, Glaser and Strauss described grounded theory as involving 'the discovery of theory from data' (p. 1). The use of the term 'discovery' suggests that the researcher uncovers something that is already there. Similarly, the concept of 'emergence' (of categories, of theory) also plays down the creative role of the researcher in the research process. Here, the researcher is like a midwife, who delivers the fully formed baby. It has been argued, however, that such a view of the research process in grounded theory is heavily influenced by a positivist epistemology and not compatible with 'big Q' qualitative methodology (see Chapter 1). This is because the suggestion that categories and theories can simply 'emerge' from data, and that it is possible for a researcher to avoid the imposition of categories of meaning onto the data, reflects the belief that phenomena create their own representations that are directly perceived by observers. Charmaz (1990, 2000, 2002, 2006) introduced a *social constructionist* version of grounded theory that argues that categories and theories do not *emerge* from the data, but are *constructed* by the researcher through an interaction with the data. According to this version, 'The researcher creates an explication, organisation and presentation *of* the data rather than discovering order *within* the data. The discovery process consists of discovering the ideas the *researcher* has about the data after interacting with it' (Charmaz 1990: 1169, emphasis in original).

Here, it is acknowledged that the researcher's decisions, the questions that he or she is asking of the data, the way he or she is using the method, as well as his or her (personal, philosophical, theoretical, methodological) background shape the research process and, ultimately, the findings. As a result, the theory produced constitutes one particular reading of the data rather than the only truth about the data. Pidgeon and Henwood (1997) substitute the term *theory generation* for *discovery* to capture the constructive element in the process of theory development. See also Clarke (2003, 2005, 2006) for more on constructionism in grounded theory.

Mapping social processes versus studying individual experience

Originally, grounded theory was developed to allow researchers in the social sciences to study, and theorize, localized social processes, such as chronic illness management, the socialization of nurses or the dying trajectory, within particular settings (e.g. the hospital, the family). The aim of the emerging theories was to clarify and explain such social processes and their consequences. These processes could be social psychological or social structural in nature. In order to identify and explicate relevant processes and their consequences, researchers engaged in the full cyclical interpretative inquiry (i.e. the *full version*). More recently, researchers have used grounded theory as a method of data analysis only (i.e. the *abbreviated version*). Here, interview transcripts have been subjected to grounded theory-inspired coding in order to produce a systematic representation of the participant's experience and understanding of the phenomenon under investigation (e.g. chronic pain, relationship break-ups, undergoing gender reassignment) through the identification of categories of meaning and experience.

This use of grounded theory shares some features with phenomenological research (see Chapter 4). Thus, while a focus on social processes takes a more contextualized and dynamic approach, whereby the researcher attempts to identify and map social processes and relationships and their consequences for participants, a focus on participants' experiences is more psychological in that the researcher is concerned with the texture and quality of the participant's perspective rather than its social context, causes or consequences. The former approach takes a view 'from the outside in', whereas the latter proceeds 'from the inside out' (see Charmaz 1995: 30–31). It is, of course, possible to combine the two perspectives and to attempt to capture the lived experience of participants *and* to explain its quality in terms of wider social processes and their consequences. It could be argued that this would indeed be required in order to gain a full understanding of social psychological phenomena.

Limitations of grounded theory as a method for psychological research

As is the case with all research methods, grounded theory does have a number of limitations. The most widely raised criticism of the grounded theory method concerns its epistemological roots. It has been argued that grounded theory subscribes to a positivist epistemology and that it sidesteps questions of reflexivity. For researchers in psychology, another shortcoming of grounded theory is its preoccupation with uncovering social processes, which limits its applicability to more phenomenological research questions. These two limitations will be discussed in turn.

The problem of induction or 'what grounds grounded theory?'

The original purpose of grounded theory was to allow new theories to *emerge* from data. In other words, grounded theory works with *induction,* whereby observations give rise to new ideas. This was meant to liberate the researcher from the straitjacket of *hypothetico-deductive* research. One of the problems associated with induction is that it pays insufficient attention to the role of the researcher. It is assumed that the data speaks for itself. However, as critics of *positivism* have argued convincingly, all observations are made from a particular perspective, that is, they are standpoint-specific. Whatever emerges from a field through observation depends on the observer's position within it. In the same way, whatever emerges from the analysis of a set of data is theoretically informed because all analysis is necessarily guided by the questions asked by the researcher. As Dey (1999: 104) puts it, 'Even if we accept the (doubtful) proposition that categories are discovered, what we discover will depend in some degree on what we are looking for – just as Columbus could hardly have "discovered" America if he had not been looking for the "Indies" in the first place.' Thus, grounded theory has been criticized for not addressing questions of *reflexivity* satisfactorily.

Stanley and Wise (1983: 152) have argued that as long as it does not address the question of 'What grounds grounded theory?', the grounded theory method remains a form of inductivist positivism. *Social constructionist* versions of grounded theory (e.g. Charmaz 1990, 2006) address these concerns and attempt to develop reflexive grounded theory. Here, it is recognized that categories can never 'capture the essence' of a concept in its entirety (see Dey 1999: 66) and that categories do not simply emerge from the data because they do not exist before the process of categorization; rather, they are constructed by the researcher during the research process.

Pidgeon and Henwood (1997) recommend that grounded theory researchers document, carefully and in detail, each phase of the research process. Such documentation increases reflexivity throughout the research process and it demonstrates the ways in which the researcher's assumptions, values, sampling decisions, analytic technique, interpretations of context, and so on have shaped the research. However, social constructionist versions of grounded theory are a recent development. While they acknowledge the epistemological limitations of a purely inductivist version, it is not yet clear whether a social constructionist approach to grounded theory requires more than a recognition of the active role of the researcher in the research process. It could be argued that a social constructionist perspective would have to theorize the role of language in the construction of categories, which in turn would mean engaging with the notion of 'discourse' (see Chapters 6 and 7). Such an engagement, however, may transform the method to such an extent that it ceases to be (a version of) grounded theory. We will have to wait and see.

Suitability for psychological research

Originally, grounded theory was designed to study social processes 'from the bottom up'. That is, the method allowed researchers to trace how actions had consequences and how patterns of social interaction combined to give rise to particular, identifiable social processes. The theories generated by grounded theory research helped to explicate basic social processes (see Dey 1999: 63). It is clear that grounded theory was designed with sociological research questions in mind. Indeed, Glaser and Strauss were themselves sociologists, and much of their own grounded theory research was concerned with medical sociology.

In recent years, grounded theory has been adopted as a qualitative research method for psychological research and it now features as a key method in psychology methods textbooks (e.g. Smith et al. 1995; Hayes 1997; Murray and Chamberlain 1999). However, its suitability as a qualitative research method for psychological research may be questioned. It could be argued that, when applied to questions about the nature of experience, as opposed to the unfolding of social processes, the grounded theory method is reduced to a technique for systematic categorization. That is, studies concerned with capturing the meanings that a particular experience holds for an individual tend to use one-off interviews with participants, transcribe them and code the transcript using the principles of the grounded theory method. The result is a systematic map of concepts and categories used by the respondents to make sense of their experience. While such a map may provide us with a better understanding of the structure of our participants' experiences, it does not, in fact, constitute a *theory*. In other words, such mapping of experiences is a *descriptive* rather than an *explanatory* exercise and, as such, is not geared towards the development of theory. It could be argued that research questions about the nature of experience are more suitably addressed using phenomenological research methods (see Chapter 4). Grounded theory techniques (preferably the *full version*) could then be reserved for the study of social psychological processes. See also Charmaz and Henwood (2008: 251–4) for a critical discussion of descriptive versions of grounded theory methodology.

Three epistemological questions

To conclude this chapter on grounded theory, let us take a look at what kind of knowledge this methodology aims to produce, the assumptions it makes about the world it studies, and the way in which it conceptualizes the role of the researcher in the process of knowledge production. I address these three questions in turn.

1 *What kind of knowledge does the grounded theory method aim to produce?*
Grounded theory was designed to identify and explicate contextualized social processes. Its techniques for data-gathering and analysis are designed to allow concepts

and categories to *emerge* from the data. The researcher is encouraged to approach the data without preconceptions or pet theories. Imposition of meanings onto the data is to be avoided at all cost. The aim of grounded theory analysis is to produce theories that are truly *grounded* in the data; that is, theories that do not depend on external concepts that are brought to the data by the researcher. As Glaser (1999: 840) puts it, '[G]rounded theory *is what is*, not what should, could or ought to be' (emphasis in original). Grounded theory, therefore, has a realist orientation. The kind of know-ledge grounded theory aims to produce is knowledge of processes that reside in the data and which can emerge from the data (with a little help from the researcher). Categorization and theorizing are simply ways in which these processes are system-atically presented to a readership by the researcher. The processes identified by the researcher, however, are assumed to take place irrespective of whether or not they are documented by the researcher. In other words, potential knowledge is 'out there' and can be captured by the researcher. In this sense, grounded theory takes a positivist approach to knowledge production. However, as we have seen, grounded theory's positivist tendencies have been challenged by those who are attempting to develop a social constructionist version of the method.

2 *What kinds of assumptions does grounded theory make about the world?*
Grounded theorists are interested in the ways in which human actors negotiate and manage social situations, and how their actions contribute to the unfolding of social processes. Grounded theory assumes that social events and processes have an objective reality in the sense that they take place irrespective of the researcher and that they can be observed and documented by the researcher. This suggests a realist ontology. However, grounded theory also assumes that social realities are negotiated by human actors and that participants' interpretations of events shape their consequences. Here, grounded theory subscribes to a symbolic interactionist perspective. This means that 'the world' that is studied by grounded theorists is very much a product of human participation and negotiation. It is a changing world, which means that the methods used for studying it must be sensitive to its dynamic properties. This is what grounded theory attempts to do by focusing on 'process' and 'change'.

3 *How does grounded theory conceptualize the role of the researcher in the research process?*
In grounded theory, the researcher acts as a witness. He or she observes carefully what is going on, takes detailed notes of proceedings, questions participants in order to better understand what they are doing and why. The researcher takes care not to import his or her own assumptions and expectations into the analysis; the aim is to develop theories that do not move beyond the data. The researcher's role is to use his or her skills to represent, in a systematic and accessible fashion, a clear picture of what is going on in the slice of social reality they have chosen to study. Here, it is the researcher's skills, his or her ability to collect and analyse the data, which is seen to determine the outcome of the research. The researcher's identity and standpoint must remain secondary. Social constructionist versions of grounded theory take a different view of the role of the researcher in the research process. Here, the researcher is more than a witness; he or she actively constructs a particular understanding of the phe-nomenon under investigation. From a social constructionist perspective, grounded

theory does not capture social reality; instead, it is itself a social construction of reality (see Charmaz 1990: 1165).

This chapter has introduced the basic principles of the grounded theory method. Charmaz and Henwood (2008: 241) sum up the defining features of the process of grounded theory as follows:

> We gather data, compare them, remain open to all possible theoretical understandings of the data, and develop tentative interpretations about these data through our codes and nascent categories. Then we go back to the field and gather more data to check and refine our categories.

Despite (or perhaps because of) the apparent simplicity of the logic underpinning grounded theory, over the years a number of different versions of grounded theory have emerged. Depending on our research question, our time constraints and resources, we can choose between the *full* and the *abbreviated* versions of grounded theory. We can use grounded theory to *theorize contextualized social processes* or to *map individuals' categories of experience*. Finally, we can take an *empiricist* or a *social constructionist* approach to grounded theory research. Whichever version we choose to use, it is important that we communicate clearly to our readership the approach we have adopted and why. Grounded theory continues to evolve and it is likely that further varieties of the grounded theory method will emerge. Some of these may be more suitable for psychological research than others. I want to close this chapter by letting Pidgeon and Henwood (1997: 255) remind us that grounded theory, in whatever guise, provides us with a set of procedures, which 'are ways of putting into practice the requirement to actively engage in close and detailed analysis of your research materials, so that they can both stimulate and discipline the theoretical imagination'.

Interactive exercises

1 Work with a newspaper article about an event or situation (e.g. a report of a public disturbance or a criminal act). To begin with, read the article and write a brief summary of what you believe the article has told you. Then follow the guidelines provided in this chapter to code the article, line-by-line. Integrate low-level (descriptive) categories into higher-level (analytical) categories. Having completed the exercise, compare your initial summary of the article with the results of your coding exercise. What does the coding tell us that a simple reading of the article does not? What is its 'added value'?

2 Formulate a research question suitable for grounded theory using the guidelines provided in this chapter. Make sure that the question can be addressed by conducting research within your own environment and that it is not ethically sensitive (e.g. How do psychology students choose topics for final year research projects?). Construct a brief interview agenda that will help you to begin investigating your research question and conduct a semi-structured interview with a friend or colleague. Transcribe and code the interview. On the basis of your initial findings, where would

you have to go next in order to persue your research question? Identify potential data sources and directions of inquiry.

Further reading

Charmaz, C. (2006) *Constructing Grounded Theory: A Practical Guide Through Qualitative Analysis*. London: Sage.

Dey, I. (1999) *Grounding Grounded Theory: Guidelines for Qualitative Inquiry*. London: Academic Press.

Dey, I. (2004) Grounded theory, in C. Seale, G. Gobo, J.F. Gubrium and D. Silverman (eds) *Qualitative Research Practice*. London: Sage.

Henwood, K.L. and Pidgeon, N.F. (2006) Grounded theory, in G. Breakwell, S. Hammond, C. Fife-Shaw and J. Smith (eds) *Research Methods in Psychology*, 3rd edn. London: Sage.

Pidgeon, N. and Henwood, K. (1997) Using grounded theory in psychological research, in N. Hayes (ed.) *Doing Qualitative Analysis in Psychology*. Hove: Psychology Press.

Strauss, A.L. and Corbin, J. (1998) *Basics of Qualitative Research: Grounded Theory Procedures and Techniques*, 2nd edn. London: Sage.

Box 1 Grounded theory or full conceptual description? The debate between Glaser and Strauss

Having co-authored *The Discovery of Grounded Theory* (1967), Barney Glaser and Anselm Strauss went on to disagree about the nature of grounded theory. In 1992, Glaser published *Emergence vs Forcing: Basics of Grounded Theory Analysis*. This book was written in response to Strauss and Corbin's (1990) *Basics of Qualitative Research: Grounded Theory Procedures and Techniques*. Glaser felt that Strauss and Corbin's book presented a version of grounded theory that was too prescriptive. He argued that the method outlined in Strauss and Corbin's book was not, in fact, grounded theory at all. Instead, he proposed that what Strauss and Corbin had described was a different method altogether, a method that did not facilitate the emergence of theory from data but rather a method that produced 'full scale conceptual forced description' (Glaser 1992: 61–2). Glaser's unhappiness with Strauss and Corbin's revision of grounded theory is evident. He described Strauss and Corbin's techniques as 'fractured, detailed, cumbersome and over-self-conscious' (Glaser 1992: 60), and he argued that they interfere with, rather than facilitate, the process of discovery. Glaser disagreed with Strauss and Corbin's (1990: 38) definition of the research question as 'a statement which identifies the phenomenon to be studied'. Instead, he proposed that the focus of the research emerges in the early stages of the research itself. Glaser also disagreed with Strauss and Corbin's coding paradigm, particularly axial coding. Glaser argued that Strauss and Corbin's approach to coding introduces preconceptions into the analysis that are incompatible with the spirit of grounded theory. As Glaser (1992: 123) put it, 'If you torture the data enough it will give up! The data is not allowed to speak for itself, as in grounded theory, and to be heard from infrequently it has to scream. Forcing by preconception constantly derails it from relevance'.

Furthermore, while Glaser proposed that verification (of relationships between categories, of emerging theories) is not part of the grounded theory method, Strauss and

Corbin maintain that verificational work is built into the research process itself. Related to this disagreement is Glaser's purely inductive approach to grounded theory, which contrasts with Strauss and Corbin's incorporation of some deductive analysis and their acknowledgement of the role of existing theories in sensitizing grounded theory researchers. It is clear that there are major differences between the two versions of grounded theory advocated by Glaser and by Strauss and Corbin, respectively. But do they constitute entirely different method(ologie)s, which ought to be referred to by different names, as Glaser would have it, or is Strauss and Corbin's version merely a manifestation of the natural evolution of grounded theory, as Strauss and Corbin suggest? Is grounded theory a research method with clearly defined and agreed upon procedures, or is it rather a set of methods based on an 'approach to inquiry with several key strategies for conducting inquiry' (see Charmaz 2006)? To make up your mind, you may wish to follow up the debate in the following publications:

Charmaz, C. (2006) *Constructing Grounded Theory: A Practical Guide Through Qualitative Analysis*. London: Sage.

Dey, I. (1999) *Grounding Grounded Theory: Guidelines for Qualitative Inquiry*. London: Academic Press.

Glaser, B.G. (1992) *Emergence vs Forcing: Basics of Grounded Theory Analysis*. Mill Valley, CA: The Sociology Press.

Melia, K.M. (1996) Rediscovering Glaser, *Qualitative Health Research* (Special Issue: Advances in Grounded Theory), 6(3): 368–78.

Strauss, A.L. and Corbin, J. (1990/1998) *Basics of Qualitative Research: Grounded Theory Procedures and Techniques*. London: Sage.

4

Phenomenological methods

Phenomenology

Transcendental phenomenology, as formulated by Husserl in the early twentieth century, is concerned with the world as it presents itself to us as humans. Its aim was to return to things themselves, as they appear to us as perceivers, and to set aside, or *bracket*, that which we (think) we already know about them. In other words, phenomenology is interested in the world as it is experienced by human beings within particular contexts and at particular times, rather than in abstract statements about the nature of the world in general. Phenomenology is concerned with the *phenomena* that appear in our consciousness as we engage with the world around us.

According to a phenomenological perspective, it makes no sense to think of the world of objects and subjects as separate from our experience of it. This is because all objects and subjects must present themselves to us *as something*, and their manifestation as this or that something constitutes their reality at any one time. The appearance of an object as a perceptual phenomenon varies depending on the perceiver's location and context, angle of perception and, importantly, the perceiver's mental orientation (e.g. desires, wishes, judgements, emotions, aims and purposes). This is referred to as *intentionality*. Intentionality allows objects to appear as phenomena. This means that 'self and world are inseparable components of meaning' (Moustakas 1994: 28). Here, meaning is not something that is added on to perception as an afterthought; instead, perception is always intentional and therefore constitutive of experience itself. This means that, from a phenomenological perspective, it is not at all surprising that different people can, and do, perceive and experience (what appears to be) the 'same' environment in radically different ways. For example, for the health and safety officer the office environment constitutes a potential source of hazards and dangers. For her, the pile of dissertations left on the floor of the office represents a potential source of falls and back injuries, as staff may trip over them or move them in a way that damages their backs. For the lecturer, by contrast, the pile of dissertations constitutes work and it represents a certain number of hours that will be spent reading and marking them. For the students, the dissertations embody their thoughts and feelings and they constitute a manifestation of their knowledge and skills, and, as such, a potential source of success or failure. From a phenomeno- logical point of view, the pile of dissertations in and of itself means nothing; in fact, it does not exist as 'a pile of dissertations' until it has been perceived with intentionality.

The phenomenological method

The phenomenological method of deriving knowledge forms a central part of tran- scendental phenomenology. Husserl suggested that it was possible to transcend pre- suppositions and biases and to experience a state of pre-reflective consciousness, which allows us to describe phenomena as they present themselves to us. Husserl identified a series of steps that would take the philosopher from a fresh perception of familiar phenomena to the extraction of the *essences* that give the phenomena their unique character. Knowledge derived in this way would be free from the common- sense notions, scientific explanations and other interpretations or abstractions that characterize most other forms of understanding. It would be a knowledge of the world as it appears to us in our engagement with it.

The phenomenological method of gaining understanding involves three distinct phases of contemplation: *epoche, phenomenological reduction* and *imaginative variation* (for a detailed account of these, see Moustakas 1994). Epoche requires the suspen- sion of presuppositions and assumptions, judgements and interpretations to allow ourselves to become fully aware of what is actually before us. In phenomenological reduction we describe the phenomenon that presents itself to us in its totality. This includes physical features such as shape, size, colour and texture, as well as experien- tial features such as the thoughts and feelings that appear in our consciousness as we attend to the phenomenon. Through phenomenological reduction, we identify the constitutents of our experience of the phenomenon. In other words, we become aware of what makes the experience what it is. Imaginative variation involves an attempt to access the structural components of the phenomenon. That is, while phenomeno- logical reduction is concerned with 'what' is experienced (i.e. its texture), imaginative variation asks 'how' this experience is made possible (i.e. its structure). The aim of imaginative variation is to identify the conditions associated with the phenomenon and without which it would not be what it is. This could involve time, space or social relationships. Finally, textural and structural descriptions are integrated to arrive at an understanding of the *essence* of the phenomenon.

Phenomenology and psychology

Even though transcendental phenomenology was conceived as a philosophical system of thought, its methodological recommendations have proved to be of interest to researchers in the social sciences in general and in psychology in particular. This is because phenomenology focuses upon the content of consciousness and the individual's experience of the world. As Kvale (1996b: 53) put it:

> Phenomenology is interested in elucidating both that which appears and the manner in which it appears. It studies the subjects' perspectives of their world; attempts to describe in detail the content and structure of the subjects' consciousness, to grasp the qualitative diversity of their experiences and to explicate their essential meanings.

Empirical phenomenological research in psychology was pioneered and applied extensively at Duquesne University in the USA (see Van Kaam 1959; Giorgi 1970, 1994; Giorgi et al. 1975). Topics of phenomenological investigation included 'feeling understood' (Van Kaam 1959), 'learning' (Giorgi 1975, 1985), 'being victimized' (Fischer and Wertz 1979), 'anger' (Stevick 1971) and many other phenomena of human experience. In fact, any human experience can be subjected to phenomenological analysis. This is another reason why this approach appeals to psychological researchers. However, there are differences in focus and emphasis between *transcendental phenomenology* as a philosophy and the use of the phenomenological method in psychology.

Spinelli (1989) pointed out that phenomenological psychology is more concerned with the diversity and variability of human experience than with the identification of essences in Husserl's sense. In addition, few, if any, phenomenological researchers in psychology would claim that it is possible to suspend all presuppositions and biases in one's contemplation of a phenomenon. Rather, the attempt to *bracket* the phenomenon allows the researcher to engage in a critical examination of his or her customary ways of knowing (about) it (see *reflexivity*, p. 10). Following the philosopher Martin Heidegger who was Husserl's student and who developed phenomenological thought in highly influential ways, many researchers embrace a hermeneutic version of phenomenology according to which interpretation, and the awareness (and analysis) of what the researcher brings to the text, constitutes an integral part of phenomenological analysis. Finally, it is important to differentiate between phenomenological contemplation of an object or event as it presents itself to the researcher, and phenomenological analysis of an account of a particular experience as presented by a research participant. The former requires introspective attention to one's own experience, whereas the latter involves an attempt to 'get inside' someone else's experience on the basis of their description of it. In phenomenological psychological research, the research participant's account becomes the phenomenon with which the researcher engages.

In this chapter I introduce the two major approaches to phenomenological research in psychology – the descriptive and the interpretative. Within these broad categories there are a number of different methods for collecting and analysing data (see Langdridge 2007; Giorgi and Giorgi 2008 and Giorgi in press, for more detail on these). This chapter provides a brief characterization of each approach and identifies key differences between them. The remainder of the chapter is dedicated to a more detailed account of one of the interpretative phenomenological methods, interpretative phenomenological analysis. The chapter outlines the methodological procedures associated with interpretative phenomenological analysis and describes an example of a published interpretative phenomenological analysis study. This is followed by a critical appraisal of interpretative phenomenological analysis in particular and of phenomenological methods in general. The chapter closes with a discussion of phenomenological research in relation to the three epistemological questions.

Descriptive phenomenology

Descriptive phenomenology remains firmly within the tradition of transcendental phenomenology by positing that perception can be more or less infused with ideas and judgements. Although descriptive phenomenologists acknowledge that interpretation plays an important role in the ways in which people perceive and experience the world, they believe that it is possible to minimize interpretation and to focus on 'that which lies before one in phenomenological purity' (Husserl 1931: 262). This means that for Husserl, and for descriptive phenomenologists, 'description is primary and that interpretation is a special type of description' (Giorgi and Giorgi 2008: 167). Descriptive phenomenology requires the researcher to adopt a phenomenological attitude in which she or he brackets all past knowledge (both lay or everyday knowledge as well as expert knowledge and theories) about the phenomenon under investigation. The researcher attempts to be truly present to the phenomenon as it manifests itself in a particular instance (e.g. a research participant's account of it). The focus of the research is the phenomenon as it is experienced by the research participant rather than the phenomenon as a material reality. Giorgi and Giorgi (2003a, 2003b) provide detailed guidelines for descriptive phenomenological research. In summary, their version of descriptive phenomenology involves the following steps (see also Giorgi and Giorgi 2008: box 10.1, p. 170):

1 Obtain a concrete description of the phenomenon of interest.

2 Adopt the phenomenological attitude towards the phenomenon.

3 Read the entire description to gain an impression of the whole.

4 Reread the description and identify 'meaning units' that capture different aspects or dimensions of the whole.

5 Identify and make explicit the psychological significance of each meaning unit.

6 Articulate the general structure of the experience of the phenomenon.

There are several versions of descriptive phenomenology all of which share the focus on description although they differ in the extent to which they foreground particular dimensions of experience (e.g. psychological or existential). Some of the most widely cited sources include Colaizzi (1978), Moustakas (1994) and Ashworth (2003). Langdridge (2007, chapter 6) also provides a detailed account of how to conduct descriptive phenomenological research.

Interpretative phenomenology

Interpretative phenomenology also aims to gain a better understanding of the nature and quality of phenomena as they present themselves. However, this version of phenomenology does not separate description and interpretation; instead, it draws on insights from the hermeneutic tradition and argues that all description constitutes a form of interpretation. As Van Manen (1990: 180, cited in Giorgi and Giorgi 2008: 168) puts it:

> (. . .) the (phenomenological) 'facts' of lived experience are always already meaningfully (hermeneutically) experienced. Moreover, even the 'facts' of lived experience need to be captured in language (the human science text) and this is inevitably an interpretive process.

Similarly, understanding cannot take place without us making some preliminary assumptions about the meaning of what we are trying to understand. There is a circularity built into the process of meaning-making that is referred to as the 'hermeneutic circle' (Schleiermacher 1998). This means that '(. . .) parts can only be understood from an understanding of the whole, but that the whole can only be understood from an understanding of the parts' (Schmidt 2006: 4). On the most basic level, this can be demonstrated in relation to understanding a simple sentence. We cannot understand the whole sentence until we have made sense of the parts (i.e. the words) that make up the whole (the sentence). However, at the same time, we cannot make sense of a word's specific meaning until we have understood the sentence as a whole. This means that understanding requires a circular movement from presupposition to interpretation and back again. Our presuppositions are tested in the light of the evolving meaning of what we are trying to understand. Therefore, instead of attempting to bracket presuppositions and assumptions about the world, the interpretative phenomenological researcher works with, and uses, them in an attempt to advance understanding.

As with descriptive phenomenology, there are several versions of this approach including Packer and Addison (1989), Van Manen (1990) and Smith (e.g. Eatough and Smith 2008). Again, Langdridge (2007: chapter 7) provides a detailed account of how to conduct interpretative phenomenological research.

Interpretative phenomenological analysis (IPA)

Interpretative phenomenological analysis is a version of the phenomenological method that accepts the impossibility of gaining direct access to research participants' life worlds. Even though it aims to explore the research participant's experience from his or her perspective, it recognizes that such an exploration must necessarily implicate the researcher's own view of the world as well as the nature of the interaction between researcher and participant. As a result, the phenomenological analysis produced by the researcher is always an *interpretation* of the participant's experience.

Interpretative phenomenological analysis shares the aims of other, more descriptive, phenomenological approaches to data analysis in that it wishes to capture the quality and texture of individual experience. However, it recognizes that such experience is never directly accessible to the researcher. Its founder, Jonathan Smith (1997: 189), characterizes interpretative phenomenological analysis as 'an attempt to unravel the meanings contained in . . . accounts through a process of interpretative engagement with the texts and transcripts'. Such engagement is facilitated by a series of steps that allows the researcher to identify themes and integrate them into meaningful clusters, first within and then across cases.

The systematic nature of its analytic procedure and the provision of detailed descriptions of the analytic process (e.g. Smith 1991, 1999; Flowers et al. 1997, 1998; Jarman et al. 1997; Osborn and Smith 1998; Smith et al. 1999) have meant that interpretative phenomenological analysis has become an increasingly attractive research method for psychologists (for reviews of studies see Reid et al. (2005), and Brocki and Wearden (2006)). In the next section, I introduce the basic methodological procedures associated with interpretative phenomenological analysis. This is followed by an illustration of the method's application to the study of nine women's experiences of chronic pain (Osborn and Smith 1998).

Doing interpretative phenomenological analysis

Interpretative phenomenological analysis works with transcripts of semi-structured interviews. Smith (1995b) provides guidance on how to conduct interviews that will generate data suitable for phenomenological analysis. In general, interviewing for interpretative phenomenological analysis shares the principles and practices associated with semi-structured interviewing as introduced in Chapter 2. Since phenomenological research requires the researcher to enter the life world of the research participant, it is extremely important that the questions posed to the participant are open-ended and non-directive. Their sole purpose is to provide participants with an opportunity to share their personal experience of the phenomenon under investigation with the researcher. Focused and/or specific questions should be used to encourage participants to elaborate rather than to check whether they agree or disagree with particular claims or statements. Even though semi-structured interviews are the most widely used method of data collection in phenomenological research, it is also possible to ask participants to produce accounts of their experiences through alternative means, such as the use of diaries (audio, video or written) or various forms of writing. Whatever type of data collection method is used, interpretative phenomenological analysis works with texts generated by participants. These are analysed one by one. Interpretative phenomenological analysis takes an *idiographic* approach whereby insights produced as a result of intensive and detailed engagement with individual cases (e.g. transcripts, texts) are integrated only in the later stages of the research (see also Chapter 5).

Analysis of an individual case

The first stage of analysis in interpretative phenomenological analysis involves the reading and rereading of the text. At this stage, the researcher produces wide-ranging and unfocused *notes* that reflect the initial thoughts and observations he or she may wish to record in response to the text. These could include associations, questions, summary statements, comments on language use, absences, descriptive labels, and so on. Notes produced at this stage constitute the most open form of annotation and are quite different from 'open coding' as used in grounded theory (see Chapter 3). These notes are simply a way of documenting issues that come up for the researcher upon his or her initial encounter with the text. Smith recommends that these are recorded in the left margin of the text.

The second stage of analysis requires the researcher to identify and label *themes* that characterize each section of the text. These are recorded in the right margin. Theme titles are conceptual and they should capture something about the essential quality of what is represented by the text. Psychological terminology may be used at this stage. For example, themes that emerged from an interview with a chronic pain sufferer included 'loss', 'social comparison' and 'sense of self' (Smith et al. 1999).

The third stage involves an attempt to introduce structure into the analysis. The researcher lists the themes identified in stage two and thinks about them in relation to one another. Some of the themes will form natural clusters of concepts that share meanings or references, whereas others will be characterized by hierarchical relationships with one another. For example, themes such as 'childhood memories', 'going to school' and 'relationship with mother' could form a 'childhood' cluster, while 'attending Spanish classes', 'watching Spanish movies' and 'practising Flamenco' would be subordinate to 'interest in Spain'. Clusters of themes need to be given labels that capture their essence. These could be *in vivo* terms used by the respondents themselves, brief quotations or descriptive labels. For instance, our cluster comprising 'childhood memories', 'going to school' and 'relationship with mother' could be called 'when I was little' (*in vivo*/quote) or 'early years' (descriptive). It is important to ensure that clusterings of themes identified at this stage make sense in relation to the original data. This means that the researcher needs to move back and forth between the list of themes he or she attempts to structure and the text that generated the themes in the first place. The connections between themes identified on paper need to be reflected in the detail of the respondent's account.

The fourth stage of analysis involves the production of a summary table of the structured themes, together with quotations that illustrate each theme. The summary table should only include those themes that capture something about the quality of the participant's experience of the phenomenon under investigation. This means that some of the themes generated during stage two will have to be excluded. These may be themes that are not well-represented within the text or which are marginal to the phenomenon. The researcher's decision about which themes should be retained and which should be abandoned is inevitably influenced by his or her interests and orientation. The summary table needs to include the cluster labels together with their subordinate theme labels, brief quotations and references to where relevant extracts may be found in the interview transcript (i.e. page and line numbers). A summary table could look like this:

Cluster label 1
- theme label   quote/keyword (*in vivo*)   page and line numbers
- theme label   quote/keyword (*in vivo*)   page and line numbers
- theme label   quote/keyword (*in vivo*)   page and line numbers

Cluster label 2
- theme label brief   quote/keyword (*in vivo*)   page and line numbers
- theme label brief   quote/keyword (*in vivo*)   page and line numbers
- theme label brief   quote/keyword (*in vivo*)   page and line numbers
- theme label brief   quote/keyword (*in vivo*)   page and line numbers

Cluster label 3
- theme label brief   quote/keyword (*in vivo*)   page and line numbers
- theme label brief   quote/keyword (*in vivo*)   page and line numbers

The numbers of clusters and themes identified can vary widely and depend entirely on the text being analysed. Some clusters consist of many themes, whereas others are much more narrowly focused. At the same time, there may be very many quotations that support a particular theme, while others are less frequently invoked in the text. The summary table should reflect the meanings that structure the participant's account rather than the researcher's expectations of what constitutes an acceptable number of clusters and themes.

Worked example

To obtain a sense of how to approach a text from an interpretative phenomenological perspective, let us look at a short extract from a young man's diary. The diary was written to document a process of change that he underwent over a period of time. The phenomenon of interest was, therefore, the experience of change and transformation. Here is what he writes:

1 I am on a train, or that's how I feel. Excited, alive, elated and a little
2 out of control; on the edge of control, like riding on a wave. Also
3 hungry, for experiences and impressions and seemingly insatiable.
4 I thought about manic states and how people say they feel like Napoleon –
5 and I thought, no, I don't want to rule the world, I just want to eat it!
6 The other day, I read something interesting about different stages in life.
7 It said that in one's youth, everything is still possible; opportunities arise
8 and can be taken up. Later in life, one learns to accept the place one has
9 arrived at and makes the most of it. That sounds about right to me.

10 I don't want to plan ahead or commit myself to anything in the long term,
11 because I want to be able to respond to new opportunities and challenges
12 which I expect to encounter. For me, there has to be movement all the time;
13 I feel that I am moving forward and changing. I need to feel free to change;
14 not to be pulled along by change but to move with it. Freedom and control
15 together – the freedom to respond to events and influences so as to change
16 in a way which is acceptable to me.

Stage 1: The researcher's initial encounter with the text

Upon initial reading, I was struck by the way in which the author uses powerful metaphoric images to communicate his feelings ('I am on a train', 'riding on a wave', 'hungry', 'Napoleon'). However, while the first part of the diary entry (lines 1–5) employs lively and colourful language, the remainder is written in a calmer style, using more abstract or conceptual terminology (e.g. 'stages in life', 'opportunities and challenges', 'freedom and control'). The author attempts to make sense of his experiences by reference to psychological concepts such as psychopathology ('manic states') and lifespan development ('stages in life'). The closing part of the diary entry grapples with the relationship between freedom and control. The author wants to experience movement and change without losing control. He wants to 'move with change'. This invokes the image of a surfer and echoes the metaphor deployed earlier in the text ('riding on a wave', line 2).

Stage 2: Identification of themes

Following the initial open engagement with the text, the researcher moves on to a more systematic reading. The aim is to capture what is represented in the text through thematic labels. Working through the text line-by-line, I was able to identify the following themes:

1 Strong feelings (of arousal, of hunger, of excitement, of movement) [lines 1–3].
2 Psychopathology ('manic states') [line 4].
3 Hunger (for stimulation, experiences, impressions, for the world) [lines 3–5].
4 Life stages ('youth' vs. 'later in life') [lines 6–9].
5 Need for movement and change ('For me, there has to be movement all the time') [lines 12–13].
6 Need for freedom ('I don't want to plan ahead or commit myself', 'I need to feel free to change') [lines 10–12 and line 13].
7 Control/agency ('a little out of control; on the edge of control', 'Freedom and control together . . .') [line 2 and lines 14–16].

Stage 3: Clustering of themes

Some of the themes identified in stage two of the analysis share reference points and some of them constitute different manifestations of a particular condition or state. For example, themes 2 and 4 invoke psychological concepts, while themes 5 and 6 refer to a variety of needs. An examination of the seven themes in relation to one another allowed me to construct three clusters of themes. These capture the main categories of meaning that the author is using in his account of change and transformation. They are as follows:

- Cluster 1: Psychological states (themes 1, 2 and 4).
- Cluster 2: Needs (themes 3, 5 and 6).
- Cluster 3: Control (theme 7).

Stage 4: Production of a summary table

Finally, to obtain a clear and systematic overview of the themes that constitute clusters, together with keywords and the locations of relevant quotations, the researcher produces a summary table. The summary table for my analysis of the young man's diary entry about transformation and change looks like this:

Cluster 1: Psychological states
- Psychopathology   'manic states'   line 4
- Life stages   'youth' vs. 'later in life'   lines 6–9
- Strong feelings   'excited, alive, elated . . . hungry'   lines 1–3

Cluster 2: Needs
- Hunger   'insatiable'   lines 3–5
- Movement   'there has to be movement'   lines 12–13
- Freedom   'I need to feel free to change'   lines 10–13

Cluster 3: Control
- Loss of control   'out of control; on the edge of control'   line 2
- Freedom and control   'freedom and control together'   lines 14–16

Integration of cases

There are two ways in which the researcher may approach integration. Having produced summary tables for each individual participant, the researcher may attempt to integrate these into an inclusive list of master themes that reflects the experiences of the group of participants as a whole. Data collection for interpretative phenomenological analysis is usually based on *purposive sampling*, whereby participants are selected according to criteria of relevance to the research question. This means that the group of participants is *homogeneous* to the extent that they share the experience of a particular condition, event or situation (e.g. suffering from chronic pain, becoming a mother, having been victimized), which they are asked to describe to the researcher. It therefore makes sense to look across the entire corpus of data (i.e. all cases) to obtain a more generalized understanding of the phenomenon. As in stage three above, it is important that the process of integration is carried out in a cyclical manner, whereby any emerging higher-order themes are checked against the transcripts. Integrative themes need to be grounded in the data just as much as lower-level conceptual themes are.

An alternative strategy for the integration of cases involves the use of the summary table for the first participant in the analysis of subsequent cases. Here, the original list of themes is used to code the other interviews, adding or elaborating themes in the process. Again, a cyclical movement is required so that themes that emerge in later transcripts can be checked against earlier transcripts. This allows the researcher to see whether newly emerging themes are merely new manifestations of old themes or whether they do, in fact, introduce genuinely new meanings or concepts. As a result of this process, a progressively integrated list of themes develops over time until, with the analysis of the final transcript, it reaches completion.

Irrespective of the approach used, integration should generate a list of master themes that captures the quality of the participants' shared experience of the phenomenon under investigation, and which, therefore, also tells us something about the *essence* of the phenomenon itself. The list of master themes should include the labels of superordinate themes and their constitutent themes, together with identifiers that indicate which of the participants invoked them and where they did so (page and line numbers). A list of master themes could look like this:

Master theme 1

	Participant 1	Participant 2	Participant 3
• Constituent theme	page/line nos	page/line nos	page/line nos
• Constituent theme	page/line nos	page/line nos	page/line nos
• Constituent theme	page/line nos	page/line nos	page/line nos
• Constituent theme	page/line nos	page/line nos	page/line nos

Master theme 2

	Participant 1	Participant 2	Participant 3
• Constituent theme	page/line nos	page/line nos	page/line nos
• Constituent theme	page/line nos	page/line nos	page/line nos
• Constituent theme	page/line nos	page/line nos	page/line nos
• Constituent theme	page/line nos	page/line nos	page/line nos
• Constituent theme	page/line nos	page/line nos	page/line nos
• Constituent theme	page/line nos	page/line nos	page/line nos

Master theme 3

	Participant 1	Participant 2	Participant 3
• Constituent theme	page/line nos	page/line nos	page/line nos
• Constituent theme	page/line nos	page/line nos	page/line nos
• Constituent theme	page/line nos	page/line nos	page/line nos
• Constituent theme	page/line nos	pageyline nos	page/line nos

Again, the numbers of master themes and constitutent themes identified in any one study vary and should reflect the data from which they are derived. The researcher cannot know beforehand how many master themes will be identified through the analysis. However, it is important to ensure that analysis continues until the point at which full integration of themes has been achieved. In other words, interpretative phenomenological analysis is not complete until that which is shared between participants has been identified and captured in superordinate themes (master themes). This means that, even though we do not know exactly how many themes we will generate, we must not stop until all subordinate themes have either been integrated into or dropped from the analysis.

Interpretation

Much research using interpretative phenomenological analysis stops with the construction of the table of master themes. However, more recently researchers have begun to move beyond this and have completed their analysis with a more explicit interpretation of the themes identified in the research. This may involve drawing upon existing theoretical constructs and formulations (see Larkin et al. 2006). Eatough and Smith (2008) advocate the adoption of two distinct levels of interpretation (see also Smith 2004). The first one, a more descriptive, empathic level, aims to allow the researcher to enter the participant's world, whereas the second critically interrogates the participant's account in order to gain further insight into its nature, meaning and origin. The second level of interpretation, therefore, takes the researcher beyond the participant's own words and understanding(s). Clearly, this second level is more tentative and speculative than the first, and should not be held too rigidly. While higher levels of interpretation enrich the research by generating new insights and understanding, they also give rise to ethical issues around the imposition of meaning and giving/denying voice to research participants (see also Willig and Stainton Rogers (2008): chapter 1).

Writing up

Following an introduction to the substantive area of research and the specific research question (Introduction), the report needs to provide an account of the methodological rationale and process associated with interpretative phenomenological analysis (Method). This is followed by a presentation of the themes identified in the analysis together with illustrative quotations from participants (Analysis/Results). The Analysis/Results section of the report may be structured around master themes. Each theme is introduced and its various manifestations are discussed. Quotations from participants are included to illustrate the ways in which themes are mobilized. Relationships between themes should also be addressed. The presentation of the results can be supported by the inclusion of a table of themes or a diagram showing the relationships between themes. Either way, the presentation of results should be organized around the themes that emerged from the analysis. The aim of this section is to provide a convincing account of the nature and quality of the participants' experience of the phenomenon under investigation. It is important to be clear about the distinction between participants' comments and the researcher's interpretation of those comments. *Reflexivity* issues should be addressed within this context. Finally, the Discussion section of an interpretative phenomenological analysis report considers the themes identified in the analysis in relation to the existing literature in the field. Implications for future research and theoretical developments are addressed. Phenomenological research can also inform recommendations for improved practice, particularly in the areas of health and counselling psychology.

An example of interpretative phenomenological analysis
The personal experience of chronic benign lower back pain (Osborn and Smith 1998)

Aims

The aim of this study was to explore the experience of chronic pain as it is mediated by the personal meanings that sufferers attribute to it. The experience of chronic low back pain is not a simple product of organic pathology, and psychological factors appear to play a crucial role in determining a sufferer's levels of distress and disability. In this study, interpretative phenomenological analysis was chosen as a suitable method to 'explore explicitly the psychological processes that determine and maintain the dynamic relationship between the participant's chronic pain, distress and disability' (Osborn and Smith 1998: 67).

Data collection

Semi-structured interviews with nine female patients at a hospital out-patient back clinic were carried out and transcribed. The women were aged 25–55 years, they had suffered from chronic back pain for at least five years, and their pain experiences were characterized by high levels of distress and disability. The interview schedule was constructed with the aim of letting the participant tell her own pain story and to allow her to give expression to the psychological experience of her chronic pain.

Analysis

The interview transcripts were analysed in accordance with the principles of interpretative phenomenological analysis. Interview transcripts were analysed one by one. Each transcript was read and reread before themes were identified. These were tentatively organized and then explored in more detail. Each theme's relation to other themes was also examined, and interrelationships between them were established. Finally, themes were integrated across transcripts in order to identify shared themes that captured the essence of the participants' experience of chronic pain.

The researchers were interested in the psychological experience of chronic pain, which meant that the psychological content of the pain experience constituted the analytical focus of the study. This is where the researchers' *interpretative* engagment with the texts becomes apparent. Their research interests lead them to ask certain kinds of question, which take the analytic process in a particular direction. As a result, interpretative phenomenological analysis does not claim to produce a definitive, or 'true', reading of participants' accounts; instead, the results of such analysis are necessarily 'a co-construction between participant and analyst in that it emerges from the analyst's engagement with the data in the form of the participant's account' (Osborn and Smith 1998: 67).

Findings

Four superordinate themes emerged from the analysis: 'searching for an explanation', 'comparing this self with other selves', 'not being believed' and 'withdrawing from others'. 'Searching for an explanation' refers to participants' motivation to understand and explain their situation. The need to know why they are suffering together with the absence of a meaningful explanation for their pain was experienced as frustrating and bewildering. This search for meaning pervaded the women's accounts and reappears throughout their accounts, thus forming a part of all other themes. 'Comparing this self with other selves' captures participants' tendency to engage in social comparisons with past and future selves as well as with other people. Participants made favourable as well as unfavourable comparisons. They talked about their losses (of mobility, of activity, of social life, etc.) by invoking what they used to be able to do (comparison with past selves) and by highlighting what other people are capable of doing (comparison with others). They also compared themselves with those who were even more unfortunate than themselves (e.g. the terminally ill, the severely disabled) to emphasize their existing strengths; however, these comparisons were often experienced as counterproductive as they made participants worry about their own future prognosis. The uncertainty and ambiguity associated with lower back pain and the participants' frustrated 'search for an explanation' meant that social comparisons tended to emphasize loss and grief. 'Not being believed' refers to participants' concern about other people's views of their illness status. Participants were aware that, since it is invisible and without a clear clinical diagnosis, chronic pain may be perceived as 'not real' or as a form of 'malingering'. As a result, participants experienced guilt and shame in relation to their disability. They also felt the need to show signs of being in pain (e.g. through appearance and demeanor) so as to be believed. 'Withdrawing from others' was a consequence of participants' fear of rejection and awkwardness in social settings. Not wishing to be perceived as 'a burden' or 'boring' in company, participants chose to withdraw from social involvement and to stay at home.

Discussion

The authors suggest that participants' failure to relieve their feelings of uncertainty and confusion was partly the result of their application of a purely medical model that does not provide a clear explanation for the occurrence of chronic lower back pain. Participants would be helped by gaining access to an explanation that allowed them to establish a basis for taking therapeutic action, to retain a sense of control over their pain and to gain a sense of legitimacy in relation to their suffering and disability. The use of social comparison and its association with a pervasive sense of loss and grief indicates that participants had not developed a positive self-concept in the face of chronic illness. Instead, they were preoccupied with their past, idealized selves and with what they had lost through their illness. To repair the disruption to their sense of self, participants would need to be able to make sense of it within the context of their life story. Participants' inability to make sense of their pain led to feelings of guilt and shame in relation to their claims to illness status and the adoption of the sick role. To assert legitimacy for their suffering, participants felt obliged to appear ill by display-ing signs of distress and disability. In addition, they withdrew from social engagement with others in order to avoid misunderstanding and rejection. The authors conclude that chronic pain patients could benefit if the themes that emerged from this study were addressed within the context of chronic pain management programmes. They propose that patients and their loved ones may be helped 'to understand their condi-tion in less self-persecutory ways and realise greater benefits in the longer term through better adjustment and accommodation' (Osborn and Smith 1998: 80). However, they acknowledge that issues around guilt, shame and denial may also require substantial psychotherapeutic input.

Limitations of interpretative phenomenological analysis

Interpretative phenomenological analysis is concerned with experiences and mean-ings. It looks at phenomena from the point of view of those who experience them. Its aim is to capture an experience and to unravel its meaning(s). To this end, it provides researchers with clear and systematic guidelines, which allow them to identify and progressively integrate themes. Ideally, upon completion, it will have generated a table of master themes that captures (something of) the essence of the phenomenon under investigation. The introduction of interpretative phenomenological analysis into psychology has made phenomenological methodology accessible to those who do not have a philosophical background. Smith and colleagues take care to provide detailed descriptions of the analytic process (e.g. Smith et al. 1999), which means that those new to the method are encouraged to use it in their own research. Like all forms of phenomenological research, it does suffer from several conceptual and practical limi-tations. These concern the role of language, the suitability of accounts, and explan-ation versus description. These limitations will be discussed in turn.

The role of language

Phenomenological analysis works with texts. Data collection techniques used in it include semi-structured interviews, diaries and other forms of accounts such as descriptions of events or situations. This indicates that language is the means by which participants (attempt to) communicate their experiences to the researcher. Since phenomenological research is interested in the actual experience itself, it must assume that language provides participants with the necessary tools to capture that experience. In other words, phenomenological analysis relies upon the represen-tational validity of language. However, as will be discussed in Chapters 6 and 7, it can be argued that language constructs, rather than describes, reality. That is, the words we choose to describe a particular experience always construct a particular version of that experience. The same event can be described in many different ways. This means that language can never simply give expression to experience. Instead, it adds meanings that reside in the words themselves and, therefore, makes direct access to someone else's experience impossible. From this point of view, an interview transcript or a diary entry tells us more about the ways in which an individual *talks about* a particular experience within a particular context, than about the *experience itself* (see Chapter 6). Alternatively, it may be that the availability of a particular way of talking about an issue also provides the categories of experience, and that, as a result, language *precedes* and therefore *shapes* experience (see Chapter 7). From this perspective, language does not constitute the means by which we express something we think or feel; rather, language prescribes what we can think and feel. Either way, the conceptualization of language in much phenomenological research can be criticized for not engaging sufficiently with its constitutive role (see also Willig 2007 for more on this).

Suitability of accounts

Phenomenology is concerned with the texture of experience. The aim of phenomenological analysis is to explore the quality of experience and to obtain a better understanding of *what it is like* to live a particular moment or situation. In its original formulation, transcendental phenomenology attemped to bracket abstract (scientific, common sense and conventional) knowledge about a phenomenon in order to better understand the essence of the phenomenon as it revealed itself in a particular experience. Even though interpretative phenomenological analysis is more modest in its aims, it also attempts to capture the experiences and meanings associated with a phenomenon rather than to identify people's opinions about it. But while phenomenology as philosophy works with introspection, whereby the philosopher explores his or her own experiences through phenomenological meditation, phenomenology as social scientific research method relies upon participants' descriptions of their experiences. This raises difficult questions. To what extent do participants' accounts constitute suitable material for phenomenological analysis? How successfully are participants able to communicate the rich texture of their experience to the researcher? And how many people are able to use language in such a way as to capture the subtleties and nuances of their physical and emotional experiences?

For example, Moustakas (1994: 177) reports that, in a phenomenological study of coronary artery bypass surgery, participants were asked to provide 'vivid, accurate and comprehensive portrayals of what these experiences were like for you: your thoughts, feelings and behaviours, as well as situations, events, places, and people connected with your experience'. It could be argued that such descriptions are very difficult to produce, particularly for participants who are not used to expressing their thoughts, feelings and perceptions in words. Similarly, in a study of the phenomenology of patients' experience of care in an Accident and Emergency Department (Lemon and Taylor 1997), patients who had sustained head injuries, suffered convulsions or taken drugs were excluded from the study. Again, this demonstrates that phenomenological research methods are not suitable for the study of the experiences of those who may not be able to articulate them in the sophisticated manner required by the method. This limits the applicability of the phenomenological method.

Explanation versus description

Phenomenological research, including interpretative phenomenological analysis, focuses upon *perceptions*. It aims to gain a better understanding of how the world appears to participants, of how participants perceive and experience the world, from their own perspectives. Here, 'the important reality is what people perceive it to be' (Kvale 1996b: 52). Phenomenological research is concerned with *how* the world presents itself to people as they engage with it in particular contexts and with particular intentions. It does not make claims about the nature of the world itself. In fact, from a phenomenological point of view, it does not make sense to conceive of 'the world' and 'the person' as separate entities. Instead, there is only 'experience of the world' based upon a relational unit of self/world (see also O'Connor and Hallam 2000). As a result, while it is able to generate detailed, rich descriptions of participants' experiences of situations and events, such research does not tend to further our understanding of *why* such experiences take place and *why* there may be differences between individuals' phenomenological representations. That is, phenomenological research describes and documents the lived experience of participants but it does not attempt to explain it.

It could be argued that an exclusive focus on appearances, without regard for their cause or origin, limits our understanding of phenomena. Much of what human beings perceive is not a direct reflection of the conditions that give rise to the perception. Our visual perception of the stars in the sky at night, for instance, does not reflect the ideal standpoint of geometric projection (cf. Holzkamp 1983). The same applies to social and psychological perceptions and experiences such as pain, love or prejudice. If we want to move beyond sharing an experience with our participants, and understand their experiences well enough to explain them, we need to be aware of the conditions that gave rise to these experiences in the first place. Such conditions can lie far beyond the moment and location of the experience itself. They may be found in past events, histories or the social and material structures within which we live our lives (see also Willig 1999a).

Is there a place for cognition in phenomenology?

Smith (1996: 263) argues that interpretative phenomenological analysis is concerned with *cognition* because it is concerned with understanding 'what the particular respondent thinks or believes about the topic under discussion'. He proposes that interpretative phenomenological analysis is compatible with a social cognition paradigm because it subscribes to 'a belief in, and concern with, the chain of connection between verbal report, cognition and physical state' (Smith et al. 1999: 219). In other words, Smith's version of the phenomenological method implies a Cartesian conceptualization of the individual as the owner of a set of cognitions (ideas, beliefs, expectations, etc.), which he or she uses to make sense of the world and to act in the world.

From this perspective, an understanding of a person's cognitive register should allow us to make sense of his or her experiences and actions. However, it could be argued that an emphasis upon cognition is not, in fact, compatible with some aspects of phenomenological thought. This is because phenomenologists challenge the subject/object distinction implied by cognitive theory. They aim to transcend the separation between 'the knower' and 'the known', between 'person' and 'world'. Phenomenology is concerned with knowledge that is non-propositional; in other words, its objective is to capture the way in which the world presents itself to the individual in an immediate (unmediated) sense, including 'vague feelings, pleasures, tastes, hunches, moods and ideas on the margin of consciousness' (O'Connor and Hallam 2000: 245). These precognitive aspects of experience are seen as central precisely because they are inarticulate and unfocused. IPA is open to questioning because it has used the term 'cognition' to refer to the subjective quality of experience. Smith and Eatough (2006) have described this as 'hot cognition'. The role of 'cognition' in phenomenology requires further exploration.

Three epistemological questions

To conclude this chapter, let us look at interpretative phenomenological analysis' position in relation to our three epistemological questions about the kind of knowledge it produces, the assumptions it makes about the world it studies, and the role of the researcher in the research process.

1 *What kind of knowledge does interpretative phenomenological analysis aim to produce?*
Interpretative phenomenological analysis aims to gain an understanding of how participants view and experience their world. Although it acknowledges that it is impossible to obtain direct, unmediated access to someone else's personal world, interpretative phenomenological analysis researchers are urged to engage with participants' accounts in such a way as to encourage an insider perspective. The objective of the analysis is to obtain an insight into another person's thoughts and beliefs in relation to the phenomenon under investigation. Interpretative phenomenological analysis starts from the assumption that people's accounts tell us something about their private thoughts and feelings, and that these in turn are implicated in people's experiences. It aims to produce knowledge of what and how people think about the phenomenon under investigation. In this, it could be said to take a *realist* approach to knowledge production. At the same time, however, interpretative phenomenological analysis recognizes that a researcher's understanding of participants' thoughts is necessarily influenced by his or her own ways of thinking, assumptions and conceptions. However, these are not seen as 'biases' to be eliminated; instead, they are seen as a necessary precondition for making sense of another person's experience. In other words, understanding requires interpretation. Here, interpretative phenomenological analysis is influenced by *hermeneutic* versions of phenomenology, such as Gadamer's philosophical hermeneutics (see Moran 2000: chapter 8). The knowledge produced by it is, therefore, also *reflexive* in so far as it acknowledges its dependence on the researcher's own standpoint.

2 *What kinds of assumptions does interpretative phenomenological analysis make about the world?*

Interpretative phenomenological analysis is concerned with the ways in which individuals perceive the world. It is interested in participants' subjective experience of the world rather than the objective nature of this (social or material) world. It also assumes that individuals can experience the same 'objective' conditions (e.g. a particular disease process or a social event) in radically different ways. This is because experience is mediated by the thoughts and beliefs, expectations and judgements that the individual brings to it. In other words, people attribute meanings to events that then shape their experiences of these events. Interpretative phenomenological analysis does not share the positivist view that the external world directly determines our perception of it. In fact, interpretative phenomenological analysis does not make any claims about the external world. It does not ask whether participants' accounts of what happened to them may be 'true' or 'false' or to what extent their perception of an event corresponds to an external 'reality'. What matters to interpretative phenomenological analysis is how participants *experience* the situation or event. In this sense, it subscribes to a *relativist ontology*. However, at the same time, it recognizes that the meanings people ascribe to events are the product of interactions between actors in the social world. This means that people's interpretations are not entirely idiosyncratic and free-floating; instead, they are bound up with social interactions and processes that are shared between social actors. Such a *symbolic interactionist* perspective ensures that interpretative phenomenological analysis does not slide into methodological solipsism.

3 *How does interpretative phenomenological analysis conceptualize the role of the researcher in the research process?*

Interpretative phenomenological analysis acknowledges that any insights gained from the analysis of a text are necessarily the product of *interpretation*. Although the aim of interpretative phenomenological analysis is to understand better the participant's psychological world, researchers accept that such understanding can only be gained through the researcher's engagement with and interpretation of the participant's account. This means that the researcher is necessarily implicated in the analysis. As a result, the analysis is both *phenomenological* (that is, it aims to represent the participant's view of the world) and *interpretative* (that is, it is dependent on the researcher's own conceptions and standpoint). In this sense, interpretative phenomenological analysis requires a *reflexive* attitude from the researcher. However, it does not *theorize* reflexivity. In other words, it recognizes the importance of the researcher's perspective but it does not actually tell us how to incorporate this insight into the research process and it does not show us how exactly the researcher's own conceptions are implicated in a particular piece of analysis. Thus, although interpretative phenomenological analysis research does not claim privileged, or direct, access to participants' meanings and experiences, the terminology used in the presentation of its findings invokes a sense of discovery rather than of construction: Themes are said to *emerge* and categories are *identified* in a way that invokes grounded theory methodology rather than social constructionism (see also Box 2: What's new?).

Conclusion

It is important to bear in mind that interpretative phenomenological analysis is but one version of phenomenological research methodology, which in turn grew out of a rich tradition of philosophical thought. Phenomenology as philosophy is itself by no means a unified system; there are diverse strands of phenomenology, including existentialist, transcendental and hermeneutic varieties (see Spinelli 1989; Moran 2000; Schmidt 2006). Each of these makes different assumptions about issues, such as the role of language and interpretation, the nature of being and human action. As a result, to describe an approach as *phenomenology* or as *phenomenological* means different things to different people. It is, therefore, important to be specific about which version of phenomenological thought one is referring to. Interpretative phenomenological analysis constitutes one way in which phenomenological ideas have inspired research practice. There are, however, many others. Nevertheless, I want to close by drawing attention to what unifies, rather than what separates, empirical phenomenological research. To this end, Kvale (1996b: 38–9) reminds us that, 'A phenomenological perspective includes a focus on the life world, an openness to the experiences of the subject, a primacy of precise description, attempts to bracket foreknowledge, and a search for invariant essential meanings in the description'.

Interactive exercises

1 Select an everyday activity (e.g. a bus journey or eating a meal). Before you engage in it the next time, adopt the phenomenological attitude and see how this changes your experience of the activity and what you can learn from this about your experience. Remember that the phenomenological attitude requires you to put aside, as far as possible, your knowledge, assumptions and expectations (e.g. do not think about what you know about the calorific value of the food you are eating or how it has been obtained and cooked, and focus instead upon the flavour and texture of it). It also means staying in the present as far as possible and trying not to project yourself forward in time (e.g. do not think about the end of your bus journey and what you are going to do when you get there). Be warned that adopting the phenomenological attitude can turn your experience of an everyday activity from something mundane and routine into something unsettling and potentially disturbing.

2 Select an experience you have had recently (e.g. an enjoyable evening out with a friend or a disappointing visit to the theatre). Describe the experience phenomenologically. You can either do this in writing or you can tape-record and then transcribe a verbal account of it. Remember that a phenomenological account needs to stay close to the quality and texture of the experience. This means focusing on what was going on inside of you as you underwent the experience rather than on what you know about it (e.g. if two hours in the theatre felt like an eternity then, phenomenologically, this is what matters). Having produced the account, read and reread it line-by-line. Ask yourself what makes the experience what it is? What is its essence (e.g. What is the essence of boredom in the theatre)? Which features of the experience need to be

present to make it what it is (e.g. What makes time with your friend enjoyable – is it the food you had? The wine you drank? The way your eyes met?)? Which are redundant?

Further reading

Eatough, V. and Smith, J.A. (2008) Interpretative phenomenological analysis, in C. Willig and W. Stainton Rogers (eds) *The Sage Handbook of Qualitative Research in Psychology*. London: Sage.

Langdridge, D. (2007) *Phenomenological Psychology: Theory, Research and Method*. London: Pearson Prentice Hall.

Larkin, M., Watts, S. and Clifton, E. (2006) Giving voice and making sense in interpretative phenomenological analysis, *Qualitative Research in Psychology*, 3: 102–20.

Osborn, M. and Smith, J.A. (1998) The personal experience of chronic benign lower back pain: an interpretative phenomenological analysis, *British Journal of Health Psychology*, 3: 65–83.

Smith, J.A. (1991) Conceiving selves: a case study of changing identities during the transition to motherhood, *Journal of Language and Social Psychology*, 10: 225–43.

Smith, J.A. (1999) Towards a relational self: social engagement during pregnancy and psychological preparation for motherhood, *British Journal of Social Psychology*, 38: 409–26.

Smith, J.A., Jarman, M. and Osborn, M. (1999) Doing interpretative phenomenological analysis, in M. Murray and K. Chamberlain (eds) *Qualitative Health Psychology: Theories and Methods*. London: Sage.

Box 2 What's new? The relationship between interpretative phenomenological analysis and grounded theory

---

Interpretative phenomenological analysis is a recently developed, and still evolving, approach to qualitative research in psychology. It is associated with the work of Jonathan Smith, who is interested in conducting qualitative research that is compatible with a social cognitive paradigm. Smith (1996) argues that qualitative methods can be used to access underlying cognitions, such as beliefs and attitudes, and that this may help us shed light upon a person's behaviour and experience. Interpretative phenomenological analysis is increasingly being used as a qualitative method, particularly in health psychology research (see Smith et al. 1999).

Interpretative phenomenological analysis and (the abbreviated version of) grounded theory share many features. Both aim to produce something like a cognitive map that represents a person's or a group's view of the world. Both proceed by systematically working through a text in order to identify themes and categories that are progressively integrated until higher-order units (core categories, master themes) are established that capture the essence or nature of the phenomenon under investigation. Both interpretative phenomenological analysis and grounded theory start with individual cases, which are then integrated to obtain a composite picture that tells us more about the phenomenon than any individual case would have been able to. Finally, both methods use categorization in order to achieve systematic data reduction, which, it is hoped, will produce some form of general understanding or insight into the fundamental process (grounded theory) or essence (interpretative phenomenological analysis) that characterizes the phenomenon of interest.

Smith himself frequently acknowledges the affinity between interpretative phenomenological analysis and grounded theory. For example, in his writings about interpretative phenomenological analysis, he recommends the use of analytic techniques 'commonly associated with grounded theory' (Smith 1999: 232; see also Smith 1997: 193) and he directs readers to grounded theory literature for guidance because it 'adopts a broadly similar perspective' (Smith 1995b: 18). In addition, interpretative phenomenological analysis shares much of its analytic terminology with grounded theory; it talks about *themes* and *categories* that *emerge* through analysis, and it works with concepts such as *saturation, negative case analysis, analytic induction* and *memo-writing*. In line with grounded theory, interpretative phenomenological analysis is conceptualized as a *cyclical process* that involves the *constant comparison* of data and their codes, leading to a continuous process of assignment and reassignment of data to evolving categories.

So what is it that interpretative phenomenological analysis offers the researcher that grounded theory cannot provide? Why should psychologists choose to use interpretative phenomenological analysis when they have access to grounded theory, which is, after all, a more established and better known qualitative method? There are two possible answers to this question. First, while grounded theory was developed to allow researchers to study basic social processes, interpretative phenomenological analysis was designed to gain insight into individual participants' psychological worlds. In other words, interpretative phenomenological analysis is a specifically psychological research method. Even though more recently grounded theory has been used to produce systematic representations of participants' experiences (the *abbreviated version*, see p. 45), it could be argued that it is better suited to address sociological research questions. This is because grounded theory aims to identify and explicate contextualized social processes that *account for phenomena*. By contrast, interpretative phenomenological analysis is concerned with gaining a better understanding of the quality and texture of individual experiences; that is, it is interested in the *nature or essence of phenomena*.

The second reason why psychological researchers may prefer to use interpretative phenomenological analysis is that grounded theory is now associated with so many debates and controversies as to make its application something of a challenge. There are now several versions of grounded theory (e.g. full vs. abbreviated, Straussian vs. Glaserian, realist vs. social constructionist) that suggest different directions for grounded theory research. The researcher needs to engage with these debates before he or she can choose the version of grounded theory that is most appropriate to his or her research question. By contrast, interpretative phenomenological analysis is a new and developing approach that leaves more room for creativity and freedom to explore on the part of the researcher who uses it.

5

Case studies

Research methods for psychological case studies • Types of design for case study research • Procedural issues • An example of case study research • Limitations of case study research • Three epistemological questions • Conclusion • Interactive exercises • Further reading

The case study is not itself a research method. Instead, it constitutes an approach to the study of singular entities, which may involve the use of a wide range of diverse methods of data collection and analysis. The case study is, therefore, not characterized by the methods used to collect and analyse data, but rather by its focus upon a particular unit of analysis: the *case*. A case can be an organization, a city, a group of people, a community, a patient, a school, an intervention, even a nation state or an empire. It can be a situation, an incident or an experience. Bromley (1986: 8) describes cases as 'natural occurrences with definable boundaries'. The case study involves an in-depth, intensive and sharply focused exploration of such an occurrence. Case studies have a long and varied history. They have been used in many different disciplines, including sociology, political theory, history, social anthropology, education and psychoanalysis. Case studies can make use of both qualitative and quantitative research methods. However, despite such diversity, it is possible to identify a number of defining features of case study research. These include:

1 *An idiographic perspective.* Here, researchers are concerned with the particular rather than the general. The aim is to understand an individual case, in its particularity. This can be contrasted with a nomothetic approach, which aims to identify general laws of human behaviour by averaging out individual variation (for a more detailed discussion of idiography, see Smith et al. 1995).

2 *Attention to contextual data.* Case study research takes a holistic approach, in that it considers the case within its context. This means that the researcher pays attention to the ways in which the various dimensions of the case relate to or interact with its environment. Thus, while particular cases need to be identified as

the focus of the study, they cannot be considered in isolation (for a discussion of the role of the 'ecological context' in psychological case studies, see Bromley 1986: 25).

3   *Triangulation.* Case studies integrate information from diverse sources to gain an in-depth understanding of the phenomenon under investigation. This may involve the use of a range of data collection and analysis techniques within the framework of one case study. Triangulation enriches case study research because it allows the researcher to approach the case from a number of different perspectives. This in turn facilitates an appreciation of the various dimensions of the case as well as its embeddedness within its various (social, physical, symbolic, psychological) contexts.

4   *A temporal element.* Case studies involve the investigation of occurrences over a period of time. According to Yin (1994: 16), '[E]stablishing the how and why of a complex human situation is a classic example of the use of case studies'. Case studies are concerned with processes that take place over time. This means that a focus on change and development is an important feature of case studies.

5   *A concern with theory.* Case studies facilitate theory generation. The detailed exploration of a particular case can generate insights into social or psychological processes, which in turn can give rise to theoretical formulations and hypotheses. Freud's psychoanalytic case studies constitute a clear example of the relationship between case studies and theory development. Hamel (1993: 29) goes as far as to claim that '[A]ll theories are initially based on a particular case or object'. In addition, case studies can also be used to test existing theories or to clarify or extend such theories, for example by looking at deviant or extreme cases.

In this chapter, I focus on case studies that are concerned with psychological phenomena and that use qualitative research methods to investigate them. For the purposes of this chapter, I adopt Bromley's (1986: ix) definition of the term 'case study', which suggests that: '[T]o the psychologist it means the study of an individual person, usually in a problematic situation, over a relatively short period of time'.

In the remainder of the chapter, I provide an overview of a range of qualitative research methods that are compatible with case study research. This is followed by a discussion of the different types of case study design that are available to the qualitative researcher. These include *intrinsic* versus *instrumental* case studies, *single-* versus *multiple-*case studies, and *descriptive* versus *explanatory* case studies. I then address procedural issues associated with case study research, including selection of cases, selection of methods for data collection and analysis, the role of theory, writing up and ethics. Ulric Neisser's (1981) case study of 'John Dean's Memory' will provide an illustration of case study research in psychology. Having discussed some of the limitations of case studies as an approach to research in psychology, the chapter concludes by addressing three epistemological questions in relation to case studies.

Research methods for psychological case studies

Since the case study is not itself a research method, researchers need to select methods of data collection and analysis that will generate material suitable for case studies. Many methods can be used in case study research. Some of these are well-known qualitative techniques, such as *semi-structured interviewing, participant observation* and *diaries*, and these are discussed in detail in Chapter 2. Data for case studies can also be generated on the basis of *personal* (e.g. letters, notes, photographs) or *official* (e.g. case notes, clinical notes, appraisal reports) *documents*. The data can be analysed in a number of different ways, including grounded theory (see Chapter 3) and interpretative phenomenological analysis (see Chapter 4). Alternatively, various forms of text interpretation, including thematic coding and global analysis, can also be used (for a detailed account of such techniques, see Flick 1998). In addition, Smith (1993) identifies two further methods, the Twenty Statements Test and Repertory Grids, as suitable analytic techniques for case study research. Although these methods can be used qualitatively, they do not constitute what has been referred to as 'big Q' methodology (see p. 9). This is because they work with preconceived categories, which are then filled with content specific to the case under investigation. However, they are idiographic in that they focus upon the individual case without reference to a comparison group. Let us take a brief look at the Twenty Statements Test and Repertory Grids.

Twenty Statements Test (Gordon 1968)

Here, the participant is asked to give 20 answers to the question, 'Who or what are you?' Each answer begins with the words 'I am . . .'. The participant's response can be explored in terms of content (e.g. what types of categories are deployed) or sequence (e.g. which aspects of self are mentioned first/last, etc.). In addition, the test can be repeated at different points in time to identify changes in self-perception.

Repertory Grids (Kelly 1955)

The Repertory Grid is designed to elicit from the participant the constructs he or she uses to make sense of the social world. To do this, the participant is asked to generate about 10 elements (e.g. roles for the self or others, activities, careers) which he or she then compares with one another. For example, if the elements are 'self as friend', 'self as lover', 'self as parent', 'self as worker', and so on, the participant would be asked in what way any two of them are similar and how they are different from a third (e.g. 'self as friend' and 'self as lover' may be described as 'warm' and contrasted with 'self as worker', which is described as 'businesslike'). Each comparison generates a construct – that is, terms of reference that the person uses to think about his or her social roles (e.g. warm vs. businesslike). This process of comparison continues until the participant finds it difficult to generate new constructs. Finally, the participant rates each element in relation to each construct (e.g. 'self as friend' and 'self as lover' as 'warm' but not 'businesslike', 'self as parent' as 'warm' and 'businesslike', 'self as worker' as not 'warm' but 'businesslike', and so on). When the grid is completed, it provides a visual display of patterns and association between elements and constructs. This in turn provides insight into the ways in which the participant construes personal meanings to make sense of the social world. (For more information on how to use Repertory Grids, see Banister et al. 1994: chapter 5; Smith 1995a; Bannister and Fransella 1986.)

Types of design for case study research

Individual cases may be studied for different reasons. A researcher may focus on a particular case because it is interesting in its own right or because it is seen as representative of a particular kind of situation. He or she may wish to explore a single case in as much depth as possible, or may seek to compare a number of cases with one another in order to arrive at a more general understanding of a phenomenon. The researcher's investigation of the case may be purely exploratory or it may be designed to test an existing theory. In addition, it may be predominantly descriptive or it may aim to generate explanations for occurrences. There are a number of different designs for case study research, each of which allows the researcher to address different sorts of question in relation to the case(s) under investigation. These include *intrinsic* versus *instrumental* case studies, *single-* versus *multiple-*case studies and *descriptive* versus *explanatory* case studies. In addition, Chamberlain et al. (2004) distinguish between *naturalist* and *pragmatic* approaches to case study research. Let us look at each of these in turn.

Intrinsic versus instrumental case studies

Intrinsic case studies represent nothing but themselves. The cases in intrinsic case studies are chosen because they are interesting in their own right. The researcher wants to know about them in particular, rather than about a more general problem or phenomenon. Cases for intrinsic case studies can be said to be pre-specified in the sense that their intrinsic interest pre-exists the research. For example, patients with rare diseases or clients with unusual problems would constitute suitable cases for intrinisic case studies. By contrast, in *instrumental case studies* the cases constitute exemplars of a more general phenomenon. They are selected to provide the researcher with an opportunity to study the phenomenon of interest. Here, the research question identifies a phenomenon (e.g. bereavement, fame, recovery from illness) and the cases are selected in order to explore 'how the phenomenon exists within a particular case' (Stake 1994: 242). In this design, individuals who are experiencing the phenomenon of interest (e.g. the bereaved, the famous, the recovering patient) constitute suitable cases for analysis (for more information on intrinsic and instrumental case studies, see Stake 1994, 1995).

Single- versus multiple-case studies

Case studies can consist of a detailed exploration of a single case or they can involve the comparison of a series of cases. Yin (1994) identifies three reasons for choosing a single-case design. First, the case may constitute a critical test for a well-formulated theory. Second, it may represent a unique or extreme case that is of intrinsic interest to the researcher. Third, the case in question may be revelatory in the sense that it was previously inaccessible. *Single-case studies* are, therefore, either of intrinsic interest to the researcher or they provide an opportunity to test the applicability of existing theories to real-world data. The *multiple-case study* design, by contrast, provides the researcher with an opportunity to generate new theories. Here, theoretical formulations are developed and refined on the basis of the comparative analysis of a series of cases. Analysis of the first case leads the researcher to formulate tentative hypotheses, which can then be explored in the light of subsequent cases. With each new case, the emerging theory is modified in order to be able to account for all instances associated with the phenomenon under investigation. Smith (1997: 193–4) likens this process to that of analytic induction (see also Flick 1998: 230–31). Multiple-case studies are, therefore, instrumental in nature (for a detailed discussion of multiple-case studies, see Yin 1994: 44–51).

Descriptive versus explanatory case studies

Even though all case studies should include descriptions of the cases under investigation, some case studies remain purely descriptive, whereas others aim to be explanatory. *Descriptive case studies* are concerned with providing a detailed description of the phenomenon within its context. Here, the case is not explored in terms of existing theoretical formulations; instead, it is hoped that the detail provided by the description will generate new insights into, and a better understanding of, the nature of the phenomenon under investigation. By contrast, *explanatory case studies* aim to generate explanations for the occurrences with which they are concerned. Here, descriptions of what is going on are accompanied by attempts to deploy explanatory concepts within the account. The explanatory case study 'goes beyond mere narrative or description' (Bromley 1986: 32). However, it is important to bear in mind that accuracy in matters of detail and the provision of sufficient evidence are of paramount importance in both descriptive and explanatory case study research (for a detailed discussion of types of case study, see Yin 1993: chapter 1).

Naturalist versus pragmatic case studies

Chamberlain et al. (2004) distinguish between *naturalist* and *pragmatic* approaches. Naturalistic case study research (e.g. Stake 1995) is carried out in naturalistic, real-world contexts and it focuses on a single case as the unit of analysis. The researcher approaches the case with an open mind and without previously defined hypotheses, allowing patterns, propositions and formulations to emerge from the data. By contrast, pragmatic case study research (e.g. Yin 1994) is more focused, beginning with a well-defined research question that guides data collection and analysis. It works with a set of propositions that identify key areas of interest and which function as (tentative and flexible) hypotheses. These are tested and revised during the course of the research. Both the selection of relevant data sources and analytic techniques are driven by the research questions and the propositions. The aim of pragmatic case study research is to produce a set of revised propositions (see

Chamberlain et al. 2004 for more information about how to conduct pragmatic case study research).

Procedural issues

Case study research can take different forms. We have seen that case studies can employ a range of different methods of data collection and analysis, and a number of different types of design for case study research have been identified. The case study researcher needs to make a series of decisions about what (the unit of analysis, the case), how (methods of data collection and analysis) and why (intrinsic interest or theoretical reasons) he or she is to conduct the research. While case study research allows the researcher to make his or her own decisions about these matters, there are a number of procedural issues that need to be addressed by all case study research. It is important to remember that the freedom and diversity associated with case studies does not mean that such research requires less planning and preparation. In fact, the opposite is likely to be the case. To ensure that the researcher maintains clarity of design and appropriateness of methods throughout, the case study needs to be carefully arranged. Bromley (1986: 14) argues that, 'in order to be useful it has to be restricted in scope and sharply focused'. *Selection of cases, methods of data collection and analysis, the role of theory, strategies for writing up* and *ethical concerns* need to be considered if the research is to generate new insights into, and/or improve our understanding of, a particular phenomenon or occurrence.

Selection of cases

Stake (1994: 236) suggests that a '[C]ase study is not a methodological choice, but a choice of object to be studied'. While not all case study researchers would agree with this statement (e.g. Yin 1994: 17), it does draw attention to the importance of the selection of the appropriate unit of analysis, that is *the case*. Hamel (1993: 41–4) differentiates between 'the object of study' and 'the case'. The object of study constitutes the phenomenon of interest to the researcher (e.g. recovery from heart surgery, divorce, being promoted), whereas the case is its concrete manifestation (e.g. the heart surgery patient, the divorcee, the person who gained promotion).

Hamel argues that the case should be selected to understand better the object of study. This conceptualization presupposes an *instrumental case study* design whereby the case constitutes an exemplar of a more general phenomenon. Here, the aim of selection of cases is to identify 'the ideal case to grasp the object of study' (Hamel 1993: 43). In *intrinsic case studies*, the case does not represent a more general phenomenon. Instead, it is chosen as a result of its intrinsic interest to the researcher. However, in both intrinsic and instrumental designs, the researcher needs to establish the boundaries of the case study and its terms of reference. This can be difficult.

Bromley (1986) draws attention to the fact that cases always exist within a context and that, therefore, the boundaries of a case study are always somewhat arbitrary. He provides the following example to illustrate his point: 'A case-study which, for one Investigator, concerns the rehabilitation of a particular drug addict, for another concerns a particular neighbourhood where narcotics are available' (Bromley 1986: 4). In addition, contexts can be social, economic, historical, biological, and so on. This means that the case can be explored in terms of a wide range of both proximal (i.e. immediate) and distal (i.e. remote) factors. To be able to establish the boundaries of the case study, the researcher needs to clearly identify its terms of reference. That is, he or she needs to be explicit about what it is (about the case) that he or she is interested in. The same case can be discussed in relation to a number of different situations and concerns. For example, a serial killer may be described in terms of his psychopathology, his childhood experiences and early development, his social location and relationships, or his subjective perceptions and worldview. It is important to remember that case studies are of necessity partial accounts of a person in a situation; they can never capture the individual in his or her entirety.

Selection of methods of data collection and analysis

The research methods to be used in a particular case study should be selected in the light of the research question that motivated the study. For example, if the researcher is interested in the ways in which an individual experiences a particular life event, then a combination of *semi-structured interviewing* and *diaries* would be an appropriate method of data collection. The data could be analysed in a variety of ways, including interpretative phenomenological analysis and grounded theory (see Chapters 3 and 4). If, however, the researcher wishes to establish an individual's educational trajectory in order to try to understand better his or her choice of career later in life, he or she would have to consult documents such as school reports and assessments as well as the individual's own account of their educational experiences. It would also be a good idea to conduct semi-structured interviews with the individual's former teachers and, if possible, also peers. Analysis of such data could include a search for recurrent *themes* (e.g. in teacher's reports) as well as grounded theory. Case study research should always involve a certain amount of *triangulation*. Since case studies concern themselves with the complex relationship between the contextual and temporal dimensions of an event or phenomenon, it is unlikely that the use of a single research method would generate data that do justice to this complexity. Flick (1998: 230) points out that triangulation is a way of 'enriching and completing knowledge and [towards] transgressing the (always limited) epistemological potentials of the individual method'. This makes triangulation an ideal way of approaching case study research, which should, ideally, throw light on the ways in which bounded, yet integrated systems function over time (see Stake 1994).

The role of theory

The role of theory in case study research is twofold. First, case studies are based upon what has been referred to as 'initial theory' (Hamel 1993: 44) or 'study propositions' (Yin 1994: 21), which direct the researcher's attention to what is to be examined within the framework of the study. In other words, the researcher's selection of a case and the questions he or she chooses to ask about it are theoretical in that they identify particular concepts as relevant. For example, we may ask questions about the effects of childhood experiences upon choices made later in life, or we may wish to explore the ways in which social relationships influence people's experience of particular life events. Other concepts of interest may be psychological symptoms, social beliefs or personal expectations. The methods chosen to collect and analyse data for the case study are those which are capable of obtaining meaningful information about these concepts. This means that theory features in the design of the case study itself. Yin (1994: 28) suggests that the design of a case study 'embodies a "theory" of what is being studied'. In order to be clear and explicit about their theoretical bases, Yin (1994: 29) proposes that all case studies should be preceded by statements about what is to be explored, the purpose of the exploration and the criteria by which it will be judged.

Second, case studies have implications for theory development. They can be designed to test an existing theory or they can constitute the starting point for the generation of a new theory. When used to test existing theory, case studies can advance knowledge through *falsification* (see Chapter 1). A single case that demonstrates an occurrence that is not compatible with exisiting theoretical predictions would be sufficient to question the applicability of the theory. In this way, single-case studies can function in the same way as experiments – namely, to establish the limits of generalizability (see also Bromley 1986: 286–96; Yin 1994: chapters 1 and 2). As Stake (1994: 245) puts it:

> Case study is part of scientific method, but its purpose is not limited to the advance of science. Whereas single or a few cases are poor representation of a population of cases and poor grounds for advancing grand generalization, a single case as negative example can establish limits to grand generalization. For example, we lose confidence in the generalization that a child of separated parents is better off placed with the mother when we find a single instance of resultant injury.

When used to generate new theory, case studies can facilitate conceptual refinement of emerging theoretical formulations or they can lead to the discovery of new insights and interpretations. For example, the researcher's immersion in the detail and specificity of an *intrinsic case study* can give rise to the formulation of an entirely new hypothesis about the processes involved in the case. Alternatively, a *multiple-case study* of an instrumental nature allows the researcher to consider a series of cases in relation to one another in order to develop a conceptual framework that accounts for them all. Bromley (1986) compares this process to the emergence of case law in jurisprudence. Case study researchers hold different views about the extent to which and the ways in which case study research allows for generalizability of its findings. These arguments are taken up in Box 3 at the end of this chapter.

Writing up

Like most qualitative research, case studies can be written up in a variety of ways. There is no standard format for the presentation of a psychological case study. The length, structure and style of the report will be influenced by the methods used in the case study and by the findings generated by the research. In line with all qualitative research reports, the case study report should include some information about the participant(s), a clear and detailed account of the methods used to collect and analyse the data, and a discussion of the implications of the findings. In addition, such a report should identify the purpose of the study and its terms of reference. It is important to acknowledge that the case study was carried out in response to a particular concern or question on the part of the researcher. It can only provide a partial understanding of how and why certain individuals experience and behave as they do, within a particular situation. The case study report can never claim to 'sum up' a person or to paint a 'complete picture' of a person. Again, in line with most qualitative research, it is difficult to think of the analysis and writing-up phases of case study research as separate activities. Instead, '[C]ase content evolves in the act of writing itself' (Stake 1994: 240).

Researchers disagree about the extent to which case study research ought to move beyond detailed descriptions of the case and provide explanations for its occurrence. Some (e.g. Bromley 1986; Hamel 1993) argue that case studies ought to transcend the information that characterizes a case and introduce explanatory concepts to account for it. From this point of view, the case study report presents a 'rational and empirical argument which explains the behaviour of the person under investigation' (Bromley 1986: 37) on the basis of abstract concepts (e.g. social roles, family dynamics, cognitive structures, etc.). Others (e.g. Stake 1994) caution against too strong a desire to theorize because this may divert attention from the particulars of the case. Instead, they recommend that the case study researcher remains close to the details of the case, emphasizing its uniqueness and particularity. The aim here is 'to describe the case in sufficient descriptive narrative so that readers can vicariously experience these happenings, and draw their own conclusions' (Stake 1994: 243). Whatever approach is taken, it is important to differentiate, clearly and explicitly, between description (of events, of what participants said, of the social context) and the researcher's interpretation of these (of their causes and consequences, of their implications, of their meanings) (see also Smith et al. 1999: 227–8).

Ethics

Case studies are concerned with the details of individual participants' life events. This means that case study research needs to be particularly sensitive to issues around confidentiality and anonymity. If the circumstances of a participant's life event are such that readers of the case report would be able to identify the participant's identity, then the researcher needs to take care to introduce modifications or adjustments to the material that prevent such identification. Bromley (1986: 309) suggests that it is possible to make alterations in such a way that the particular case is rendered unrecognizable, while preserving the case study's form and content. In addition, agreements should be reached with participants about the limits of accessibility to records, documents and other materials prior to data collection. Furthermore, it is good practice to supply participants with drafts of how their cases are being written up and to take note of their feedback.

Some case study researchers (e.g. Smith 1995a) take a more interactive approach to their work with participants and involve them in an ongoing discussion of the meanings and implications of emerging interpretations. It has been suggested that such a procedure can generate therapeutic gain through reflection for the participant (Smith 1993: 263–4). Perhaps more than any other type of research, case studies require us to take note of Stake's (1994: 244) observation that, 'Qualitative researchers are guests in the private spaces of the world. Their manners should be good and their code of ethics strict'.

An example of case study research
Ulric Neisser's (1981) analysis of John Dean's testimony

In 'John Dean's memory: a case study', Neisser (1981) presents a detailed analysis of a number of documents to throw light on the ways in which John Dean remembers a series of events that took place at the White House. John Dean, who used to be a counsel to former US president Richard Nixon, testified before the Watergate Committee of the United States Senate in June 1973. The Committee's investigation took place to establish whether or not high-ranking government officials had been involved in the cover-up of a politically motivated burglary. Neisser was interested in the extent to which Dean's testimony matched up with the transcripts of tape-recordings of conversations in the White House, which emerged after Dean's interrogation had taken place. This case study was, therefore, *instrumental* in the sense that John Dean's testimony serves as an exemplar of a more general phenomenon (i.e. the workings of memory). While Neisser acknowledges that it is not possible to do full justice to John Dean's testimony within the terms of reference of a cognitively oriented case study, he proposes that the exploration of memory within a real-life context of some complexity can expand our understanding of some of the mechanisms involved in the psychology of memory. This case study is, therefore, 'a psychological study aimed at clarifying the nature of memory for conversations' (Neisser 1981: 4). It is an *explanatory, single-case study*.

Neisser uses two sources of data for his study: (1) the official transcripts of two important meetings in the president's Oval Office, which took place on 15 September 1972 and on 21 March 1973, respectively, and (2) transcripts of the Committee's cross-examination of John Dean about both of these meetings. Neisser compares the transcript of each meeting with Dean's account of the meeting during cross-examination. The purpose of these comparisons is to establish how Dean remembers the conversations that took place between himself, the president and White House aide Robert Haldeman.

Comparison between the transcript of the meeting of 15 September 1972 and Dean's account of the meeting almost one year later shows that, during his testimony, Dean reports contributions to the conversation by Nixon, Haldeman and himself, which none of them had, in fact, made. These contributions are largely self-serving in the sense that they express others' respect and recognition for Dean (e.g. a warm and cordial reception, praise for his work) and his own modesty and foresight (e.g. a reluctance to take credit, a warning about future developments in the case). Neisser suggests that Dean's testimony of the meeting of 15 September describes a conversation that Dean *wishes* had taken place rather than the one that did, in fact, take place. However, at the same time, Neisser points out that Dean's recollection of the conversation is basically accurate in that it demonstrates that president Nixon was fully aware of the cover-up of the burglary and that he approved of it. Thus, while Dean's recollection was faulty, both in terms of the words used by participants in the conversation as well as their gist, his testimony was characterized by what Neisser (1981: 13) refers to as 'a deeper level of truth'.

Comparison between the transcript of the meeting of 21 March 1973 and Dean's account of it during cross-examination tells a different story. Now Dean produces a generally accurate recollection of his conversation with president Nixon. Neisser suggests that this is because on 21 March Dean was able to present the president with a verbal report while the president listened, interjecting the occasional remarks or questions. This meant that Dean had had an opportunity to rehearse his contribution to the conversation, both before and after the meeting itself. In addition, this meeting, unlike the meeting on 15 September, had fulfilled Dean's hopes in that he had been given the opportunity to say what he wanted to say while president Nixon listened to him. This interpretation is supported by the fact that, in his testimony, Dean barely referred to the second half of the 21 March meeting during which Haldeman joined Dean and the president. Important statements made during that second half of the meeting were remembered by Dean but they were attributed to another conversation altogether. Neisser argues that Dean's memory of 21 March is dominated by his own performance and that other memories of what took place during that meeting were shifted or forgotten as a result.

On the basis of his case study, Neisser is able to identify a process of recollection that he calls 'repisodic'. He argues that, in addition to episodic memory (i.e. retrieval of autobiographical events) and semantic memory (i.e. facts, word meanings, general knowledge), it may be useful to think of memory as being 'repisodic' in that it is based upon a series of similar events that were nevertheless remembered as one representative episode. In Neisser's (1981: 20) words, 'what seems to be an episode actually represents a repetition'. 'Repisodes' embody the common characteristics of a series of events. This means that what people say about such 'repisodes' is true at a deeper level even though it is not faithful to any one particular occasion. John Dean's testimony provides an illustration of how 'repisodic memory' occurs within the circumstances of a particular historical event, which ultimately led to the resignation of president Nixon.

Limitations of case study research

Psychological case studies can be used to address a wide range of questions about the experiences and behaviours of individuals in particular situations. The different types of design available (i.e. *intrinsic* versus *instrumental, single* versus *multiple, explanatory* versus *descriptive*) allow the case study researcher to select the one that is most appropriate to the purpose of the study and its terms of reference. This means that case study research constitutes a versatile approach to qualitative investigation. It also means that rather different kinds of studies can be described as case studies. As a result, it is not always easy to be sure whether a series of related studies constitute case study research proper or whether they are no more than a collection of studies concerned with similar questions. For example, having identified a particular discursive construction, interpretative repertoire or discursive strategy within a text, discourse analysts (see Chapters 6 and 7) may explore other texts in order to find out whether the same devices are deployed there, too. Similarly, conversation analysis (e.g. Drew 1995; Heritage 1997) works with large amounts of data, drawn from a series of related conversations (e.g. telephone conversations or instances of doctor–patient communication) in order to identify consistent patterns and recurrent features of talk-in-interaction (e.g. turn-taking, closure, repair, etc.). In a sense, such research could be described as multiple-case studies. However, researchers using discourse or conversation analytic methods do not tend to see themselves as case study researchers. Thus, there is a lack of clarity in relation to what does and what does not constitute case study research. In addition, there are a number of problems that may arise when conducting case studies. These concern *epistemological* and *ethical* difficulties.

Epistemological difficulties

Triangulation

Case studies rely upon the use of *triangulation*. However, as Silverman (1993) pointed out, triangulation of methods may lead to a neglect of the role of context in the constitution of meaning. In triangulation, the researcher is using different methods of data analysis to arrive at a better understanding of what is 'really going on'. In the process, he or she integrates insights gained from the different analytic approaches. As a result, in an attempt to resolve tensions or contradictions, the researcher may lose sight of context-specific aspects of the data. In addition, it is possible that some of the methods of analysis chosen by a researcher are not, in fact, epistemologically compatible. For example, a combination of realist and relativist methods of analysis of a participant's account of a particular event cannot generate meaningful insights. This is because the two approaches imply different conceptualizations of the status of the text (see pp. 9–10). In one case, the account may be assumed to give expression to the participant's mental processes (e.g. thoughts, memories, perceptions), while in the other, it may be seen to demonstrate the deployment of discursive resources in the pursuit of a particular social objective. It is very important that methods of data collection and analysis used in triangulation are appropriate to the research question asked (i.e. the purpose of the study) as well as epistemologically compatible with one another. Ideally, the research question posed should be clear and focused enough to ensure that the methods chosen to answer it are, in fact, compatible.

Generalizability

The extent to which case study research lends itself to *generalization* is a matter of debate (see also Box 3). While *intrinsic case studies* are explored on account of their particularity, an *instrumental case study design* does appear to aspire to a wider applicability of findings. Similarly, *multiple-case studies* are carried out to generate insights that expand our understanding of a particular phenomenon as it manifests itself across cases. Early case studies, such as Le Play's family monographs (see Hamel 1993: 5–13) or the Chicago School's life histories (see Yin 1994: 21–5), conceived of 'the case' as a micro-social unit that could tell the researcher something about the context in which it occurred (e.g. society, the city, the neighbourhood). It has also been suggested (e.g. Giddens 1984, cited in Hamel 1993) that case studies of the same phenomenon carried out in sufficient numbers can give rise to statements about general trends and the typicality of occurrences. This implies that case study research is capable of a certain 'movement from the local to the global' (Hamel 1993: 34). It means that, for many case study researchers, 'the case' represents something beyond itself. But what does it represent? To what extent can the analysis of a small number of cases tell us something about a more general phenomenon? It is clear that cases in a multiple-case study do not constitute a representative sample in the same way that participants in a survey or experiment represent a particular population. As a result, generalizations from case study research can never apply to other, as yet unexplored, cases, in any direct sense. However, case studies can be used to develop or refine theory, and this means that case study research can give rise to explanations that *potentially* apply to new cases. Case study researchers need to be very careful about the way in which they generalize from their work.

Ethical difficulties

Case study research often requires active involvement on the part of the participant. The participant is asked to talk or write about a particular aspect of their experience (a life event, a situation) in depth. Being interviewed, writing a diary or taking part in tests that involve self-reflection are likely to stimulate thoughts and feelings in the participant, which he or she may not have experienced otherwise. Although this may have positive and even therapeutic effects (see Smith 1993: 263–4), it is also possible that it could affect the participant in less desirable ways. For example, it may draw attention to beliefs and values whose precise content and implications the participant had been largely unaware of. It may prompt the participant to remember events that he or she would rather have kept out of consciousness. It may highlight contradictions between the participant's attitudes and behaviours, which he or she now feels compelled to, but at the same time unable to, resolve. It may bring to light feelings of resentment and regret, which, once recognized and labelled, come to dominate the participant's thoughts. In other words, taking part in case study research has the potential to bring about significant changes in the participant, not all of which are necessarily positive. The researcher needs to take responsibility for the effects that the study is having on the participant. However, the researcher is not always able to deal with such unintended consequences. In such cases, the participant needs to be made aware of other forms of support (e.g. counselling services, support groups, sources of information).

Furthermore, taking part in interactive case study research can engender changes in the participant that have implications for the validity of the study. In interactive case studies, the participant is actively involved in data analysis. In practice, this usually means that the researcher presents his or her emerging interpretations to the participant to obtain feedback. This is sometimes referred to as *respondent validation*

(Silverman 1993: 156). Here, the participant comments upon, elaborates, challenges or validates the analysis. While such participant involvement undoubtedly has both methodological and ethical benefits, it can give rise to problems. The researcher, especially when he or she is also a psychologist, is likely to be attributed expert status by the participant. As a result, the researcher's interpretations of the case material, especially when they are couched in psychological terminology, may be perceived by the participant as information to be understood and absorbed, rather than as interpretative suggestions to be evaluated and challenged. This means that the process of consultation during the interactive case study can miss its purpose by taking on a didactic quality. As a consequence, we do not know whether the participant's endorsement of the researcher's interpretation of the data constitutes genuine validation or simply a form of acquiescence.

Three epistemological questions

Before we close, let us think about the epistemological basis of case study research. What kind of knowledge do case studies produce? What sorts of assumptions do case study researchers need to make about the world when they approach a case? And how does such research position the researcher? Each of these questions allows us to throw some light upon the epistemological arguments that underpin case study research.

1 *What kind of knowledge do case studies aim to produce?*
Case studies are concerned with '[E]stablishing the how and why of a complex human situation' (Yin 1994: 16). They use a variety of methods of data collection and analysis in order to obtain rich and detailed information about a particular occurrence, its context and its consequences. Case study research requires the researcher to produce an accurate and comprehensive description of the characteristics of the case, within the study's terms of reference, in order to generate new insights into the phenomenon under investigation. This means that case studies are basically *realist* in orientation. They aim to improve our understanding of 'what is going on' in a particular situation. Where case studies are concerned with individuals' thoughts and feelings, they assume that it is possible to gain access to these through participants' accounts. Methods used to analyse such accounts (e.g. grounded theory, interpretative phenomenology) are based on the assumption that there is a relationship between what people say about their experiences and the nature of such experiences (see Chapters 3 and 4). Case studies take a close look at individual cases so as to understand better their internal dynamics. Cases are conceptualized as functioning systems (see Stake 1994: 236), which means that they are seen to have an existence that is independent of the researcher's view or interpretation of it. However, Radley and Chamberlain (2001: 321) argue that '(. . .) cases are made, not found', and that researchers would do well to pay attention to both their own and their participants' contribution to the construction of a 'case' as a case.

2 *What kinds of assumptions does case study research make about the world?*
Case study research takes an *idiographic* approach. Case studies focus upon the particular. They start with careful and detailed descriptions of individual cases in all

their particularity before they move on to a cautious engagement with theory development or generalization. This means that case study research is based upon the assumption that the world is a complex place where even general laws or common patterns of experience or behaviour are never expressed in predictable or uniform ways. Such a position resonates with a *critical realist* view of the world. Even general trends always manifest themselves in particular ways. Each case is unique even where it shares characteristics with other cases. In addition, case study research takes a *holistic* perspective. This means that a case can only be understood within its (physical, social, cultural, symbolic, psychological, etc.) context. The meanings of the various characteristics of the case depend on their relationship with others as well as the context(s) within which they manifest themselves. Thus, case study research perceives the world as an integrated system that does not allow us to study parts of it in isolation.

3 *How does case study research conceptualize the role of the researcher in the research process?*
The task of the researcher in case study research is to provide an accurate and detailed account of the case. He or she is expected to look closely and carefully at the evidence to produce a report that captures the characteristics of the case, within the terms of reference of the study. Even though case studies are generally expected to move beyond description and to provide insights that transcend the information that has been collected about a case, they do rely upon the collection of case material. Whether *descriptive* or *explanatory*, the case study relies upon accuracy in matters of detail and the provision of sufficient evidence in support of the researcher's interpretations. This means that the role of the researcher is that of a *witness* or a *reporter*. He or she remains close to the scene in an attempt to observe events carefully and accurately as they unfold. And he or she is expected to be an objective and neutral observer whose attempt to explain or interpret events should not interfere with his or her recording of observations. Even though case study research acknowledges the importance of theory in both the design and conduct of case studies, such studies are expected to tell us more about the case than about the researcher.

Conclusion

We have seen that the case study is an extremely versatile method of research. In fact, it may be suggested that the case study is not really a research method at all, but an approach to the study of singular entities that makes use of a wide range of methods of data collection and analysis. It is possible to characterize case study research by reference to its idiographic perspective, its attention to context, its use of triangulation, its inclusion of a temporal element and its concern with theory (see pp. 74–5). Despite such common ground, case studies can take many different forms, including *intrinsic* versus *instrumental,* *single* versus *multiple,* and *descriptive* versus *explanatory* designs (see pp. 77–9). This diversity can make it difficult to conceive of case study research as a unified approach to qualitative research. It also means that case studies cannot necessarily be compared with one another in a meaningful way. However, it seems to me that there is something which characterizes case study research above all else and which allows us to recognize a case study whatever its design. This is its concern with uniqueness and particularity. As Stake (1995: 8) puts it:

> The real business of case study is particularization, not generalization. We take a particular case and come to know it well, not primarily as to how it is different from others but what it is, what it does. There is emphasis on uniqueness, and that implies knowledge of others that the case is different from, but the first emphasis is on understanding the case itself.

Interactive exercises

1 Think about a suitable case for an intrinsic case study; if you had time, funding and the logistical support necessary, what would intrigue and interest you enough to embark upon an intrinisic case study? Remember that your unit of analysis (i.e. the 'case') can be a person (e.g. a person living with a rare disease), a community (e.g. a group of people living an alternative lifestyle) or an event (e.g. a political protest, a riot). Having selected a suitable case, think about ways in which you would approach the research. How would you collect and analyse data? What would be the role of theory in your design?

2 Think about a suitable case for an instrumental case study; if you had time, funding and the logistical support necessary, what might be a worthwhile research question driving your instrumental case study? Remember that your unit of analysis (i.e. the 'case') needs to constitute an exemplar of the phenomenon you are interested in. This means that you need to identify the phenomenon of interest before you can select the case. Having selected a suitable case, think about ways in which you would approach the research. How would you collect and analyse data? What would be the role of theory in your design? Would it make sense to conduct multiple-case studies in order to shed further light upon the phenomenon?

Further reading

Bromley, D.B. (1986) *The Case Study Method in Psychology and Related Disciplines*. Chichester: John Wiley.

Chamberlain, K., Camic, P. and Yardley, L. (2004) Qualitative analysis of experience: grounded theory and case studies, in D.F. Marks and L. Yardley (eds) *Research Methods for Clinical and Health Psychology*. London: Sage.

Hamel, J. (1993) *Case Study Methods*. London: Sage.

Radley, A. and Chamberlain, K. (2001) Health psychology and the study of the case: from method to analytic concern, *Social Science and Medicine*, 53: 321–32.

Smith, J.A., Harré, R. and Van Langenhove, L. (1995) Idiography and the case study, in J.A. Smith, R. Harré and L. Van Langenhove (eds) *Rethinking Psychology*. London: Sage.

Stake, R.E. (1994) Case studies, in N.K. Denzin and Y.S. Lincoln (eds) *Handbook of Qualitative Research*. London: Sage.

Yin, R.K. (1994) *Case Study Research: Design and Methods*. London: Sage.

Box 3   Extrapolation or generalizability?

Silverman (2000: 300) defines 'generalizability' as that characteristic of research which permits 'generalizing from particular cases to populations'. Some researchers (e.g. Giddens 1984; Hammersley 1992) have suggested that it is possible to establish the representativeness of a single case on the basis of comparisons with a larger sample of similar cases. This argument is based upon an *inductive* logic whereby the frequency of occurrences, or *cases*, serves to strengthen our confidence in the typicality of the phenomenon. Here, generalizability is achieved through accumulation of similar cases. Others (e.g. Bromley 1986; Yin 1994) argue that such a view of generalizability is not appropriate within the context of case study research. These researchers propose that case studies can give rise to theoretical insights that may be generalizable; however, they cannot be used to generalize their findings to populations of similar cases. Yin (1994) differentiates between *analytic generalization* and *statistical generalization*. He suggests that 'the case study, like the experiment, does not represent "a sample", and the investigator's goal is to expand and generalize theories (analytic generalization) and not to enumerate frequencies (statistical generalization)' (p. 10).

Yin argues that cases should not be conceived of as sampling units like subjects in an experiment or a survey. Rather, the case study can be likened to the experiment itself. This means that, while a case study can constitute a test of a theory, it can never be representative of other cases in any statistical sense. As a result, case study research can generate generalizable theoretical propositions but it cannot tell us anything about the characteristics of populations. From this point of view, case study research follows a *hypothetico-deductive* logic whereby cases help us to test the limits of our existing understanding and allow us to develop or modify theories to explain occurrences. Stake (1994: 245) sums up the argument: '[Whereas] the single or a few cases are poor representation of a population of cases and poor grounds for advancing grand generalization ... case studies are of value in refining theory and suggesting complexities for further investigation, as well as helping to establish the limits of generalizability'.

Since the argument about the nature of generalizability in case study research has not been resolved, it is important to be aware of the problems associated with both *inductive* and *hypothetico-deductive* models of generalizability. While induction can never establish certainty in relation to the universality of a phenomenon, hypothetico-deductive work relies upon, and therefore remains limited by, the use of existing theoretical frameworks (see also Chapter 1). An alternative approach to generalization in qualitative research has been proposed by Alasuutari (1995: 156–7), who recommends that we replace the term 'generalization' with 'extrapolation' to refer to the ways in which 'the researcher demonstrates that the analysis relates to things beyond the material at hand'. In this way, we can talk about the wider applicability of case study research without importing claims associated with statistical or experimental research into our arguments.

The following authors provide helpful discussions of generalizability in qualitative research:

Alasuutari, P. (1995) *Researching Culture: Qualitative Method and Cultural Studies*. London: Sage.

Bromley, D.B. (1986) *The Case Study Method in Psychology and Related Disciplines*. Chichester: John Wiley.

Silverman, D. (2000) *Doing Qualitative Research: A Practical Handbook*. London: Sage.

Yin, R.K. (1994) *Case Study Research: Design and Methods*. London: Sage.

6

Discursive psychology

The 'turn to language' • Discursive psychology and Foucauldian discourse
analysis • Discursive psychology • An example of discourse analysis
  • Limitations of discursive psychology • Three epistemological questions
  • Interactive exercises • Further reading

Chapters 6 and 7 introduce *discursive psychology* and *Foucauldian discourse analysis*, respectively. These two approaches to the analysis of discourse share important features. Some researchers argue that they are complementary and that any analysis of discourse should involve insights from both (e.g. Potter and Wetherell 1995; Wetherell 1998; see also Box 4 at the end of this chapter). However, in recent years, the two versions of discourse analysis have become increasingly differentiated.

In this chapter, I provide a general introduction to the 'turn to language' in psychology, and the emergence of the two versions of discourse analysis, discursive psychology and Foucauldian discourse analysis. The remainder of the chapter is devoted to discursive psychology. The next chapter introduces Foucauldian discourse analysis. A direct comparison between the two versions of discourse analysis is made at the close of Chapter 7.

The 'turn to language'

Psychologists' turn to language was inspired by theories and research that had emerged within other disciplines over a period of time. From the 1950s onwards, philosophers, communications theorists, historians and sociologists became increasingly interested in language as a social performance. The assumption that language provided a set of unambiguous signs with which to label internal states and with which to describe external reality began to be challenged. Instead, language was reconceptualized as productive; that is, language was seen to construct versions of social reality and it was seen to achieve social objectives. The focus of enquiry shifted from the individual and his or her intentions to language and its productive potential.

Wittgenstein's philosophy, Austin's speech act theory and Foucault's historical studies of discursive practice are important examples of such early work. However, psychology had remained relatively untouched by these intellectual developments throughout the 1950s and 1960s. Instead, it was concerned with the study of mental representations and with the rules that controlled cognitive mediation of various types of 'input' from the environment. In the 1970s, social psychologists began to challenge psychology's cognitivism (e.g. Gergen 1973, 1989), and in the 1980s the 'turn to language' gained a serious foothold in psychology. The publication of Potter and Wetherell's (1987) *Discourse and Social Psychology: Beyond Attitudes and Behaviour* played an important part in this development. Their book presents a wide-ranging critique of cognitivism, followed by a detailed analysis of interview transcripts using a discourse analytic approach. Later publications developed the critique of psychology's preoccupation with cognition and its use as an all-purpose explanatory strategy, which involved 'claiming for the cognitive processes of individuals the central role in shaping perception and action' (Edwards and Potter 1992: 13). The critique of cognitivism argues that it is based upon a number of unfounded assumptions about the relationship between language and representation. These include (1) that talk is a route to cognition, (2) that cognitions are based on perception, (3) that an objective perception of reality is theoretically possible, (4) that there are consensual objects of thought, and (5) that there are cognitive structures that are relatively enduring. Let us look at each of these assumptions in turn.

1   From a cognitive point of view, people's verbal expression of their beliefs and attitudes provides information about the cognitions that reside in their minds. For the research participant, language provides a way of expressing what is 'in their minds'; for the researcher, language provides a way of accessing participants' cognitions. In other words, *talk is a route to cognition*. As long as the researcher ensures that participants have no reason to lie, their words are taken to constitute true representations of their mental state (e.g. of the beliefs that they subscribe to or the attitudes that they hold). Discourse analysts do not share this view of language. They argue that when people state a belief or express an opinion, they are taking part in a conversation that has a purpose and in which all participants have a stake. In other words, to make sense of what people say, we need to take into account the social context within which they speak. For example, when male participants are interviewed by a female researcher with the aim of identifying men's attitudes towards sharing housework, their responses may be best understood as a way of disclaiming undesirable social identities (as 'sexist slob', as dependent on their female partners, as lazy). This is not to say that they are lying to the researcher about the amount of housework that they do (even though, of course, they may do that as well); rather, it suggests that, in their responses, participants *orient towards* a particular reading of the questions that they are being asked (e.g. as a challenge, as a criticism, as an opportunity to complain), and that the accounts they provide need to be understood in relation to such a reading. Similarly, a response to a question may orient towards what was discussed in an earlier part of the interview. For instance, having been asked about domestic violence earlier on, a participant may take care to distance himself from any

association with such practices in his responses to later questions. Indeed, a participant may orient towards events that took place outside of the immediate interview context, such as those reported in the media. This means that, from a discourse analytic point of view, people's speech is understood as social action, and it is analysed in terms of what it accomplishes within a social context. As a result, we should not be surprised to find that people's expressed attitudes are not necessarily consistent across social contexts.

2   Ultimately, cognitivism has to assume that *cognitions are based on perceptions.* Cognitions are mental representations of real objects, events and processes that occur in the world. Even though cognitions are abstractions and, therefore, often simplifications and distortions of such external events, they do constitute attempts to capture reality. In turn, once established, cognitive schemata and representations facilitate perception and interpretation of novel experiences and observations. By contrast, discourse analysts argue that the world can be 'read' in an unlimited number of ways and that, far from giving rise to mental representations, objects and events are, in fact, constructed through language itself. As a result, it is discourse and conversation that should be the focus of study, because that is where meanings are created and negotiated.

3   If cognitions are based on perceptions, as proposed by cognitivism, it follows that *an objective perception of reality is theoretically possible.* Errors and simplifications in representation are the result of the application of time-saving heuristics, which introduce biases into cognition. Given the right circumstances, it should be possible to eliminate such biases from cognitive processes. Again, discourse analysts take issue with this assumption. If language constructs, rather than represents, social reality, it follows that there can be no objective perception of this reality. Instead, emphasis is placed upon the ways in which social categories are constructed and with what consequences they are deployed in conversation.

4   Attitudes describe how people feel about objects and events in the social world, whereas attribution theory is concerned with how people account for actions and events. In both cases, researchers assume that the social object or event towards which participants have different attitudes, and which participants attribute to different causes, is itself consensual. That is, even though people hold different attitudes and attributions in relation to something (e.g. European Monetary Union, same-sex marriages, the break-up of the Soviet Union), that 'something' itself is not disputed. In other words, there are *consensual objects of thought,* in relation to which people form opinions. People agree on *what it is* they are talking about, but they disagree about why it happened (attributions) and whether or not it is a good thing (attitudes). Discourse analysts do not accept that there are such consensual objects of thought. They argue that the social objects themselves are constructed through language and that one person's version of, say, 'the break-up of the Soviet Union' may be quite different from that of another person. From this point of view, what has traditionally been referred to as 'attitudes' and 'attributions' are, in fact, aspects of the discursive construction of the object itself. For example, if we conceptualize the break-up of the Soviet Union as a consequence of macro-economic global

developments, we would attribute the event to economic processes. If, by contrast, we conceptualize it as a victory for the USA in the Cold War, we would attribute it to the superior political strategies of the US administration. Thus, what differentiates people are not their attitudes and attributions *towards* a social object or event, but rather the *way in which they construct the object or event itself*, through language.

5   Finally, cognitivism is based upon the assumption that somewhere inside the human mind there are *cognitive structures that are relatively enduring*. People are said to hold views and have cognitive styles. They access cognitive schemata and they process information in predictable ways. Cognitive structures can change, but such change needs to be explained in terms of intervening variables, such as persuasive messages or novel experiences. The assumption is that, in the normal course of events, beliefs, attitudes, attributions, and so on remain stable and predictable from day to day. Discourse analysts' conceptualization of language as productive and performative is not compatible with such a view. Instead, they argue that people's accounts, the views that they express and the explanations that they provide, depend on the discursive context within which they are produced. Thus, what people say tells us something about what they are *doing* with their words (e.g. disclaiming, excusing, justifying, persuading, pleading, etc.) rather than about the cognitive structures these words represent.

Discourse analysts' challenge to cognitivism shows that discourse analysis is not simply a research method. It is a critique of mainstream psychology, it provides an alternative way of conceptualizing language, and it indicates a method of data analysis that can tell us something about the discursive construction of social reality. Discourse analysis is more than a methodology because 'it involves a theoretical way of understanding the nature of discourse and the nature of psychological phenomena' (Billig 1997: 43).

Discursive psychology and Foucauldian discourse analysis

There are two major versions of discourse analysis (but note that Wetherell 2001 identifies as many as six different ways of doing discourse analysis). Even though they share a concern with the role of language in the construction of social reality, and are therefore critical of cognitivism, the two versions address different sorts of research question. They also identify with different intellectual traditions. *Discursive psychology* was inspired by ethnomethodology and conversation analysis and their interest in the negotiation of meaning in local interaction in everyday contexts. It is concerned with discourse practices; that is, it studies what people do with language and it emphasizes the performative qualities of discourse. *Foucauldian discourse analysis* was influenced by the work of Michel Foucault and post-structuralist writers who explored the role of language in the constitution of social and psychological life. It is concerned with the discursive resources that are available to people, and the ways in which discourse constructs subjectivity, selfhood and power relations. While discursive psychology is primarily concerned with *how* people *use* discursive resources in order to achieve interpersonal objectives in social interaction, Foucauldian discourse analysis focuses upon *what kind of* objects and subjects are constructed through discourses and *what kinds of* ways-of-being these objects and subjects make available to people.

The two versions of discourse analysis address different sorts of questions. Discursive psychology asks how participants use language in order to negotiate and manage social interactions so as to achieve interpersonal objectives (e.g. disclaim an undesirable social identity, justify an action, attribute blame). Foucauldian discourse analysis seeks to describe and critique the discursive worlds people inhabit and to explore their implications for subjectivity and experience (e.g. what is it like to be positioned as 'asylum seeker' and what kind of actions and experiences are compatible with such a positioning?). Willig (2008) applies the two versions of discourse analysis to the same interview extract in order to highlight similarities and differences between them.

Burr (1995, 2003), Parker (1997) and Langdridge (2004: chapter 18) provide detailed discussions of the distinction between the two versions of discourse analysis. However, Potter and Wetherell (1995: 81) argue that the distinction between the two versions 'should not be painted too sharply' and that a combined focus on discursive practices *and* resources is to be preferred. Wetherell (1998) also advocates a synthesis of the two versions. The debate about whether or not it is helpful to identify two distinct versions of discourse analysis is discussed in more detail in Box 4.

Discursive psychology

This version of discourse analysis was introduced into British social psychology with the publication of Potter and Wetherell's (1987) *Discourse and Social Psychology: Beyond Attitudes and Behaviour*. The label 'discursive psychology' was provided later by Edwards and Potter (1992). As the method evolved, changes in emphasis also emerged. These are largely to do with an increasing emphasis on the flexibility of discursive resources and a preference for the use of naturalistic data sources. Recent developments in discursive psychology continue to be strongly influenced by conversation analytic principles (see Wooffitt 2005). Wiggins and Potter (2008) provide a detailed account of the history and evolution of discursive psychology and its relationship with earlier formulations of discourse analytic perspectives. Discursive psychology is a *psychology* because it is concerned with psychological phenomena such as memory or identity. However, in line with the critique of cognitivism, discursive psychology conceptualizes these phenomena as *discursive actions* rather than as cognitive processes. This means that discursive psychologists are interested in references to concepts such as memory and identity within naturally occurring talk and text, and the functions and consequences of such references. Psychological activities such as justification, rationalization, categorization, attribution, naming and blaming are understood as ways in which participants manage their interests. They are discursive practices that are used by participants within particular contexts to achieve social and interpersonal objectives. In the process, participants may mobilize references to 'memory' or 'identity' (e.g. disclaiming responsibility for missing a birthday by saying 'My memory was playing up again' or justifying an impulsive act by invoking one's 'passionate nature'). As a result, psychological concepts such as prejudice, identity, memory or trust become something people *do* rather than something people *have or are.*

The focus of analysis in discursive psychology is on *how* participants use discursive resources and with what effects. In other words, discursive psychologists pay attention to the *action orientation* of talk. They are concerned with the ways in which speakers manage issues of stake and interest. They identify discursive strategies such as 'disclaiming' or 'footing' and explore their function in a particular discursive context. For example, an interviewee may disclaim a racist social identity by saying 'I am not racist but I think immigration controls should be strengthened' and legitimize the statement by referring to a higher authority: 'I agree with the Prime Minister's statement that the situation requires urgent action'. Other discursive devices used to manage interest and accountability include the use of metaphors and analogies, direct quotations, extreme case formulations, graphic descriptions, consensus formulations, stake inoculation and many more (for a detailed discussion of such devices, see Edwards and Potter 1992; Potter 1996).

Data collection

Ideally, discourse analysis should be used to analyse naturally occurring text and talk (Hepburn and Wiggins 2005; Potter and Hepburn 2005; see contributions to Hepburn and Wiggins 2007). This is because the research questions addressed by discursive psychology are concerned with how people manage accountability and stake in everyday life. Such questions are best explored by analysing conversations that are unsolicited and which take place within familiar settings (e.g. the home or the workplace). For example, tape-recordings of naturally occurring telephone conversations, police-suspect interviews, medical consultations, social work case conferences, radio interviews with politicians and counselling sessions have been used for discourse analysis. However, both ethical and practical difficulties in obtaining such naturally occurring data have led many discourse analysts to carry out semi-structured interviews to generate data for analysis (e.g. see Hepburn and Potter 2003 for a discussion of the ethical challenges involved in utilizing calls to a telephone helpline as data). The disadvantage of using semi-structured interviews is that participants invariably orient towards the interview situation and, as a result, our discursive analysis will reveal more about the ways in which the participant manages his or her stake in the interview *as an interviewee*, than about discursive strategies used in everyday life. In addition, any discourse analysis of semi-structured interviews must include an analysis of *both* interviewer's and interviewee's comments. This requires a high level of reflexivity on the part of the researcher.

An alternative way of generating data for discourse analysis is to set up a group discussion, preferably within pre-existing groups (e.g. a group of friends, colleagues, family members) (see Puchta and Potter 2004). This simulates a naturally occurring conversation, and it is likely that participants will be more relaxed and spontaneous than they would be within the context of a one-to-one interview with a researcher (see also Billig 1997: 45). Sometimes researchers decide to interview friends or acquaintances in order to reduce the artificiality of the interview situation. However, it is important to be aware that interviewing friends can be a challenging experience and that it may lead to reappraisals of one another.

Before discourse analysis can take place, the researcher needs to prepare a *transcript* of the material to be analysed. Transcription is an extremely time-consuming process. It takes at least 10 hours to transcribe a one-hour long interview. Group interviews or interviews with poor sound quality take even longer. In addition, the amount of time spent transcribing depends on the transcription style adopted. The most labour-intensive transcription style is the one used in conversation analysis (see Atkinson and Heritage 1984; Have 1999). Discourse analysts often adopt a reduced adaptation of this transcription style, which retains the key features of the original transcription notation. Here, speech errors, pauses, interruptions, changes in volume and emphasis, as well as audible intake of breath are indicated in the transcript. A full transcription notation of the reduced adaptation can be found in the appendix to Potter and Wetherell (1987) (for an account of the basic principles of transcription, see O'Connell and Kowal 1995). It is important that the transcript contains at least some information about non-linguistic aspects of the conversation, such as delay, hesitations or emphasis. This is because the way in which something is said can affect its meaning. For example, irony can often be detected only by paying attention to tone of voice. A discourse analysis that aims to trace the action orientation of talk will need to pay attention to *the way in which* things are said as well as to *what* is being said.

Given that discourse analysis is a very labour-intensive method, decisions about sample size are often strongly influenced by pragmatic considerations. That is, where research is carried out within narrow time limits, the number of interviews the researcher decides to conduct, transcribe and analyse is likely to be determined by the time available. As a result, researchers often analyse less data than they would have liked to. However, discourse analysts do not need to work with vast amounts of texts in order to produce meaningful analyses. Ultimately, the sample size required to produce valid research depends on the specific research question asked by the researcher (see also Potter and Wetherell 1987: 161–2). If the research question is concerned with the availability and use of particular discursive constructions among a group of people, a relatively large number of interviews with members of the group may be required. Similarly, if the researcher wants to know which discursive strategies people use to disclaim responsibility for an undesirable outcome, the sample size has to be large enough to allow for the identification of a range of strategies and their use within different discursive contexts. On the other hand, if our aim is to understand how a particular text (e.g. an influential political speech, a controversial advertising campaign, a celebrated scene from a movie) achieves its effect, our analysis will concentrate upon a single text.

How to do discourse analysis

I have already pointed out that discourse analysis is more than a methodology. Discourse analysis involves a conceptualization of language as *constructive* and as *functional*. Discourse analysis requires psychologists to look at language in a different way and to ask different questions about it. Instead of asking 'what do participants' responses tell us about their attitudes, beliefs or thoughts?', we need to interrogate the internal organization of the discourse itself and ask 'what is this discourse doing?' Discourse analysis can therefore be described as a particular *way of reading* – reading for action orientation (what is this text doing?) rather than simply reading for meaning (what is this text saying?). Since discourse analysis requires us to adopt an orientation to talk and text *as social action*, it cannot be learned from one day to the next and it cannot be followed like a recipe. Potter and Wetherell (1987: 175) propose that 'discourse analysis is heavily dependent on craft skills and tacit knowledge', while Billig (1997: 39) warns that discourse analysis is not a set of methodological procedures that can be learned in the absence of its wider, theoretical approach to psychology. All this means that discourse analysis needs to be understood, first of all, in terms of its 'broad theoretical framework concerning the nature of discourse and its role in social life' (Potter and Wetherell 1987: 175). On the basis of such an understanding, researchers may then approach texts for analysis. To help novices get started, leading discourse analysts have produced procedural guidelines for the analysis of discourse; for example, Potter and Wetherell (1987: 160–76) identify 'ten stages in the analysis of discourse', and Billig (1997: 54) presents a 'procedural guide for discourse analysis'. Wiggins and Potter (2008) provide detailed and comprehensive guidance regarding the practicalities of discursive psychology research. Antaki et al. (2003) identify criteria by which to evaluate discursive psychology research. However, authors tend to caution readers against following such guidelines too rigidly.

In the next section, I present some guidelines for the analysis of interview transcripts and for the production of the research report, as they pertain to discourse analysis within the discursive psychology tradition (guidelines for Foucauldian discourse analysis are presented in Chapter 7).

Procedural guidelines for the analysis of discourse

Reading
First, the researcher needs to take the time to *read* the transcripts carefully. Although the researcher will continue to read and reread the transcripts throughout the process of coding and analysis, it is important that the transcripts are read, at least once, without any attempt at analysis. This is because such a reading allows us to experience *as a reader* some of the discursive effects of the text. For example, a text may come across as an apology even though the words 'I am sorry' are not actually spoken. We may feel that a text 'makes it sound like' there is a war going on even though the topic of the transcribed speech was a forthcoming election. Reading a text before analysing it allows us to become aware of *what a text is doing*. The purpose of analysis is to identify exactly *how* the text manages to accomplish this.

It is also a good idea to listen to the tape-recordings before analysis, particularly if the transcription notation used is fairly basic.

Coding
Reading and rereading of the transcripts is followed by the selection of material for analysis, or *coding*. Coding of the transcripts is done in the light of the research

question. For example, if our research question is concerned with the ways in which heterosexual adults talk about safer sex and the risk of HIV transmission, all references to condoms, condom use and sexual safety would need to be selected (see Willig 1997). All relevant sections of text are highlighted, copied and filed for analysis. At this stage, it is important to make sure that *all* material that is potentially relevant is included. This means that even instances that are indirectly or only vaguely related to the research question should be identified. Most importantly, use of certain key words is *not* required for selection of textual material. All *implicit constructions* (MacNaghten 1993) must be included at this stage. Thus, in my study of heterosexual adults' talk about safer sex, use of the terms 'condom' or 'safer sex' was not required for inclusion; and references to sexual safety in its widest sense (e.g. talk about 'precautions' and 'safe relationships') were also selected for analysis.

The need for coding before analysis illustrates that we can never produce a complete discourse analysis of a text. Our research question identifies a particular aspect of the discourse that we decide to explore in detail. Coding helps us to select relevant sections of the texts that constitute our data. There are always many aspects of the discourse that we will not analyse. This means that the same material can be analysed again, generating further insights (e.g. Potter and Wetherell 1987; Wetherell and Potter 1992; Willig 1995, 1997, 1998).

Analysis

Discourse analysis proceeds on the basis of the researcher's interaction with the text. Potter and Wetherell (1987: 168) recommend that throughout the process of analysis the researcher asks 'Why am I reading this passage in this way? What features [of the text] produce this reading?' Analysis of textual data is generated by paying close attention to the constructive and functional dimensions of discourse. To facilitate a systematic and sustained exploration of these dimensions, *context, variability* and *construction* of discursive accounts need to be attended to. The researcher looks at how the text constructs its objects and subjects, how such constructions vary across discursive contexts, and with what consequences they may be deployed. To identify diverse constructions of subjects and objects in the text, we need to pay attention to the terminology, stylistic and grammatical features, preferred metaphors and figures of speech that may be used in their construction. Potter and Wetherell (1987: 149) refer to such systems of terms as 'interpretative repertoires'. Different repertoires are used to construct different versions of events. For example, a newspaper article may refer to young offenders as 'young tear-aways', while a defending lawyer may describe his or her clients as 'no-hope kids'. The former construction emphasizes the uncontrollability of young offenders and implies the need for stricter parenting and policing, whereas the latter draws attention to the unmet psychological and educational needs of young offenders and importance of social and economic deprivation. Different repertoires can be used by one and the same speaker in different discursive contexts in the pursuit of different social objectives. Part of the analysis of discourse is to identify the action orientation of accounts. To be able to do this, the researcher needs to pay careful attention to the discursive contexts within which such accounts are produced and to trace their consequences for the participants in a conversation. This can only be done satisfactorily on the basis of an analysis of *both* the interviewer's and the interviewee's contribution to the conversation. It is important to remember that discourse analysis requires us to examine language *in context*.

Interpretative repertoires are used to construct alternative, and often contradictory, versions of events. Discourse analysts have identified conflicting repertoires within participants' talk about one and the same topic. For example, Potter and Wetherell (1995) found that their participants used two different repertoires to talk about Maori culture and its role in the lives of Maoris in New Zealand – 'Culture-as-Heritage' and 'Culture-as-Therapy'. Billig (1997) identifies two alternative, and contrasting, accounts of the meaning of history in participants' discussions of the British royal family – 'History as National Decline' and 'History as National Progress'. The presence of tensions and contradictions among the interpretative repertoires used by speakers demonstrates that the discursive resources that people draw on are inherently dilemmatic (see Billig et al. 1988; Billig 1991). That is, they contain contrary themes that can be pitted against each other within rhetorical contexts. To understand why and how a speaker is using a particular theme, we need to look to the rhetorical context within which he or she is deploying it. Again, the analytic focus is upon variability across contexts and the action orientation of talk.

Writing

The *introduction* to a discourse analytic report often consists of a discussion of the limitations of existing psychological research in relation to the subject matter (e.g. cognitivist approaches to the study of 'prejudice' or behaviouristic conceptualizations of 'addiction'), followed by a rationale for the use of discourse analysis. However, as discourse analysis gains in popularity, researchers will have to review existing discourse analytic studies in their introductions. It is important to be aware of other discourse analytic studies of the same, or related, phenomena to ensure that one's own study is designed to extend or build upon existing research. For example, having identified the use of the phrase 'I dunno' as a way of limiting the extent to which a claim can be undermined by one's partner in conversation ('stake inoculation') in a television interview with Princess Diana, Potter (1997) goes on to show that 'I don't know' is used in the same way by a participant in a counselling session.

Similarly, having explored some of the ways in which 'trust' and 'sexual safety' were discursively constructed and deployed in conversation by heterosexual adults (Willig 1995, 1997, 1998), it would be interesting to see whether gay men or lesbians use similar discursive constructions when talking about sex, risks and relationships. Thus, while early discourse analytic studies stood alone and, by necessity, defined themselves *against* mainstream psychological research, it is now possible, and indeed necessary, for discourse analysts to discuss their work *in relation to* existing discourse analytic research (see also Potter and Wetherell 1994).

The *method* section of a discourse analytic report should provide some information about the nature of discourse analysis. This should include coverage of both theoretical as well as methodological aspects. In other words, the method used to analyse the data needs to be introduced within the context of its theoretical claims about the nature of discourse and its role in the construction of social (and psychological) realities. In addition, the method section should contain information about the ways in which the data (i.e. the texts) have been obtained or produced by the researcher, including transcription notation where appropriate. If the source of data was a semi-structured interview, there should be some discussion of the interviewing style used by the researcher. Questions to be addressed here include: Did the researcher use an interview agenda and, if so, what were the questions? Did the interviewer use an argumentative or a purely facilitative style? What kind of event did the interview constitute (e.g. a research interview, a conversation between friends that happened to be tape-recorded, a challenge to the interviewee's views)? Demographic information about participants should only be provided *where relevant*. For example, if the study is concerned with the ways in which men talk about women and work, it may well be helpful to know whether participants are themselves employed or unemployed, and whether or not they have female partners. However, provision of 'standard' demographic information (e.g. age, gender, social class, ethnicity, education) is *not* appropriate. This is because, from a discourse analytic point of view, provision of such 'information' is, in fact, a way of constructing identities. Providing such 'information' out of context and without rationale suggests that particular social categories capture the essence of people placed within them. Discourse analysis is about exploring the ways in which social reality is constructed within particular contexts through language; an imposition of social categories at the outset is not helpful.

The presentation of the *analysis* constitutes the most extensive section of a discourse analytic report. The structure of this section should reflect both the research question and the emphasis of the analysis. For example, where a study is primarily concerned with the identification of *interpretative repertoires*, the report may be structured by sub-headings that introduce the various repertoires (e.g. 'Culture-as-Heritage' and 'Culture-as-Therapy', or 'History as National Decline' and 'History as National Progress'). A discussion of their contextual deployment and effects would then be presented under the appropriate sub-heading. Alternatively, an exploration of *discursive strategies* used in, say, the negotiation of memory or identity, could be structured around the strategies themselves (e.g. disclaiming, footing) or around their effects (e.g. to enable the speaker to criticize without taking personal responsibility for the criticism and its consequences). Most discourse analytic studies will, of course, combine a discussion of interpretative repertoires and discursive strategies (and their effects). However, the structure of the analysis section will reflect the researcher's primary concern. It is a good idea also to identify this in the title of the report. For example, a title referring to 'discourses of *x*' or 'constructions of *y*' suggests that the study is primarily concerned with the nature of available repertoires, whereas a title that talks about 'negotiating *x*' or 'doing *y*' is likely to introduce a study of discursive strategies and their consequences.

Whatever the primary concern of the study, the analysis section will contain extracts from transcripts or whatever texts constitute the data. Extracts are cited verbatim in the report and they must be clearly identified (e.g. through quotation marks, a different font, or indentation). Selection of extracts for inclusion will, again, depend on the study's focus and the research question. A detailed discussion of the researcher's analysis of the extracts must be provided. It is important to remember that extracts never speak for themselves.

For the purposes of presenting discourse analytic research, it makes sense to merge *analysis* and *discussion* sections. This is because, as in most qualitative research, findings cannot be presented first and then discussed. Instead, a meaningful presentation of the analysis of data can only really take place within the context of a discussion of the insights generated by the analysis. However, it is possible to address wider issues arising out of the research, such as any broader theoretical and conceptual developments, the practical implications of the analysis or any future research indicated by the present study, in a separate *conclusion* section.

All research reports should include a *list of references*, including all authors referred to in the report. There may also be *appendices* containing additional information (e.g. transcription notation or a transcript). These should be clearly labelled and identified at relevant points in the report itself.

Finally, a word about process. Writing up discourse analytic research is not necessarily a process that is entirely separate from the analysis of the texts. Both Potter and Wetherell (1987) and Billig (1997) draw attention to the fact that writing a report is itself a way of clarifying analysis. The attempt to produce a clear and coherent account of one's research in writing allows the researcher to identify inconsistencies and tensions, which in turn may lead to new insights. Alternatively, the researcher may have to return to the data in order to address difficulties and problems raised in the process of writing. It is, therefore, a good idea to allow plenty of time for writing up a discourse analytic study.

An example of discourse analysis
(from Potter and Wetherell 1987)

In order to illustrate the way in which discourse analysts approach a text, let us look at some of the interview extracts discussed by Potter and Wetherell (1987: 46–55). All extracts are taken from transcripts of a series of open-ended interviews with white, middle-class New Zealanders. All of the extracts are concerned with participants' views of 'Polynesian immigrants'. While the analytic comments presented below are tentative and do not constitute a full discourse analysis of the interview transcripts, they do demonstrate the ways in which discourse analysts pay attention to the action orientation of talk.

> *Extract 1*
> I'm not anti them at all you know, I, if they're willing to get on and be like us; but if they're just going to come here, just to be able to use our social welfares and stuff like that, then why don't they stay home?

This extract opens with a *disclaimer* (Hewitt and Stokes 1975). A disclaimer is a verbal device that anticipates, and rejects, potentially negative attributions. In this case, 'I'm not anti them at all, you know' disclaims possible attributions of racism in the light of the comments that are about to follow: 'then why don't they stay home?' To justify the criticisms made of 'Polynesian immigrants' in this extract, the respondent uses an *extreme case formulation* (Pomerantz 1986), whereby claims or evaluations are taken to their extremes to provide an effective warrant. Here, the repeated use of the word 'just' fulfils this function: 'but if they're *just* going to come here, *just* to be able to use our social welfares'. The use of the disclaimer and the extreme case formulation allow the respondent to blame Polynesian immigrants for the hostility they encounter among white New Zealanders and to disclaim any negative attributions or charges of racism at the same time. This demonstrates that discourse has an *action orientation*; in this case, blaming and disclaiming are the tasks that have been accomplished discursively.

Extract 2
What I would li . . . rather see is that, sure, bring them into New Zealand, right, try and train them in a skill, and encourage them to go back again.

Extract 3
I think that if we encouraged more Polynesians and Maoris to be skilled people they would want to stay here, they're not um as uh nomadic as New Zealanders are [Interviewer. Haha.] so I think that would be better.

Both of these extracts are taken from the same interview transcript. The obvious contradiction in the respondent's comments makes it difficult to establish a clear attitude towards immigration; we cannot say whether the respondent is *for* or *against* Polynesians taking up permanent residence in New Zealand. However, from a discourse analytic perspective, such variability is to be expected. This is because speakers orient towards the context within which they speak. Since discourse is organized to accomplish social functions, we need to look at the surrounding text in order to be able to identify the functions to which the discourse is put.

Extract 2 (extended version)

Interviewer: [Do] you think that, say, immigration from the Pacific Islands should be encouraged [ ] to a much larger extent than it is? It's fairly restricted at the moment.

Respondent: Yes. Um, I think there's some problems in, in encouraging that too much, is that they come in uneducated about our ways, and I think it's important they understand what they're coming to. I, what I would li . . . rather see is that, sure, bring them into New Zealand, right, try and train them in a skill, and encourage them to go back again because their dependence on us will be lesser. I mean [ ] while the people back there are dependent on the people being here earning money to send it back, I mean that's a very very negative way of looking at something. [ ] people really should be trying, they should be trying to help their own nation first.

Extract 3 (extended version)
Polynesians, they are doing jobs now that white people wouldn't do. So in many sectors of the community or, or life, um, we would be very much at a loss without them, I think. Um, what I would like to see is more effort being made to train them into skills, skilled jobs, because we are without skilled people and a lot of our skilled people, white people, have left the country to go to other places. I

think that if we encouraged more Polynesians and Maoris to be skilled people they would want to stay here, they're not um as, uh, nomadic as New Zealanders are [Interviewer. Haha.] so I think that would be better.

The respondent's changing position in relation to the question of whether or not Polynesian workers should return to the Pacific Islands makes more sense now. In Extract 2 (extended version), the respondent is concerned with Polynesian society's dependence on wages earned in New Zealand, whereas in Extract 3 (extended version), the respondent discusses the problems of New Zealand's labour market. In relation to the first concern, 'dependence', the presence of Polynesian workers in New Zealand is a bad thing, whereas in relation to the second concern, 'New Zealand's labour market', it is a good thing. Discourse analysis is able to account for variability and contradictions in respondents' accounts because it focuses upon the organization of discourse and its functions. Speakers have access to a variety of contrary themes and arguments that they deploy within different discursive contexts. As Billig (1997: 44) puts it, '[E]ach person has a variety of "voices" '. Instead of mining the discourse for the respondent's underlying 'true' attitude or 'real' view, discursive psychologists view respondents' comments as discursive acts that can only be understood in context.

Extract 4
Then again, it's a problem of their racial integration. They've got a big racial minority coming in now and so they've got to get used to the way of life and, er, perhaps rape is accepted over in Samoa and Polynesia, but not in Auckland. They've got to learn that. And the problem's that a lot of people coming in with mental disease I think it is, because there is a lot of interbreeding in those islan . . . islands. And that brings a big, high increase of retards and then people who come over here, retards perhaps and they//
Interviewer: // and that causes problems?
Respondent: /And that's pretty general I know.

This extract demonstrates how discourse *constructs* the objects of which it speaks. The speaker's version of 'Polynesian immigrants' – as rapists, as retards, as products of inbreeding – contains a negative evaluation. The speaker does not simply provide a negative evaluation of a consensual object of thought; instead, the object itself is constructed in a way that *commands* a negative evaluation. In this way, description (i.e. what 'Polynesian immigrants' are like), explanation (i.e. why they are this way) and evaluation (i.e. how the speaker feels about them) are interdependent aspects of discourse.

Potter and Wetherell's (1987) brief analysis of the four interview extracts demonstrates how *context, variability* and discursive *construction* are fundamental concerns in discourse analytic work. The *context* within which an account is produced provides the analyst with information about the organization and the function of the account – that is, its *action orientation. Variability* in accounts draws attention to the requirements of the discursive context within which speakers are located and the ways in which they *orient towards* such requirements. Different discursive *constructions* of one and the same object contain different explanations and evaluations. This means that objects (people, events, processes, topics) are not *talked about* but *constituted through* discourse. Thus, discourse analysts ask 'How is participants' language constructed, and what are the consequences of different types of construction?' (Potter and Wetherell 1987: 55). Analytic attention to *context, variability* and *construction* allows the discourse analyst to trace the action orientation of talk and text.

Limitations of discursive psychology

It is possible to identify a number of limitations associated with discursive psychology. Some of these have led researchers to turn to the Foucauldian version of discourse analysis introduced in the next chapter. However, it is important to differentiate between limitations that are the result of problems inherent in the methodology, and those that are the inevitable consequence of the chosen focus of the approach. I explore both types of limitations below. Let us begin with limitations in focus.

Limitations in focus

Discursive psychology is interested in discourse and in discourse only, and has been criticized for what Langdridge (2004: 345) refers to as 'the lack of a person' (see also Burr 2002; Butt and Langdridge 2003). Potter and Wetherell (1987: 178) state that '[O]ur focus is exclusively on discourse itself: how it is constructed, its functions, and the consequences which arise from different discursive organisation. In this sense, discourse analysis is a radically non-cognitive form of social psychology'. Thus, discursive psychologists suggest that if we are interested in phenomena such as memory, social identity or the emotions, we should study the ways in which people negotiate their meanings in conversation with one another. The focus of the analysis is on language and its role in the construction of these phenomena. What is of interest to discursive psychologists is the discursive construction and negotiation of psychological concepts and processes, rather than their hypothesized referents (e.g. mental states or cognitions). This means that discursive psychology does not address questions about *subjectivity* – that is, our sense of self, including intentionality, self-awareness and autobiographical memories. This version of discourse analysis is concerned with public discourse, and it does not provide any guidance as to how we may study internalized, or private, manifestations of discourse such as thought or self-awareness. When Potter and Wetherell (1987: 180) point out that for discourse analysis 'the relationship between language and mental states is a nonissue', they do not suggest that 'mental states' or 'cognitive processes' are *necessarily* redundant concepts; in fact, they caution against 'the danger of getting involved in fruitless debates about the reality or non-reality of mental entities, which can easily end in the kind of linguistic imperialism which denies all significance to cognitive processes'.

Inherent limitations

Discursive psychology emphasizes the importance of accountability and stake in conversation (see Edwards and Potter 1992; Potter 1997). It is argued that participants orient to issues of stake and interest throughout their interactions. According to this version of discourse analysis, interpretative repertoires, discursive constructions and discursive devices are deployed strategically by participants in conversation in the pursuit of interpersonal and social objectives. Here, discourse is very much a *tool* that is used by speakers to actively manage their interactions and to pursue their objectives. The assumption is that participants in social interaction have a stake in this interaction and that they are capable of managing their stake through the use of discursive resources. However, despite its heavy emphasis upon the action orientation of talk and text, discursive psychology is unable to account for *why* particular individuals, or groups of individuals, pursue particular discursive objectives. For instance, why is it that speakers work so hard to disclaim certain attributions? Why do some work harder than others? Why is it that sometimes people appear to be using discursive strategies that do *not* work in their favour? Why do some people find it difficult to say things (such as 'Sorry' or 'I love you') even though it would be strategically useful to do so? In other words, discursive psychology assumes that all conversation is driven by stake and interest; however, it is unable to account for what motivates people to adopt, or fail to adopt, a particular stake or to pursue, or fail to pursue, a particular interest (see also Madill and Doherty 1994). Put another way, discursive psychology brackets, and yet relies upon, a notion of motivation or desire, which it is incapable of theorizing. Finally, this version of discourse analysis can be criticized for limiting its analysis of discourse to the texts that constitute its data. The assumption is that meaning is produced through/in the text and that there is, therefore, no need to look 'outside of the text' for further information. Here, what matters is the way in which speakers read one another's comments within a particular context (e.g. the radio interview or the therapy session), rather than who they are or what their words may mean in a wider social context. The problem with this view is that certain discursive and non-discursive practices, rituals, forms of dress and address, and so on, reflect and enact social and material structures. It may be necessary to be aware of such wider social meanings and functions to interpret the use of discourse in a particular context satisfactorily. For example, in order to 'read' a suspect's silence within the context of a police–suspect interview, it would help us to know whether or not the police officer was holding a gun. In recent years, discursive psychology has started to work with video recordings allowing researchers to include visual data such as gestures, gaze and physical orientation (eg. MacMartin and LeBaron 2006). However, on the whole discursive psychology, while placing a strong emphasis upon *language in context* (e.g. by insisting on the inclusion of the interviewer's comments in the analysis), tends to discard the wider social and material context in which a conversation takes place.

Three epistemological questions

To conclude this chapter on discursive psychology, let us take a look at what kind of knowledge it aims to produce, the assumptions it makes about the world it studies, and the way in which it conceptualizes the role of the researcher in the process of knowledge production. I address these three questions in turn.

1 What kind of knowledge does discursive psychology aim to produce?

Discursive psychology is concerned with *how* particular versions of reality are manufactured, negotiated and deployed in conversation. This means that discursive psychology does not seek to understand the 'true nature' of psychological phenomena such as memory, social identity or prejudice. Instead, it studies how such phenomena are constituted in talk as social action. Therefore, the kind of knowledge that discursive psychology produces is not knowledge of the nature of phenomena (such as cognitions, mental states, personality traits or whatever); rather, it is an understanding of the processes by which they are enacted in and through discourse and with what effects. In other words, discursive psychology does not seek to produce a knowledge *of things* but an understanding of the *processes by which they are 'talked into being'*. Discursive psychology is social constructionist in orientation. The knowledge it produces is about how particular constructions are brought into being through the use of interpretative repertoires and discursive devices. It does not make claims about the nature of the world, the existence of underlying causal laws or mechanisms, or entities that give rise to psychological phenomena.

2 What kinds of assumption does discursive psychology make about the world?

Discursive psychologists are interested in the ways in which language is constructive and functional. This means that they emphasize the variability and fluidity of discourse as it serves people in their performance of social actions. As a result, discursive psychologists see the world as a shifting and negotiable place that cannot be understood, or 'read', except through language. And since language is constructive and functional, no one reading can be said to be 'right' or 'valid'. This means that, from a discursive psychologist's perspective, it would be wrong to make any *a priori* assumptions about 'the nature of the world', except to note that the various possible versions of what the world may be like are themselves discursive constructions that are best understood in terms of their action orientation as they are deployed in specific conversational contexts. Discursive psychology, therefore, subscribes to a relativist position.

3 How does discursive psychology conceptualize the role of the researcher in the research process?

Given that discursive psychology emphasizes the constructive and functional nature of language, the role of the researcher is, of necessity, that of an *author* of the research. Since discursive research is an analysis of language use, which is itself, in turn, written up and thus gives rise to another text, it is impossible to see the researcher as a witness or a discoverer. Instead, discursive psychologists acknowledge their active role in the construction of their research findings. They present their research as a reading of the data that is not the only possible reading. Billig (1997: 48) draws attention to the fact that a discursive analysis of a text is never completed and that '[T]he final draft is only final in the sense that the analyst feels that for reasons of deadlines, exhaustion or boredom, no further improvements are likely to be made and that the current draft contains analyses which might be of interest to the reader'. Thus, discourse analysis can provide insights constructed by the analyst; however, it can never 'tell the truth about' a phenomenon because, according to a discursive perspective, such a thing as 'the truth' is itself not *recovered from* but rather *constructed through* language.

In this chapter, a general introduction to the 'turn to language' and discourse analytic thinking was followed by a detailed discussion of one of two major versions of discourse analysis in psychology: *Discursive psychology*. In the next chapter, we take a look at another approach to discourse analytic research. *Foucauldian discourse analysis* shares discursive psychology's critique of cognitivism and its emphasis upon the role of language in the social construction of reality. However, there are also key differences between the two approaches. These will be discussed in more detail in the following pages.

Interactive exercises

1 Construct a dialogue between yourself and a friend in which you turn down an invitation to dinner. You can either do this on your own, by thinking about how you might formulate your response to the friend's invitation and how she or he may react to your response, or you can role-play this situation with a friend or colleague and tape-record your conversation. Look at the transcript and reflect on how the refusal takes shape. How did you package your refusal and why? What did you not do? What might have happened if you had responded differently?

2 Record and transcribe 5 minutes of conversation between two characters in a soap opera. Carefully examine the transcript and think about the characters' stake in the conversation that they are having. What may be their interactional objectives and how do they use language in order to achieve them?

Further reading

Edwards, D. (2004) Discursive psychology, in K. Fitch and R. Sanders (eds) *Handbook of Language and Interaction*. Mahwah, NJ: Lawrence Erlbaum.

Hepburn, A. and Potter, J. (2003) Discourse analytic practice, in C. Seale, D. Silverman, J. Gubrium and G. Gobo (eds) *Qualitative Research Practice*. London: Sage.

Potter, J. (1997) Discourse analysis as a way of analysing naturally occurring talk, in D. Silverman (ed.) *Qualitative Research: Theory, Method and Practice*. London: Sage.

Potter, J. and Wetherell, M. (1994) Analysing discourse, in A. Bryman and R.G. Burgess (eds) *Analysing Qualitative Data*. London: Routledge.

Wetherell M., Taylor S. and Yates S.J. (eds) (2001) *Discourse Theory and Practice: A Reader*. London: Sage.

Wiggins, S. and Potter, J. (2008) Discursive psychology, in C. Willig and W. Stainton Rogers (eds) *The Sage Handbook of Qualitative Research in Psychology*. London: Sage.

Box 4   One method or two?

It has become increasingly common to differentiate between two traditions of discourse analysis in psychology. Even though most researchers emphasize the overlap and cross-fertilization between the two 'versions', they nevertheless identify two separate strands. Some discourse analysts prefer to think of these as differences in emphasis or focus (e.g. Potter and Wetherell 1995; Billig 1997), while others refer to them as different theoretical frameworks or approaches (e.g. Parker 1997; Potter 1997). For example, Potter and Wetherell (1995) differentiate between a concern with *discourse practices* – that is, with what people do with their talk and writing – and a concern with the *discursive resources*, which people draw on when they talk or write. However, according to Potter and Wetherell (1995: 80), these two concerns constitute a 'twin focus' for discourse analysis rather than representing two separate versions of discourse analysis. By contrast, both Parker (1997) and Potter (1997) suggest that there are distinct versions, or variants, of discourse analysis that have grown out of different theoretical and disciplinary traditions (post-structuralism, philosophy and literary theory versus ethnomethodology, sociology and conversation analysis).

Wetherell (1998) takes issue with such a conceptual separation between the two perspectives. She argues that a 'division of labour' with regard to a focus on discursive practices, as inspired by conversation analysis, and a focus on discursive resources, following post-structuralist theory, is counterproductive. Wetherell's (1998) paper constitutes an attempt 'to intervene in the construction within social psychology of contrasting camps of discourse analysts, and to suggest [further] reasons for preferring a more eclectic approach' (p. 405). Wetherell argues that only a synthesis of the two 'versions' – that is, an adoption of a 'twin focus' – allows the discourse analyst to produce a reading that pays attention to *both* the situated and shifting nature of discursive constructions as well as the wider social and institutional frameworks (of meaning, of practices, of social relations) within which they are produced. That is, we need to take into account *both* the availability of interpretative repertoires within a particular social and cultural formation *and* the participants' local concerns and their realization through discourse within a specific context, if we want to understand what is happening in a particular piece of social interaction. While a focus on *discursive practice* helps us to understand *how* speakers construct and negotiate meaning, a focus on *discursive resources* helps us to answer questions about *why* speakers draw on certain repertoires and not others. Wetherell (1998) presents an analysis of a segment of a group discussion in order to demonstrate how discourse analysis can integrate the two perspectives in a way that gives rise to insights that either version on its own would not have been able to generate. It could be argued that the most ambitious discourse analytic studies pay attention to *both* the situated and shifting deployment of discursive constructions, *and* the wider social and institutional frameworks within which they are produced and which shape their production (e.g. Edley and Wetherell 2001). To decide to what extent you agree with Wetherell's call for a more synthetic (that is, integrated) approach to discourse analysis, you may wish to follow up the debate in the following publications:

Parker, I. (1997) Discursive psychology, in D. Fox and I. Prilleltensky (eds) *Critical Psychology: An Introduction*. London: Sage.

Potter, J. (1997) Discourse analysis as a way of analysing naturally occurring talk, in D. Silverman (ed.) *Qualitative Research: Theory, Method and Practice*. London: Sage.

Schegloff, E.A. (1997) 'Whose text? Whose context?', *Discourse and Society*, 8(2): 165–88.

Wetherell, M. (1998) Positioning and interpretative repertoires: conversation analysis and post-structuralism in dialogue, *Discourse and Society*, 9(3): 387–413.

7

Foucauldian discourse analysis

Selecting texts for analysis • Procedural guidelines for the analysis of discourse • An illustration of the application of the six stages to an interview extract • Limitations of Foucauldian discourse analysis • Three epistemological questions • Key differences between discursive psychology and Foucauldian discourse analysis • Interactive exercises • Further reading

The Foucauldian version of discourse analysis was introduced into Anglo-American psychology in the late 1970s. A group of psychologists who had been influenced by post-structuralist ideas, most notably the work of Michel Foucault, began to explore the relationship between language and subjectivity and its implications for psychological research. Some of their work was published in the pages of the journal *Ideology and Consciousness*. The publication of *Changing the Subject: Psychology, Social Regulation and Subjectivity* in 1984 provided readers with a clear illustration of how post-structuralist theory could be applied to psychology. In the book, the authors – Julian Henriques, Wendy Hollway, Cathy Urwin, Couze Venn and Valerie Walkerdine – critically and reflexively examine psychological theories (e.g. of child development, of gender differences, of individual differences) and their role in constructing the objects and subjects that they claim to explain. *Changing the Subject* became a highly influential publication, which inspired many discourse analytic research projects, including doctoral theses, throughout the 1980s and 1990s. A second edition of *Changing the Subject* was published in 1998.

Foucauldian discourse analysis is concerned with language and its role in the constitution of social and psychological life. From a Foucauldian point of view, discourses facilitate and limit, enable and constrain what can be said, by whom, where and when (see Parker 1992). Foucauldian discourse analysts focus upon the availability of discursive resources within a culture – something like a discursive economy – and its implications for those who live within it. Here, discourses may be defined as 'sets of statements that construct objects and an array of subject positions' (Parker 1994: 245).

These constructions in turn make available certain ways-of-seeing the world and certain ways-of-being in the world. Discourses offer *subject positions*, which, when taken up, have implications for subjectivity and experience. For example, from within a biomedical discourse, those who experience ill-health occupy the subject position of 'the patient', which locates them as the passive recipient of expert care within a trajectory of cure. The concept of *positioning* has received increasing attention in recent years (see Harré and Van Langenhove 1999). Foucauldian discourse analysis is also concerned with the role of discourse in wider social processes of legitimation and power. Since discourses make available ways-of-seeing and ways-of-being, they are strongly implicated in the exercise of power. Dominant discourses privilege those versions of social reality that legitimate existing power relations and social structures. Some discourses are so entrenched that it is very difficult to see how we may challenge them. They have become 'common sense'. At the same time, it is in the nature of language that alternative constructions are always possible and that *counter-discourses* can, and do, emerge eventually. Foucauldian discourse analysts also take a historical perspective and explore the ways in which discourses have changed over time, and how this may have shaped historical subjectivities (see also Rose 1999). This is what Foucault (1990) did in his three volumes on *The History of Sexuality*. Finally, the Foucauldian version of discourse analysis also pays attention to the relationship between discourses and institutions. Here, discourses are not conceptualized simply as ways of speaking or writing. Rather, discourses are bound up with institutional practices – that is, with ways of organizing, regulating and administering social life. Thus, while discourses legitimate and reinforce existing social and institutional structures, these structures in turn also support and validate the discourses. For instance, being positioned as 'the patient' within a biomedical discourse means that one's body becomes an object of legitimate interest to doctors and nurses, that it may be exposed, touched and invaded in the process of treatment that forms part of the practice of medicine and its institutions (the hospital, the surgery) (see also Parker and the Bolton Discourse Network 1999: 17).

The Foucauldian version of discourse analysis is concerned with language and language use; however, its interest in language takes it beyond the immediate contexts within which language may be used by speaking subjects. Thus, unlike discursive psychology, which is primarily concerned with interpersonal communication, Foucauldian discourse analysis asks questions about the relationship between discourse and how people think or feel (subjectivity), what they may do (practices) and the material conditions within which such experiences may take place.

In the remainder of this chapter, I identify suitable texts for Foucauldian discourse analysis, formulate procedural guidelines for analysing discourse in this way and work through an example of such analysis. This is followed by a discussion of the limitations of Foucauldian discourse analysis. Its responses to the three epistemological questions are also identified. The chapter closes with a direct comparison between discursive psychology and Foucauldian discourse analysis.

Selecting texts for analysis

Foucauldian discourse analysis can be carried out 'wherever there is meaning' (Parker and the Bolton Discourse Network 1999: 1). This means that we do not necessarily have to analyse words. While most analysts will work with transcripts of speech or written documents, Foucauldian discourse analysis can be carried out on any symbolic system. Parker (1992: 7) recommends that we 'consider all tissues of meaning as texts'. This means that '[S]peech, writing, non-verbal behaviour, Braille, Morse code, semaphore, runes, advertisements, fashion systems, stained glass, architecture, tarot cards and bus tickets' all constitute suitable texts for analysis (p. 7). In *Critical Textwork*, Ian Parker and the Bolton Discourse Network (1999) present discursive analyses of a wide variety of 'texts' including cities and gardens. Foucauldian discourse analysis, therefore, allows us to engage with an extremely wide range of materials.

To select texts for analysis that will generate answers to our research question(s), we need to be clear about what kinds of text are available to us. We need to ask questions about the object status of the text: is it an account, or a narrative, or a part of a conversation (see also Harré 1997)? Or is it part of a campaign, a set of rules or a ritual? How was it produced and who has access to it? Is it language-based or does it use other types of symbolic system? The selection of suitable texts for analysis is informed by the research question. For example, if we wanted to know how the discipline of health psychology has constructed its subject(s), we would need to analyse health psychology textbooks, research papers and perhaps also conversations between health psychologists (see Ogden 1995). If we want to find out how contemporary discourses of pain and pain management position sufferers of chronic pain, and with what consequences, we may analyse literature that discusses biopsychosocial theories of pain, information and guidance given to chronic pain patients (e.g. leaflets, booklets, videotapes), and perhaps also doctor–patient consultations at a pain clinic (see Kugelmann 1997). If, however, we want to find out how ordinary people construct meaning in relation to a particular topic (e.g. the menopause, divorce, national identity), we can work with transcripts of semi-structured interviews or focus group discussions alone. Where researchers are interested in exploring the relationship between public or expert discourses and the ways in which lay people take up (and possibly transform) such discourses, they need to analyse a variety of texts, including documents, published papers and official publications (to identify expert discourses), as well as interview transcripts, group discussions or diaries (to generate lay accounts for analysis).

Procedural guidelines for the analysis of discourse

In chapter one of *Discourse Dynamics: Critical Analysis for Social and Individual Psychology*, Parker (1992) identifies 20 steps in the analysis of discourse dynamics. These 20 steps take the researcher from the selection of a text for analysis (steps 1 and 2) through the systematic identification of the subjects and objects constructed in them (steps 3–12) to an examination of the ways in which the discourse(s) that structure the text reproduce power relations (steps 13–20). Parker provides us with a detailed and wide-ranging guide, which helps us to distinguish discourses, their relations with one another, their historical location and their political and social effects (see Langdridge 2004: 339 for an abridged version of Parker's steps). Other guides to Foucauldian discourse analysis (e.g. Kendall and Wickham 1999: 42–6) rely on fewer steps but presuppose a more advanced conceptual understanding of Foucault's method. In this section, I set out six stages in the analysis of discourse. These stages allow the researcher to map some of the discursive resources used in a text and the subject positions they contain, and to explore their implications for subjectivity and practice (see Box 5 at the end of this chapter for a checklist of key questions to ask of a text in order to facilitate analysis). This is followed by an illustration of how the six stages may be worked through in relation to a short interview extract. Please bear in mind, however, that these six stages do not constitute a full analysis in the Foucauldian sense. In particular, Foucault's concern with the historicity and evolution of discursive formations over time (their genealogy) is not addressed here. For more guidance on how to address key Foucauldian concerns such as genealogy, governmentality and subjectification, see Arribas-Ayllon and Walkerdine (2008).

Stage 1: Discursive constructions

The first stage of analysis is concerned with the ways in which discursive objects are constructed. Which discursive object we focus on depends on our research question. For example, if we are interested in how people talk about 'love' and with what consequences, our discursive object would be 'love'. The first stage of analysis involves the identification of the different ways in which the discursive object is constructed in the text. This requires that we highlight all instances of reference to the discursive object. As mentioned in the previous chapter, it is important that we do not simply look for keywords. Both implicit and explicit references need to be included. Our search for constructions of the discursive object is guided by shared meaning rather than lexical comparability. The fact that a text does *not* contain a direct reference to the discursive object can tell us a lot about the way in which the object is constructed. For example, someone may talk about a relative's terminal illness without directly naming it. Here, references to 'it', 'this awful thing' or 'the condition' construct the discursive object (i.e. terminal illness) as something unspeakable and perhaps also unknowable.

Stage 2: Discourses

Having identified all sections of text that contribute to the construction of the discursive object, we focus on the differences between constructions. What appears to be one and the same discursive object can be constructed in very different ways. The second stage of analysis aims to locate the various discursive constructions of the object within wider discourses. For example, within the context of an interview about her experience of her husband's prostate cancer, a woman may draw on a biomedical discourse when she talks about the process of diagnosis and treatment, a psychological discourse when she explains why she thinks her husband developed the illness in the first place, and a romantic discourse when she describes how she and her husband find the strength to fight the illness together. Thus, the husband's illness is constructed as a biochemical disease process, as the somatic manifestation of psychological traits, and as the enemy in a battle between good (the loving couple) and evil (separation through death) within the same text.

Stage 3: Action orientation

The third stage of analysis involves a closer examination of the discursive contexts within which the different constructions of the object are being deployed. What is gained from constructing the object in this particular way at this particular point within the text? What is its function and how does it relate to other constructions produced in the surrounding text? These questions are concerned with what has been referred to as the *action orientation* of talk and text in the previous chapter. To return to our example of a wife talking about her husband's cancer, it may be that her use of biomedical discourse allows her to attribute responsibility for diagnosis and treatment to medical professionals and to emphasize that her husband is being taken good care of. Her use of romantic discourse may have been produced in response to a question about her own role in her husband's recovery after surgery and may have served to emphasize that she is, in fact, contributing significantly to his recovery. Finally, psychological discourse may have been used to account for her husband's cancer in order to disclaim responsibility for sharing in a carcinogenic lifestyle (e.g. 'I told him to slow down and take better care of himself but he wouldn't listen'). A focus on action orientation allows us to gain a clearer understanding of what the various constructions of the discursive object are capable of achieving within the text.

Stage 4: Positionings

Having identified the various constructions of the discursive object within the text, and having located them within wider discourses, we now take a closer look at the *subject positions* that they offer. A *subject position* within a discourse identifies 'a location for persons within the structure of rights and duties for those who use that repertoire' (Davies and Harré 1999: 35). In other words, discourses construct *subjects* as well as objects and, as a result, make available positions within networks of meaning that speakers can take up (as well as place others within). For example, Hollway's (1989) 'discourse of male sexual drive' contains the subject position of the instinct-driven male sexual predator, positions both men and women as highly socialized moral actors. Subject positions are different from roles in that they offer discursive locations from which to speak and act rather than prescribing a particular part to be acted out. In addition, roles can be played without subjective identification, whereas taking up a subject position has direct implications for subjectivity (see Stage 6 below).

Stage 5: Practice

This stage is concerned with the relationship between discourse and practice. It requires a systematic exploration of the ways in which discursive constructions and the subject positions contained within them open up or close down opportunities for action. By constructing particular versions of the world, and by positioning subjects within them in particular ways, discourses limit what can be said and done. Furthermore, non-verbal practices can, and do, form part of discourses.

For example, the practice of unprotected sex has been found to be bound up with a marital discourse that constructs marriage and its equivalent, the 'long-term relationship', as incompatible with the use of condoms (Willig 1995). Thus, certain practices become legitimate forms of behaviour from within particular discourses. Such practices in turn reproduce the discourses that legitimate them. In this way, speaking and doing support one another in the construction of subjects and objects. Stage 5 of the analysis of discourse maps the possibilities for action contained within the discursive constructions identified in the text.

Stage 6: Subjectivity

The final stage in the analysis explores the relationship between discourse and subjectivity. Discourses make available certain ways-of-seeing the world and certain ways-of-being in the world. They construct social as well as psychological realities. Discursive positioning plays an important role in this process. As Davies and Harré (1999: 35) put it:

> Once having taken up a particular position as one's own, a person inevitably sees the world from the vantage point of that position and in terms of the particular images, metaphors, storylines and concepts which are made relevant within the particular discursive practice in which they are positioned.

This stage in the analysis traces the consequences of taking up various subject positions for the participants' subjective experience. Having asked questions about what can be said and done from within different discourses (Stage 5), we are now concerned with what can be felt, thought and experienced from within various subject positions. For example, it may be that positioning himself within a discourse of male sexual drive allows a man not only to publicly disclaim responsibility for an act of sexual aggression, but to actually *feel* less guilty about it as well.

An illustration of the application of the six stages to an interview extract

The following extract is taken from a transcript of a semi-structured interview with a woman who had recently experienced the break-up of an intimate relationship. The extract represents an exchange between the interviewer (I) and the respondent (R) that occurred about halfway through the hour-long interview (see Willig in press for a discursive psychology analysis of the same extract).

1 I: And when you made the decision um when you were actually working towards
2   finishing it did you talk to friends about it?
3 R: Oh of course

4 I: Yeah

5 R: All the time yeah it would always be a case of how do I do it

6 I: Ah right

7 R: How do I say it what do I say I know I've got to do it how do I go about doing
8   it you know and and just sort of role playing it through and and you know
         just
9   sort of just preparing myself to actually say to him I don't want to go out
         with
10   you anymore because it's so hard even though you know it's got to be done
11   It is just so hard because there's all these you know ties and emotional
         baggage
12   which is which you're carrying and you you you're worrying about the
         other
13   person and you're thinking you invested you know he's invested maybe two
14   years in me

15 I: Yes

16 R: by going out with me and suddenly I'm dumping him what if he doesn't
         find
17   anyone else to go out with

18 I: Oh right yes

19 R: You you start taking responsibility for them and for how they'll cope
20   afterwards you know maybe to the detriment to your own personal sort of
         well
21   being

22 I: Right

23 R: And it was a case of how is he going to cope what's going to happen to him
24   what if no-one goes out with him what if this and what if that and it's all a
         case
25   of ifs anyway and you know as far as I was concerned I was I was more
26   concerned about him and how he would be [. . .] (and a little later in the
         interview)

27 I: [. . .] if you sort of think about it as going on through time um was there
28   anything that changed in the way you behaved towards each other or sex
         life or
29   anything like that? Could you say you know something changed or

30 R: No it was the way I saw it was would I want to marry him was the sort
         of um
31   you know foundation I would use

32 I: Right

33 R: because I thought OK we've been going out for two nearly two years if we
         were
34   going out for another two years would I want to marry him and the answer
35   was no

36 I: Right

37 R: And even though [. . .] I had no intentions of getting married say for
         another you

38   know four five whatever amount of years it was on that basis I was using
      the
39   criteria of my wanting to continue going out with him
40 I: Right
41 R: because it was a case of where is this relationship going and as far as I was
42   concerned it had hit the the brick wall and it wasn't going any further

Stage 1: Discursive constructions

Let us focus on 'the relationship' as our discursive object. Since the study from which the interview extract is taken was concerned with how people describe and account for the break-up of an intimate relationship (see Willig and dew Valour 1999, 2000), it makes sense to ask questions about the ways in which 'the relationship' is constructed through language. In the extract above, 'the relationship' is referred to as something that can be 'finished' (line 2), as something that involves 'going out with' someone (line 9), as something that involves 'ties and emotional baggage' (line 11), as something that requires 'investment' (line 13), as something that provides security (lines 16–19 and lines 23–6), as something that can be stable or change (lines 27–9), as something that requires a foundation or *raison d'être* (lines 30–1 and lines 38–9), as something associated with marriage (lines 30–9) and as something that requires a future (lines 41–2). These nine references construct 'the relationship' as a clearly identifiable social arrangement with a beginning and an end, which offers security in return for investment of time and emotion (lines 2–26). In the second half of the extract, 'the relationship' is also constructed as a step on the way to marriage (lines 30–42).

Stage 2: Discourses

In the interview extract, the relationship is constructed in at least two different ways. On the one hand, the relationship is constructed as a social arrangement between two people who agree to invest resources (e.g. time and emotion) to gain mutual support and security. Such an arrangement is hard to extricate oneself from ('It's hard [. . .] it's just so hard', lines 10–11) because 'ties and emotional baggage' have grown over time. On the other hand, the relationship is constructed as a testing ground for, and a step on the way to, a superior form of involvement, namely marriage. Here, the relationship has to be 'going somewhere' for it to be worthwhile ('[. . .] it had hit the brick wall and it wasn't going any further', lines 41–2), and its quality is judged in the light of its future direction ('And even though [. . .] I had no intentions of getting married for another you know four five whatever amount of years it was on that basis I was using the criteria of my wanting to continue going out with him', lines 37–9).

Let us attempt to locate these two constructions of the relationship (as 'social arrangement' and as 'a step on the way') within wider discourses surrounding intimate relationship. The construction of interpersonal relationships as mutually beneficial social arrangements resonates with *economic discourse*. Notions of investment of resources in return for long-term security and the expectation that social actors exchange goods and services with one another are prominent in contemporary talk about the economy. For example, the term 'partner', now widely used to refer to one's significant other, also describes those we share business interests with. By constructing the relationship through discursive resources derived from economic discourse, we map a picture of intimate relationships that contains assumptions, expectations, legitimate practices and subject positions that give rise to a particular version of intimate relationships. This version is mobilized in the construction of the relationship as a 'social arrangement'. By contrast, the construction of the relationship as 'a step on the way' to marriage draws on a *romantic discourse*. Here, the relationship is not conceptualized as a mutually beneficial arrangement but rather as a way of moving towards the ultimate goal: marriage. Marriage itself is not defined or explored within the text. It is interesting that there appears to be no need to account for *why* the respondent uses suitability for marriage as a 'foundation' (line 31), a 'basis' (line 38) and 'the criteria' (line 39) in her account. She even points out that she has no intention of actually getting married in the near future. However, marriage as a goal forms part of a romantic discourse in which 'love', 'marriage' and 'monogamy' are inextricably linked with one another. By invoking one, we invoke them all. That is, from within a romantic discourse, references to marriage imply the presence of love and monogamy, while references to love imply monogamy as a practice and marriage as a goal. As a result, suitability for marriage becomes a legitimate basis for making decisions about intimate relationships even where there is no suggestion that marriage is a realistic option in the near or medium future.

Stage 3: Action orientation

A closer examination of the discursive context within which the two different constructions of the relationship are deployed allows us to find out more about them. What are their implications for the speaker's interactional concerns? To what extent do they fulfil functions such as assign responsibility or promote one version of events over another? How do they position the speaker within the moral order invoked by the construction (see also Stage 4: Positionings)?

The portion of text that constructs the relationship as a 'social arrangement' is produced in response to a question about the involvement of friends in the decision-making process (I: 'And when you made the decision um when you were actually working towards finishing it did you talk to friends about it?'; lines 20–2). This question in turn is preceded by an account of how the respondent's friends had 'taken a dislike' to her ex-partner and how they had 'talked about him with disdain'. As a result, the respondent pointed out, 'everyone was glad when I'd finished it with him'. The respondent's use of a discursive construction of the relationship as a 'social arrangement' could be seen, within this context, as a way of emphasizing her sense of responsibility for her ex-partner's well-being. Talk about her friends' dislike of her ex-partner and their joy at seeing the relationship break up may have created the impression that he, disliked and rejected, was the victim of a callous act of abandonment on the respondent's part. To counteract such an impression, a construction of the relationship as a 'social arrangement' draws attention to its mutually supportive nature and to the respondent's awareness of the emotional significance of the break-up ('It's hard [. . .] it's just so hard', lines 10–11).

The portion of text that constructs the relationship as a 'step on the way' is produced following the respondent's account of how her ex-partner 'didn't think there was a problem that couldn't be worked out', including the respondent's unhappiness with the relationship. The use of romantic discourse at this point allows the respondent to ward off the charge that she did not give her ex-partner a chance to 'work out' the problems and to save the relationship. From within a romantic discourse, no amount of work can transform 'liking' into 'love', or an 'OK-relationship' into 'the real thing'. The acid-test of romantic love ('would I want to marry him?', line 30) renders redundant attempts to work out problems, because if marriage is not a goal that can be envisaged, the relationship is not worth saving ('and as far as I was concerned it had hit the brick wall and it wasn't going any further', lines 41–2). From within a romantic discourse, the respondent cannot be blamed for not trying hard enough to make the relationship work.

Stage 4: Positionings

What are the subject positions offered by the two discursive constructions of 'the relationship'? A construction of relationships as 'social arrangement' positions partners as highly dependent on one another. Involvement in such a relationship undermines the individual's freedom and mobility; partners are tied to one another through investments, history and emotions ('there's all these you know ties and emotional baggage which . . . you're carrying', line 11). As a result, whoever decides to withdraw from the arrangement is going to cause the other person considerable disruption, inconvenience and probably also a great deal of distress. The subject positions offered by this construction are, therefore, those of responsible social actors who depend on one another for support and who are faced with the difficult task of realizing their interests within relationships of interdependence.

The romantic construction of intimate relationships as 'a step on the way' offers provisional subject positions to lovers. While involved in unmarried relationships, lovers are not fully committed to the relationship. Their involvement contains an opt-out clause that allows them to withdraw from the relationship without penalty. Everything that occurs between lovers within such an arrangement is permanently 'under review' and there is no guarantee that the relationship has a future. Therefore, the subject positions offered by this construction are those of free agents who reserve the right to withdraw from the relationship at any time and without moral sanction.

Stage 5: Practice

What are the possibilities for action mapped by the two discursive constructions of relationships? What can be said and done by the subjects positioned within them? Constructions of relationships as 'social arrangements' and their subject positions of responsible social actors require those positioned within them to act responsibly and with consideration for the consequences of their actions. Being part of a mutually beneficial social arrangement means that whatever we do has effects on the other party within the arrangement, and that we need to take responsibility for these effects. The respondent's account of how she rehearsed breaking-up (lines 5–10) and how hard it was for her to 'actually say to him I don't want to go out with you anymore' (lines 9–10) demonstrates her positioning as a responsible social actor. Taking responsibility for one's partner's well-being (line 19) and breaking up in a way that demonstrates concern for their future are practices that support a construction of relationships as 'social arrangements'. By contrast, being positioned within a relationship as 'a step on the way' does not require the same preoccupation with the other's well-being. Note that the section of text that constructs the relationship as 'a step on the way' (lines 30–42) does not contain any references to the respondent's ex-partner. Instead, it talks about the nature of the relationship and the criteria by which to assess its value. The subject position of a free agent who reserves the right to withdraw from the relationship at any time and without moral sanction involves a focus upon the self and its interests. The free agent is required to make (the right) choices and (good) decisions; he or she is free to choose but receives no help in making decisions. This means that the subject position of the free agent is associated with careful deliberation and a consideration of the effects of potential decision and choices upon the self alone. This is demonstrated in lines 30–42 (note the consistent use of the first person singular and the references to 'foundation', 'basis' and 'criteria' for decision-making in this section).

Stage 6: Subjectivity

This stage in the analysis is, of necessity, the most speculative. This is because here we are attempting to make links between the discursive constructions used by participants and their implications for subjective experience. Since there is no necessary direct relationship between language and various mental states (see the critique of cognitivism in Chapter 6), we can do no more than to delineate what *can* be felt, thought and experienced from within various subject positions; whether or not, or to what extent, individual speakers actually *do* feel, think or experience in these ways on particular occasions is a different question (and one we probably cannot answer by using discourse analysis alone; see 'Limitations of Foucauldian discourse analysis' below).

So, what kinds of subjective experience may be made available by constructions of relationships as 'social arrangements' and their subject positions of responsible social actors? And what kinds of psychological reality may be constructed by a romantic discourse that positions subjects as free agents in search of the ideal relationship? It could be argued that feelings of guilt and regret are available to those positioning themselves within a construction of relationships as 'social arrangements' ('You start taking responsibility for them and for how they'll cope afterwards you know maybe to the detriment to your own personal sort of well-being', lines 19–21), while taking up a position as a free agent within a construction of relationships as 'a step on the way' may involve a sense of time-urgency in relation to decision-making ('because I thought OK we've been going out for two nearly two years if we were going out for another two years would I want to marry him and the answer was no', lines 33–5).

The six stages in the analysis of discourse outlined and illustrated in the preceding sections help us to approach a text and to explore the ways in which it constructs its objects and subjects. In addition, working through the six stages allows us to trace some of these constructions' implications for practice and subjectivity. They can also provide a structure for the presentation of discourse analytic research within the framework of a research paper or report (see Chapter 6 for general guidelines for writing up discourse analytic work). However, it is important to point out that the six stages do not constitute a full analysis in the Foucauldian sense. Foucault was concerned with the relationships between discourse, history and governmentality (see Rose 1999). His methodology involved much more than the analysis of isolated texts and included 'archaeology' and 'genealogy' (for an accessible introduction to these terms, see Kendall and Wickham 1999: 24–31). Critical discourse analysis (e.g. Fairclough 1995; Wodak 1996) stays closer to Foucault's methods by paying attention to the relationship between a particular discursive event and the institutions and social structures that frame it. Parker's (1992) 20 steps in the analysis of discourse dynamics also include those that focus on the historical origins of discourses and their relationships with institutions, power and ideology (steps 13–20).

The six stages identified in this chapter are designed to provide a 'way in' to Foucauldian discourse analysis; a fuller understanding of the social, historical and material dimensions of discourse can only be gained by engaging with the other aspects of Foucault's methods (see, for example, Kendall and Wickham 1999).

Limitations of Foucauldian discourse analysis

The Foucauldian version of discourse analysis conceives of 'text' in its widest sense as containing networks of meaning (discourses) that construct social and psychological realities. It is more ambitious than discursive psychology in that it claims to have something to say about the relationship between symbolic systems (including language), human subjectivity and social relations, rather than being concerned only with language use in interpersonal communication. However, addressing issues such as subjectivity, ideology and power raises a number of difficult theoretical questions for Foucauldian discourse analysts. These include questions about the extent to which we can theorize subjectivity on the basis of discourse alone, and the relationship between discourse and material reality. Let us look at each of these in turn.

Can subjectivity be theorized on the basis of discourse alone?

The Foucauldian version of discourse analysis attributes to discourse the power to construct subjects. Here, discourse is implicated in the process by which 'human beings are made subjects' (Foucault 1982: 208) and, as a result, gain access to particular ways-of-seeing the world and ways-of-being in the world. The availability and uptake of subject positions in discourse gives rise to (social, cultural and grammatical) selves, including that of the unitary rational subject (see Henriques et al. 1984; Harré and Gillett 1994). Discourse analysts agree that discourse is implicated in the construction of selves and subjectivity; however, it is less clear whether discourse is *all* that is required for a sense of personal identity to be formed.

There are some who argue that the mere availability of subject positions in discourse cannot account for the emotional investments individuals make in particular discursive positions and their attachment to those positions. For example, Urwin (1984) emphasizes the role of fantasy, identification and separation in the production of subjectivity. Hollway (1989) uses psychoanalytic concepts such as projection to account for the motivational basis upon which particular positions in discourse are taken up. Hollway and Jefferson (2000) develop this approach and propose the notion of the 'defended subject' whose positionings in discourse are the product of attempts to ward off anxiety (see *British Journal of Social Psychology*, volume 44, for a debate about the use of psychoanalytic concepts in order to unpick discursive positionings). Frosh and colleagues (e.g. Frosh et al. 2003; Frosh and Saville Young 2008) advocate a psychosocial approach that applies psychoanalytic interpretative strategies in order to 'thicken' the discursive reading. Here, biographical information (e.g. about the participant's early life experiences, sibling relationships, etc.) as well as the researcher's observations about the participant's way of relating to the researcher (e.g. an interviewee's questions about how they compare to other interviewees; an interviewee's ability to make the interviewer think of them as special, etc.) can be used as data to provide insights into participants' emotional investments in particular discourses and subject positions. Other discourse analysts (e.g. Davies and Harré 1999) do not feel the need to invoke such theoretical constructs and attempt to account for emotional meanings attached to particular positions in terms of individual life histories and experiences (e.g. of having been located in these positions or of having related to someone in that position). Such an account in turn raises a question about the stability of subject positions and the effects of contradictory positionings on the sense of self. For example, Harré and Van Langenhove (1999) propose that it is only the singularity of our selfhood, expressed through the use of devices such as the first-person pronoun 'I', which remains stable. However, the same singularity (or self) can take up a wide range of subject positions in discourse and thus present a wide range of public personas. These in turn can be internalized and give rise to psychological states, including thoughts and feelings (see Harré and Gillett 1994). But how stable are such internalized states? To what extent can a particular subject position be taken up habitually and to what extent is positioning something that is entirely context-dependent? How can we explain individual differences in preferred subject positions and why do people sometimes position themselves in ways that limit their opportunities for action? These questions need to be addressed more fully by those who use the Foucauldian version of discourse analysis, particularly where they do not wish to invoke theoretical constructs from outside of a discursive framework, such as psychoanalysis (for a more detailed discussion of these questions, see also Willig 2000).

What is the relationship between discourse and material reality?

Discourse analysts agree that discursive constructions have 'real' effects. That is, the way in which we talk about things has implications for the ways in which we experience the world, both physically and psychologically. As Parker (1992: 8) put it, '[D]iscourse constructs "representations" of the world which have a reality almost as coercive as gravity, and, like gravity, we know of objects through their effects'. Religious discourse, for example, illustrates this process very well. However, there is less clarity about the way in which social and material reality in turn may impact upon discourse. If discourse does, indeed, *construct reality*, then to what extent can 'reality' be said to constrain discourse? To put it another way, are there limits to what discourse can do, and if so, what are they? And can we conceive of 'reality' as something separate from, or outside of, discourse? These questions have been addressed by discourse analysts and they have generated strong disagreements between 'relativists' and 'realists' (see Box 6: What, if anything, exists outside of discourse? at the end of this chapter).

While most would agree that 'reality' is of necessity mediated by discourse, and that we do not have direct access even to material reality, there are different views about the extent to which discourse is constrained by social and material structures. Some discourse analysts hold that discourses are produced within a particular set of material conditions and that they can only construct versions of reality that are compatible with these conditions. Others refuse to assign primacy to either discourse or material reality, and emphasize the interdependency between discourses, institutions and social practices. These disagreements have implications for our conceptualization of *power*. If we take the first position, power is maintained and enacted through discourse (among other things such as police forces, armies and weapons), but it is not where power originates. If, however, we take the second position, power is actually produced by discourse; it is an aspect of discursive relations rather than a resource controlled by a particular group of people. Whatever position we take, the relationship between discourse and material reality is a complex one, and it requires further elaboration within discourse analytic work in psychology (for a more detailed discussion of these issues, see Parker 1998; see also Sims-Schouten et al. 2007 for an argument in favour of critical realist discourse analysis followed by a counter-argument by Speer 2007).

Three epistemological questions

Before we make a direct comparison between discursive psychology and Foucauldian discourse analysis, let us take a look at the epistemological orientation of the latter. The three questions below will help us to focus on the kind of knowledge produced by Foucauldian discourse analysis, the assumptions it makes about the world and the role of the researcher in the research process.

1 *What kind of knowledge does Foucauldian discourse analysis aim to produce?*
Foucauldian discourse analysis aims to map the discursive worlds people inhabit and to trace possible ways-of-being afforded by them. Some discourse analysts also ask questions about the historical origin of discourses and their relationship with institutions and social structures. Like discursive psychologists, Foucauldian discourse analysts do not seek to understand the 'true nature' of psychological phenomena, but rather the ways in which particular *versions* of such phenomena are constructed through language (and other symbolic practices). However, unlike discursive psychology, this approach to discourse analysis is also concerned with the social, psychological and physical effects of discourse. Foucauldian discourse analysis aims to produce knowledge about the discursive economy within which we find ourselves,

how it got to be this way (historically) and what this means for us as human subjects (for our sense of self, for our subjectivity, for our experiences). Foucauldian discourse analysis is *social constructionist* in orientation; however, the more realist versions of this approach also aspire to an understanding of the underlying mechanisms that give rise to conditions that make possible the formation of particular discourses (see Box 6). This means that some Foucauldian discourse analysts subscribe to a *critical realist* epistemology (e.g. Parker 1992; Willig 1999a; Sims-Schouten et al. 2007).

2 *What kinds of assumption does Foucauldian discourse analysis make about the world?*
According to this approach, there is no one 'world' that can be described and studied; rather, there are numerous *versions* of the world, each of which is constructed through discourses and practices. Some of these are more widely used, more strongly supported by institutions and, therefore, constitute more legitimate ways-of-seeing. However, no version of the world remains dominant for ever because the social construction of reality through discourse is characterized by change and transformation. Thus, Foucauldian discourse analysis makes very few assumptions about the nature of the world. It takes as its starting point the proposition that multiple readings are always possible and that objects and subjects are not represented by, but rather constructed through, language. Its aim is to identify and map these readings and their consequences. Foucauldian discourse analysis is based on the assumption that discourse plays a fundamental role in the construction of meaning and that human subjectivity is (largely or wholly) structured through language.

3 *How does Foucauldian discourse analysis conceptualize the role of the researcher in the research process?*
From a Foucauldian perspective, *all* forms of knowledge are constructed through discourse and discursive practices. This includes scientific knowledge. As a result, the reports and papers produced by a researcher are themselves discursive constructions that cannot be evaluated outside of a discursive framework. As with discursive psychology, here the researcher *authors*, rather than discovers, knowledge. A reflexive awareness of the problematic status of one's own knowledge claims, and of the discourses used to construct them, is, therefore, an important component of discourse analytic research.

Key differences between discursive psychology and Foucauldian discourse analysis

Both versions of the discourse analytic method share a concern with the role of language in the construction of social reality. However, as I hope has become clear in this and the previous chapter, there are also important differences between the two approaches. To conclude the two chapters dedicated to the discourse analytic method, I want to make a direct comparison between the two versions of discourse analysis. Key differences between them are presented under three headings: 'Research questions', 'Agency' and 'Experience'.

Research questions

Discursive psychology and Foucauldian discourse analysis are designed to answer different sorts of research question. Discursive psychology projects typically ask, 'How do participants use language to manage stake in social interactions?', while Foucauldian discourse analysis is used to find out 'What characterizes the discursive worlds people inhabit and what are their implications for possible ways-of-being?'

Agency

Discursive psychology and Foucauldian discourse analysis emphasize different aspects of human agency. Discursive psychology conceptualizes the speaker as an active agent who uses discursive strategies to manage stake in social interactions. By contrast, Foucauldian discourse analysis draws attention to the power of discourse to construct its objects, including the human subject itself. The availability of subject positions constrain what can be said, done and felt by individuals.

Experience

Discursive psychology questions the value of the category 'experience' itself. Instead, it conceptualizes it (along with others such as 'subjectivity' and 'identity') as a discursive move whereby speakers may refer to their 'experiences' to validate their claims (e.g. 'I know this is hard because I've been there!'). Here, 'experience' is just another discursive construction, to be deployed as and when required. Anything more than this is seen to constitute a return to cognitivism and this would, therefore, not be compatible with discursive psychology. By contrast, Foucauldian discourse analysis does attempt to theorize 'experience' (and 'subjectivity'). According to this approach, discursive constructions and practices are implicated in the ways in which we experience ourselves (e.g. as 'sick' or 'healthy', as 'normal' or 'abnormal', as 'disabled' or 'able-bodied', and so on). As a result, an exploration of the availability of subject positions in discourse has implications for possibilities of selfhood and subjective experience.

Discourse analysis is a relatively recent arrival in psychology. However, despite its short history, it has already generated a large body of literature. As researchers use discourse analytic approaches within different contexts, they encounter new challenges that lead them to develop new ways of applying a discursive perspective. For example, early work in discourse analysis tended to concern itself with social psychological topics such as prejudice. More recently, health psychologists have started to use the method, which has led to the formulation of a material-discursive approach (Yardley 1997), while others have attempted to find ways in which discourse analysis could inform social and psychological interventions (Willig 1999b). Wetherell (2001) identifies as many as six different ways of doing discourse analysis. This demonstrates that discourse analysis is not a method of data analysis in any simple sense. Rather, it provides us with a way of thinking about the role of discourse in the construction of social and psychological realities and this in turn can help us approach research questions in an innovative and original way. The two versions of discourse analysis introduced in this book constitute ways of approaching texts rather than recipes for producing 'correct analyses'. The choice of approach should be determined by the research question(s) we wish to address; in some cases this means that a combination of the two approaches is called for.

Interactive exercises

1 Obtain a transcript of the lyrics of your favourite song. Using the transcript as your data, work through the six stages of Foucauldian discourse analysis as outlined in this chapter. Having identified the discursive constructions, discourses and subject positions contained within the song, reflect on their implications for subjectivity and practice. What are the possibilities for action mapped out by the lyrics? What can be said and done, felt, thought and experienced by the subjects positioned within it? Moving on to a psychosocial analysis, you may want to ask yourself why it is that you like the song so much. What is it about you and your personal history that makes you respond to the discourses invoked by the lyrics in the way that you do? On a more political level of analysis, you may want to think about the extent to which the lyrics are empowering or disempowering – do they offer subject positions from within which to challenge oppressive or limiting social practices or do they reinforce them? Having deconstructed the lyrics, is it still your favourite song?

2 Write a short piece about yourself (around 300 words) in response to the question 'Who am I?'. Using the text you have generated as your data, work through the six stages of Foucauldian discourse analysis as outlined in this chapter. Identify the discursive constructions, discourses and subject positions that structure your account and reflect on their implications for subjectivity and practice. Reflect also on what you have not included and why. Again, you may want to take the analysis further and think about your emotional investments into your preferred discourses and positionings, and to reflect on their political implications.

Further reading

Burr, V. (2003) *Social Constructionism*, 2nd edn. London: Routledge.

Carabine, J. (2000) Unmarried motherhood 1830–1990: a genealogical analysis, in M. Wetherell, S. Taylor and S.J. Yates (eds) *Discourse as Data: A Guide for Analysis*. London: Open University Press.

Fairclough, N. (1995) *Critical Discourse Analysis: The Critical Study of Language*. London: Longman.

Kendall, G. and Wickham, G. (1999) *Using Foucault's Method*. London: Sage.

Parker, I. (1992) *Discourse Dynamics: Critical Analysis for Social and Individual Psychology*. London: Routledge.

Parker, I. and the Bolton Discourse Network (1999) *Critical Textwork: An Introduction to Varieties of Discourse and Analysis*. Buckingham: Open University Press.

Willig, C. (1998) Constructions of sexual activity and their implications for sexual practice, *Journal of Health Psychology*, 3(3): 383–92.

Box 5   Key questions driving Foucauldian discourse analysis (adapted from Vingoe, 2008)

Key Questions	Corresponding Analytic Stage
How is the discursive object constructed through language? What type of object is being constructed?	Stage 1: Discursive Constructions
What discourses are drawn upon? What is their relationship to one another?	Stage 2: Discourses
What do the constructions achieve? What is gained from deploying them here? What are their functions? What is the author doing here?	Stage 3: Action Orientation
What subject positions are made available by these constructions?	Stage 4: Positionings
What possibilities for action are mapped out by these constructions? What can be said and done from within these subject positions?	Stage 5: Practice
What can potentially be felt, thought and experienced from the available subject positions?	Stage 6: Subjectivity

---

Box 6   What, if anything, exists outside of discourse?

Discourse analysts argue that discourse constructs reality. It is not surprising that such a radical claim has given rise to challenges from those who feel that there is more to social and psychological life than language and its various uses. Discourse analysts have responded to such challenges in different ways. In fact, there is an ongoing debate among psychologists who use discourse analytic methods about the extent to which there is such a thing as the extra-discursive. Even though there are many positions and arguments that characterize this debate, its most well-known protagonists are probably Jonathan Potter and Ian Parker.

Potter identifies with a *relativist* position, whereas Parker has argued for a *critical realist* stance. Parker (1992, 1998) has expressed concern that some versions of discourse analytic research may appear to suggest that discursive constructions are entirely independent of the material world. Such a view is idealistic in the sense that it attributes primacy to ideas (expressed in language) rather than to matter (as manifested in structures that exist independently of what we may think of, or say about, them). Parker advocates a critical realist position that acknowledges that our knowledge of the world is necessarily mediated by, and therefore also constructed through, language (i.e. epistemological relativism) while maintaining that there are underlying structures and mechanisms that generate phenomena, versions of which we then construct through language (i.e. ontological realism). This means that discursive constructions of reality are not free-floating but that they are grounded in social and material structures, such as institutions and their practices. Therefore, Parker (1992: 28) argues, 'discourse analysis needs to attend to the conditions which make the meanings of texts possible'.

By contrast, in 'Death and furniture: the rhetoric, politics and theology of bottom line arguments against relativism', Edwards et al. (1995) defend a radical form of *relativism* that refuses to accept 'a bottom line, a bedrock of reality that places limits on what may be treated as epistemologically constructed or deconstructible' (p. 26). In their article, they present a discourse analytic examination of realist arguments in order to demonstrate that even references to 'death and furniture' (i.e. physical and material realities) are themselves discursive constructions rhetorically deployed in the course of a debate. They argue that even thumping a table to appeal to its materiality is a semiotically mediated communicative act and, therefore, a discursive move. Tables can be described in different ways, for different purposes. We may refer to their uses, to their status as a cultural artefact, to the materials they are made of, their consistency at a molecular or even atomic level, and so on. Hitting the table does not give it an extra-discursive essence. Similarly, they point out that death can take many forms (e.g. natural death, terminal disease, murder, manslaughter, capital punishment, fatal accident, suicide, etc.) and it can be conceptualized in different ways (resurrection, afterlife, brain death, spiritual death, etc.). In this way, the authors reinforce their claim that 'it is language itself that provides the tools for constructing a reality beyond words' (p. 31).

Both critical realists and relativists have criticized the implications of each other's arguments. Critical realists have accused relativists of being unable to take up a moral or political position in relation to anything at all. It is argued that if everything is discursively constructed, then we have no grounds for adjudicating between different views. As a result, all views are equally valid and 'anything goes'. Relativists in turn have pointed out that realists' commitment to 'bottom line' arguments means that certain truth claims are ruled out of bounds and cannot be challenged. A principled questioning of all truth claims is, therefore, not possible within a realist framework. It is this, however, relativists argue, which is required to promote a genuine spirit of enquiry.

The debate between realists and relativists has produced many publications. To find out more about the various arguments and positions involved, you may wish to start with the following:

Burman, E. (1990) Differing with deconstruction: a feminist critique, in I. Parker and J. Shotter (eds) *Deconstructing Social Psychology*. London: Routledge.
Edwards, D., Ashmore, M. and Potter, P. (1995) Death and furniture: the rhetoric, politics and theology of bottom line arguments against relativism, *History of the Human Sciences*, 8(2): 25–49.

Parker, I. (1992) *Discourse Dynamics: Critical Analysis for Social and Individual Psychology*. London: Routledge.

Parker, I. (ed.) (1998) *Social Constructionism, Discourse and Realism*. London: Sage.

Potter, J. (1992) Constructing realism: seven moves (plus or minus a couple), *Theory and Psychology*, 2: 167–73.

Potter, J. (1998) Fragments in the realization of relativism, in I. Parker (ed.) *Social Constructionism, Discourse and Realism*. London: Sage.

8
Working with memories

Narrative psychology • Memory work • Why memories? • Data collection
and analysis • 'Saying sorry': an example of data analysis in memory work
• Limitations of memory work • Three epistemological questions • Conclusion
• Interactive exercises • Further reading

Much, perhaps most, qualitative research involves working with memories in one way or another. When research participants provide accounts, be it through interviews, diaries, everyday conversations or focus groups, they tend to invoke past experiences. In some contexts, participants are directly invited to tell stories about their past (e.g. in life history research) whereas in other contexts, memories will play a subsidiary role (e.g. in focus group discussions about a policy issue). Whatever the focus of the research, it is common for participants to make reference to their past experiences, to contextualize and to anchor their observations and opinions within accounts of the past. When we encounter memories within the context of qualitative research, we need to think about what these memories represent and we need to decide how to interpret them. In other words, we need to engage with questions around 'the status of the text' (see Chapter 1, pp. 9–10). Do memories provide us with information about what actually happened to our participants? Or do they tell us something about how our participants construct their life story from the vantage point of their present situation? Does reference to a particular memory within the context of an interview (or focus group discussion or diary entry) fulfil a function, such as to justify or excuse current problem behaviours or difficulties? Or perhaps invoking a memory is part of a bigger project of identity work or collective remembering (see also Middleton and Brown 2005)? There are many ways in which we can approach and 'read' memories, and much has been written about the 'status of memories' within psychotherapeutic work (e.g. see Karson 2006 for a review). It is important that, as qualitative researchers, we are aware of the interpretative options available and that we are clear and explicit about which of them we have chosen to adopt in any particular research project.

So far, I have argued that, whatever the explicit focus of their research, qualitative researchers are likely to come across memories in their data and that they need to engage with questions around the status of such accounts of the past within their analysis. This means that memories as data cannot be avoided in qualitative research. However, there are some qualitative methods whose sole purpose it is to elicit, analyse and interpret accounts of the past and it is to these that we now turn. In this chapter, I introduce two approaches to the analysis of accounts of the past: *narrative psychology* and *memory work*. There are a number of versions of narrative psychology. These are briefly introduced and their common features are identified. This is followed by a more detailed discussion of memory work. The chapter describes data collection and analysis techniques used in memory work. Crawford and coworkers' (1992) research on emotion and gender are introduced to illustrate their application. I also draw attention to some of the limitations of memory work as a research method. The chapter concludes with a discussion of the epistemological position associated with memory work.

Narrative psychology

Narrative psychology is interested in the ways in which people organize and thus bring order to experience. Through constructing narratives about their lives, people make connections between events and interpret them. Telling a story about what has happened to us allows us to give coherence and meaning to what may otherwise feel like a confusing and disorganized sequence of events. Murray (2003: 113) defines narrative as 'an organized interpretation of a sequence of events [which] involves attributing agency to the characters in the narrative and inferring causal links between the events'. In addition, narrative provides us with an opportunity 'to define ourselves, to clarify the continuity in our lives and to convey this to others' (ibid.: 116). Clearly, researching narratives can tell us much about the ways in which people construct meaning in (and for) their lives. Narrative researchers share a belief in the importance of stories, and they share an interest in the structure and form of the stories people tell (sometimes referred to as 'story grammar', see Langdridge 2007). However, narrative researchers differ in the ways in which they approach the study of story grammar. They show interest in different features of narratives and they ask different questions of the narrative during analysis. Ultimately, it does not matter which approach is taken as long as the narrative analysis is systematic and clear, and as long as it generates insights into the structure of the narrative, its functions and its social and/or psychological implications.

When we begin narrative analysis, it is useful to take a look at the types of plots and story forms that have been identified by narrative researchers in the past. Most stories have a beginning, a middle and an end. Stories can also be categorized into romance, comedy, tragedy and satire (see Hiles and Čermák 2008: 156). Gergen and Gergen (1986) identify three types of narrative – progressive (where events progress towards a goal), regressive (where things unravel) and stable (where there is little or no movement in the plot) – which organize many narratives. Frank (1995) describes three kinds of illness narrative – the restitution narrative (where restored health is the goal and assumed/preferred endpoint of the story), chaos narrative (where events do not make sense and no one is in control) and the quest narrative (where the illness experience transforms the sufferer and extends his or her experiential range). Elsbree (1982) identifies five narrative plots, including the journey, the contest, the experience of suffering, pursuing consummation and establishing a home (see Langdridge 2007: 131). It is important, however, that the narrative researcher does not simply sort the narratives that constitute his or her data into an existing framework of types of plot or story forms. The identification of a typology of plots ought to be the outcome of the research rather than its starting point. The types of story identified in the research may or may not resonate with existing typologies.

Narrative researchers work with narrative accounts of particular experiences. These can be obtained through narrative interviewing or by using existing documents such as published memoirs (see Murray 2003 for more information on data collection for narrative analysis). Langdridge (2007) as well as Hiles and Čermák (2008) have formulated helpful guidelines for narrative analysis. They recommend that the narrative researcher applies a range of *interpretative perspectives* to the narrative. This means working through the text repeatedly, asking different questions of the narrative. One set of questions concerns the content of the narrative: What type of story is being told? Who are the protagonists and what happens to them? Does the story have a clear direction (e.g. is it progressive or regressive) or does it meander and fizzle out? Another set of questions is concerned with the tone of the narrative: How is the story being told? What kind of language is being used? Is the delivery flat or emotional? Is the story's tone optimistic or pessimistic? Comic or tragic? Does the speaker seek agreement from the listener(s)? What may be the rhetorical functions of the narrative (e.g. does it aim to persuade, excuse, justify, entertain)? A further set of questions focuses on the themes that are invoked within the narrative: What are the thematic priorities of the text? What are its key themes? How do they relate to one another? Do they support or contradict one another? Finally, we need to ask questions about the social and psychological functions of the narrative: What kind of identities are constructed in the narrative? How does the narrative position the protagonist? How does it position other people in relation to the protagonist? How much agency does the narrative offer its protagonist? Who is and who is not powerful within the story? In whose interest do events unfold in the narrative? Who gains and who loses as a result?

For further information about how to conduct narrative research in psychology see Crossley (2000) and Langdridge (2007).

Memory work

Memory work is a method of inquiry that was developed in the 1980s by Frigga Haug and her colleagues in West Germany (see Haug 1987). Haug's research group was interested in the ways in which individuals appropriate and internalize social relations and practices, or in Haug's words, 'the way they enter into pre-given structures within which they produce both themselves and the categories of society' (Haug 1987: 40). Haug and her colleagues needed a research method that would allow them to study the formation of identities in a way that acknowledged the importance of social structures as well as the participation of individuals in the process of socialization. This required a new approach to the study of self and identity:

If we refuse to understand ourselves simply as a bundle of reactions to all-powerful structures or to the social relations within which we have formed us, if we search instead for possible indications of how we have participated actively in the formation of our past experience, then the usual mode of social scientific research, in which individuals figure exclusively as objects of the process of research, has to be abandoned.

(Haug 1987: 35)

In memory work, the distinction between those who conduct the research (i.e. the researchers) and those who are being studied (i.e. the subjects, the respondents, the participants) disappears. Instead, the researchers themselves generate the data that they then analyse. By working with their own memories, researchers are able to explore their own role in the construction of their unique, yet socially contingent, sense of self. Memory work is designed to trace the process of the construction of individual selves within a predetermined social space.

Why memories?

Haug and her colleagues wanted to understand the processes of socialization by which 'practices of femininity' (Haug 1987: 39) had become incorporated into their own bodies and selves. They wanted to know how they themselves had played an active part in the construction of their identities as 'women', even where this involved subordination. Haug and her research group were not content to invoke social roles and norms to explain why people reproduce oppressive social relations. Instead, they wanted to explore the complex ways in which individuals process the social world, over time, in an attempt to find meaning and pleasure in their interaction with it. Memories play an important role in this process. They provide 'the material out of which we have made ourselves' (Haug 1987: 48). It is important to understand that memory work does not claim that it is the events of the past themselves that make us who we are; rather, as in *narrative psychology*, it is the process by which we have attempted to assimilate the unfamiliar, to resolve contradictions and conflict, and to construct a particular version of the past, and of ourselves, which is decisive. It is in this sense that '[E]xperience may be seen as lived practice in the memory of a self-constructed identity' (Haug 1987: 42). Memory work is designed to uncover the traces of the process of identity formation. It does this by working with memories of particular situations in a way that pays attention to detail rather than using biographical narratives or lengthy accounts. This is because memories of specific situations are more likely to contain evidence of contrasts and contradictions, ambiguities and inconsistencies, that is, the 'rough edges' that can tell us something about the *process* of self-construction. By contrast, autobiographical stories tend to have been rehearsed and recounted many times, and they will have become more and more coherent and stereotyped in the process. It could be argued that, as a result, they tell us more about the *product* of our self-formation.

Another important feature of memory work is its *collective* nature. Memories are produced and analysed by a group of people – a collective – who attempt to trace the social nature of the production of these memories. Thus, while acknowledging that each memory is unique and individual, memory work is concerned with what memories tell us about the social relations within which their meanings were constructed. Ideally, memory work should 'involve[s] the co-researchers in a re-appraisal of these meanings in the light of their common experience' (Crawford et al. 1992: 50). See Stephenson and Kippax (2008) for a detailed account of the theoretical underpinnings of memory work and a review of studies using memory work.

Data collection and analysis

Memory work challenges familiar distinctions – between researcher and researched, between data collection and analysis, between academic and everyday knowledge. The method involves a process of group work during which co-researchers remember, compare, discuss and theorize. Memory work research can take many months or even years to complete, and it can generate diverse insights. While memory work groups differ in their composition, the time they take to complete their research and even the procedures according to which they generate and analyse memories, it is a good idea to follow a set of guidelines, developed by Haug (1987) and elaborated by Crawford et al. (1992), to facilitate systematic analysis and theorizing. In chapter three of *Emotion and Gender: Constructing Meaning from Memory*, Crawford et al. (1992: 43–52) present a clear and comprehensive guide to the memory work process. They split the research process into three phases. Phase one is concerned with the writing of the memories, phase two produces analysis of the memories, and phase three involves integration and theory-building. We can identify a series of steps that need to be taken within each phase.

Phase 1: Generating memories

Step 1: Form a *memory work* group
Memory work groups can have between four and eight members. Crawford et al. (1992) recommend that the members of such a group share characteristics that may be regarded as relevant in relation to the topic under investigation. For example, with topics such as emotions or sexual practices (and their role in the formation of selves), single-sex groups may be preferable. For some topics, a group of friends may be best, whereas other issues may be best discussed within an atmosphere of relative anonymity. The most important requirement, however, is mutual trust and a feeling of safety within the group. In addition, status differences within the group (e.g. the existence of a clear 'leader') are not helpful, since they are likely to undermine equal and active participation by all group members.

Step 2: Choose a trigger
To prompt group members to write memories, the group needs to agree on a suitable *trigger*. The trigger is a word or a short phrase that is expected to generate memories that are relevant to the topic under investigation. For example, where the topic under investigation is 'emotions' (as it was for Crawford et al. 1992), suitable triggers

would be 'saying you are sorry', 'danger' and 'crying'. It is not always easy to find a trigger that will work. Crawford et al. draw attention to the fact that triggers which call up well-rehearsed, scripted memories (e.g. 'first love' or 'being angry') are not as useful as those that prompt more problematic and contradictory memories (e.g. 'touching' or 'saying no'). This is because memory work is interested in tracing the *process* by which selves are constructed within a social space rather than simply in gaining access to the social constructions that dominate that social space. Useful triggers also tend to refer to specific events or episodes rather than generalized or abstract concepts.

Step 3: Write memories
Each member of the group writes a memory in response to the trigger. The writing of memories can take place either within the context of the group meeting itself or outside of it. Crawford et al. (1992: 48) suggest that writing a memory is 'a process that often requires a week's gestation' and is therefore better done outside of the group. To ensure that the memories are written in a way that renders them suitable for memory work analysis, they should be written in the third-person singular and include as much circumstantial detail as possible. This could be references to sounds, tastes and smells that appear to be inconsequential or trivial in terms of the event being remembered. It is important to avoid censoring apparently irrelevant information and to avoid interpretation or justification. The style of writing should be purely descriptive but rich in detail. This is because a first-person account, which includes autobiographical explanations and justifications of events, would be less likely to contain contradiction, conflict and ambiguity. When we are called to account for events, we tend to try to produce a coherent and intelligible version of events that warrants what we did. Writing in the first-person singular encourages this. If, however, we are given an opportunity to describe things from an outside perspective and in great detail, we may be able to reduce such evaluation and justification (e.g. compare the following account in the first person: 'I hit my little sister because I was so angry about the way in which she always took my things without asking first' with the detailed third-person description of the same event: 'It was hot in the room and she felt herself getting more and more angry. Her little sister was clutching her favourite scarf in her chocolate-stained hands. Suddenly, she reached out, tore the scarf from the little girl and flung her hand across her pink cheeks'). Group members may also agree on whether to write early or recent memories. Again, such a decision will depend on the topic under investigation.

Phase 2: Analysis of the memories

Step 4: Textual analysis
The memory work group reconvenes, with members bringing along their written memories. Initially, each individual memory is analysed separately. Each member of the group is handed a typed copy of each memory that has been produced. The memories are then examined, one by one, in terms of the sequences of actions, role relations, clichés and contradictions, statements made and absences that characterize

them. This step in the analysis shares some features with Stage 1 of Foucauldian discourse analysis (see p. 115), in that it aims to identify the social construction of meaning contained in each memory.

Step 5: Cross-sectional analysis

Here, the co-researchers compare their memories with one another. They look for similarities, differences, recurring themes and common patterns. The focus is upon the social relations within which the memories may be located and the cultural meanings on which they may draw. Group members explore the pool of memories as a manifestation of the social space within which they were generated and within which they are being discussed. This means invoking cultural imperatives, popular conceptions, sayings and images that resonate with the memories. It is also important to discuss what is *not* written in the memories and what might have been expected to be included. This step in the analysis aims to uncover the processes involved in the construction of common-sense understandings.

The group discussions surrounding textual (Step 4) and cross-sectional (Step 5) analysis are tape-recorded and transcribed. These transcripts constitute data for further analysis in Phase 3 (see below).

Step 6: Rewriting the memories

At this point in the process of analysis, it may be helpful for group members to return to their memories and to rewrite them in the light of the textual and cross-sectional analysis. Rewriting memories can be a way of becoming more acutely aware of the processes of meaning construction because it requires us to think of *different* ways of making sense of the 'same' event. This is where memory work connects with consciousness-raising.

Phase 3: Integration and theory-building

Step 7: Analysis of transcripts and memories

Now it is time to compare and contrast the memories produced in response to several triggers. The transcripts of the group discussions of the memories constitute further data for integrative analysis. The ideas generated by the group in relation to particular social constructions are themselves subjected to critical appraisal and further theorizing. Existing theories and models are also explored in the light of the group's insights. To what extent can existing psychological theories account for the group's observations? Do the data generated through memory work fit psychological constructs? How may existing models be modified to accommodate the data? What kinds of new theory may be needed to account for the group's observations? In addition, everyday notions and common-sense perceptions (e.g. of what it means to 'feel' something) are also subjected to critical reappraisal. Again, we can see that memory work challenges received categories and distinctions. In memory work, the transcripts of the group's textual and cross-sectional analysis are used as data, while psychological theories and everyday notions are subjected to the same critical appraisal. The data collection and analysis phases are not clearly differentiated (as in grounded theory, see Chapter 3), while both academic and everyday discourse are engaged with.

Step 8: Writing memory work

The process of writing up memory work is still part of Phase 3. Writing both requires and facilitates integration of material. It is also likely that theoretical formulations will be clarified, and even revised, during the process of writing. Since memory work is a collective enterprise, writing cannot be separated from further discussion (another challenge to a familiar distinction). Drafts of papers will have to be read and discussed by the co-researchers, and this may generate new ideas and changes to the original analysis. It is hard to be sure when a memory work project has been completed, and writing it up does not necessarily achieve a sense of closure. As Crawford et al. (1992: 51) observed: 'Writing this book has led us to reflect once again and to ask ourselves when *if ever* the process of reappraisal and reflection will end' (my emphasis).

Memory work research can be written up in different ways. Following the introduction and methodology sections, the presentation of findings can be structured around *constructions* (e.g. 'Women as Objects', 'Women as Monogamous' and 'Women as Seductive'; see Kippax et al. 1990), *themes* (e.g. 'Condom Visibility', 'Pill Invisibility' and 'The Long-term Relationship'; see Harden and Willig 1998) or *topics* (e.g. 'The Hair Project', 'The Body Project', 'The Slavegirl Project' and 'The Legs Project'; see Haug 1987). In all cases, this is followed by an integrative discussion section in which the theoretical implications of the research are addressed in some detail.

'Saying sorry': an example of data analysis in memory work (Crawford et al. 1992)

In *Emotion and Gender: Constructing Meaning from Memory*, Crawford et al. (1992) discuss the social construction of emotions such as happiness and hurt, fear and joy, guilt and shame, anger and rage. In their book, they present memories written within the context of a memory work group. The group's collective analysis of these memories attempts to trace the processes by which group members developed their emotions. To generate memories for analysis, Crawford et al. used several relevant triggers, such as 'being happy', 'danger', 'crying', 'play', 'holidays', 'being praised' and 'fear'. In this section, I illustrate the process of analysis in memory work by looking at the memories produced by Crawford et al. in response to the trigger 'saying sorry'. The group produced five memories that constituted the pool of memories for cross-sectional analysis. This is Ann's memory:

> She was aged between 4 and 6. It was evening, her mother in the kitchen cooking dinner. She was playing on the carpet near her father's feet. He was reading the paper, sometimes talking to her, sometimes responding to her questions or comments. It was a warm night, he had taken off his suit coat. Absorbed in her game she didn't notice him falling asleep until he failed to respond to one of her remarks. His hands were tucked behind his head, his mouth slightly open, he was snoring lightly. She crept to him giggling to herself, anticipating his delight as she

initiated one of their tickling games, watchful as to whether he was *really* asleep. He pretended a lot. At the first touch of the cotton shirt covering his armpits his eyes startled open, his mouth erupted an 'ugh' of anger, his hand stung across her face: 'Don't you *ever* do that again'. She cried loudly enough so her mother heard (or perhaps she heard him shout) and came in. 'What happened?' And after the explanation: 'She didn't mean to upset you'.

The group's *textual analysis* of Ann's memory drew attention to the memory's emotional tone, which is characterized by sharp contrasts and contradiction. Delight is quickly transformed into fright and surprise. We are presented with an image of a loving father who plays 'reciprocal games', yet his response to being tickled is anger and violence. The role relations presented in the memory are characterized by a discrepancy in power between Ann and her father. Even though the tickling game is described as 'reciprocal', Ann is punished when she attempts to initiate it. Her apology (which is, in fact, not explicitly referred to in this memory) is a way of placating the father to prevent further punishment, rather than an expression of regret or an acceptance of guilt. The reference to 'her mother in the kitchen cooking dinner' while her father is 'reading the paper' invokes traditional gender roles. The mother's intervention to restore harmony also reflects a gendered social cliché. Finally, the mother's defence of Ann – 'she didn't mean to upset you' – constitutes an apology on Ann's behalf and is therefore also an attribution of responsibility to Ann for the incident. As a result, Ann is positioned as being responsible for her father's anger.

The other group members' memories of 'saying sorry' reflected many of the themes that emerged from Ann's memory. *Cross-sectional analysis* of the five memories led to the identification of common patterns. First, the group members' expectations that memories of 'saying sorry' would contain references to emotions such as guilt, shame, repentance or regret were not met. Instead, the memories invoked feelings of confusion, fear and indignation. 'Saying sorry' was not an expression of regret but rather an attempt to deflect adults' anger. Second, the sequences presented in the memories suggested that no wrong-doing had been intended. Instead, protagonists' attempts to behave in an 'adult' fashion had been interpreted as a challenge to authority. In four of the five memories, the protagonist had acted in what she perceived to be a reasonable, even mature manner (e.g. initiating a game, reading the newspaper, saying a prayer, defending a club house) only to be met with disapproval by adults (father, grandmother, mother, parents). 'Saying sorry' was a way of recognizing that adults had power over children (to punish them, to hurt them, to make them apologize) but not that they were right. As a result, a sense of injustice and feelings of humiliation prevailed.

The identification of these common patterns led the group to ask questions about the social relations within which their experiences had been constituted. To what extent and in what ways did the protagonists' actions challenge the social relations within which they took place? What kind of commentary did they make on these relations? What purpose was served by making them apologize for their actions? A discussion of these questions allowed the group to move to a more *theoretical* level of analysis.

Here, group members attempted to contextualize their memories and to understand the wider meanings of their actions at the time. For example, in Fay's memory her mother reprimands her for reading her aunt's newspaper without permission. Fay is made to apologize to her aunt. Fay's actions were embedded in a specific set of social relations. She and her mother shared a house with her aunt and two other female relatives during the war years. The aunt was the breadwinner. She occupied a powerful position within the household. Although 'difficult', the aunt was treated with respect by the other women who tried not to annoy her. Within this context, Fay's actions constituted a challenge to her aunt's authority. Fay's apology to the aunt was necessary to restore power relations within the household: 'For the sake of "oiling the social mechanism" it was essential that Fay be made to apologise' (Crawford et al. 1992: 63).

Similar processes could be observed in the other memories. In three of the five memories, 'saying sorry' served the purpose of restoring the existing web of social relationships. In addition, all the memories positioned the protagonists as being responsible for other people's well-being. By being made to apologize, the girls were taught to accept responsibility for the effects that their actions had on others, even where these were unintended. Crawford et al. (1992) proposed that this process is gendered, in that adult women tend to feel responsible for other people's emotional well-being even when they have no power to control it. The episodes remembered by the group can, therefore, be understood as instances of female socialization.

Overall, Crawford and co-workers' (1992: 73–4) analysis of memories of 'saying sorry' suggested that:

> children construct a number of emotions – anger, defiance, glee, shame, guilt . . . in the context of a complex of relations around issues of responsibility and autonomy. In most of the memories discussed, our actions are actions of children trying out our wings, pushing at the boundaries. We try to be adult amongst adults, or we try to be one with our peers; we act as we believe others expect us to act, we reciprocate, we test our competence. Adults often respond to these actions by punishing us . . . Our actions are viewed as irresponsible and incompetent . . . Children define transgression in terms of adult punishment. Our autonomy is threatened by the punishment and the implicit (and often explicit) admonition not to repeat the action.

Limitations of memory work

Memory work is a recently developed research method with a relatively short history and a limited range of applications. Introduced to English-speaking readers by Haug and colleagues in 1987, it has inspired Australian researchers in particular (e.g. Kippax et al. 1988, 1990; Crawford et al. 1992; Pease 2000). Its domain of application so far has been the gendered body and its practices (e.g. Crawford et al. 1994; Harden and Willig 1998; Koutroulis 2001; Gillies et al. 2004). As the method is gaining in popularity, a number of theoretical and practical limitations will have to be addressed, which include the following.

Theoretical limitations

The relationship between past and present

Memory work uses memories of past events because these events, together with the way they are subsequently constructed, are seen to play an important part in the construction of the self. One of the challenges that faces memory work researchers is to clarify the relationship between the subjectively significant event that gave rise to the memory and the memory that is subsequently written about it. Memory work researchers are not concerned with the *accuracy* of the written memory. It is not important whether or not what is described really happened in just the way that it is recounted. Rather, what matters is the extent to which the written memory captures the *meanings* that were invoked by the event at the time. If, as Crawford et al. (1992: 40) propose, 'The task of memory-work is to uncover and lay bare the earlier understandings in the light of current understandings, thus elucidating the underlying processes of construction involved', then it is imperative that we can clearly differentiate between 'earlier' and 'current' understandings.

But to what extent is this possible? How can we know whether a particular written memory does indeed reflect the meanings attributed to the event at the time? To what extent can a memory produced *now* ever capture what was *then*? For instance, from a discursive psychology perspective (see Chapter 6), a text such as a written memory tells us much more about the requirements of the context within which it is written than about the past. Memory work researchers may counter that there are differences between memories that capture earlier meanings and those that reflect current understandings. For example, Crawford et al. (1992) note that their childhood memories had an immediacy that was not present in their adult memories. The former made less use of clichés and cultural imperatives, and they seemed to be less rehearsed. This suggests that, even though both childhood and adult memories are (re)constructions of past events, there are differences in the extent to which they are 'worked over'. However, despite the relevance of this observation, memory work is left with the question of how to differentiate, systematically and theoretically, between *then* and *now*.

The nature of memories

Memory work is based on the assumption that memories of events that involved conflict and contradiction, novelty and unfamiliarity, can tell us most about the processes of self-formation. This is because such events require reflection and reappraisal in relation to what had been taken for granted previously. These events are significant because they throw light on what was socially constructed as problematic at the time, how perceived contradictions may have been resolved and with what consequences for the individual's sense of self. It could be argued, however, that habitual, routine events, which are repeated many times and which require little or no reflection, may also impact significantly upon our developing sense of self. It may be that, precisely because we do *not* reflect on some of our everyday activities, they have the power to shape who we are. It may be that those practices that we engage in unthinkingly are the ones that make us 'grow into' our embodied subjectivities. Crawford et al. (1992:

154) do draw attention to the fact that 'problematic' and 'habitual, mundane, ordinary' events are, in fact, interdependent in that the former are necessarily defined
in relation to the latter. That is, mundane events 'and their habitual nature form the
context from which "problematic" events derive their problematic nature'. However,
memory work does not engage directly with memories of events (or activities/
practices) that were expected, unproblematic or routinized.

Practical limitations

Problems with group work
Memory work takes place in a group setting. One of the strengths of memory work is
its ability to allow participants to analyse and theorize their memories collectively.
Individual memories are explored in detail (*textual analysis*) before they are compared
with the other memories within the pool (*cross-sectional analysis*). This approach to
analysis ensures that both the richness of individual memories as well as their social
embeddedness are recognized and theorized. However, group work creates its own
problems.

First, the emergence of group norms within the memory work collective is likely
to influence both production and analysis of memories. However comfortable group
members feel with one another, it is likely that certain memories will be deemed either
inappropriate or irrelevant by members and will, therefore, not be written (or not be
written in a particular way). In addition, expectations of what kind of memories
should be written, or what kind of features written memories should contain, are likely
to develop as the research progresses. For example, Ann's memory of 'saying sorry'
discussed earlier is actually a second version that Ann wrote after reflecting on the fact
that her mother had not featured in the first version. The fact that Ann noticed her
mother's absence in particular (as opposed to other absences) was probably a result of
the group's interest in emotion and *gender*. It is interesting to note, within this context,
that Crawford et al. (1992) dedicated their book 'to our mothers'. This is not to say
that such a focus leads to bias; in fact, remembering without a focus is not possible.
However, we need to recognize that what is remembered and how it is remembered is
not independent of the group's concerns. Similarly, contributions to the group discussions during textual and cross-sectional analysis are also likely to be influenced by
emerging group norms.

Second, the ideal of running a group without status differences in membership
can be difficult. The person who decides to set up the group may be a more experienced researcher than those who join the group. Also, having initiated a memory work
research project, such a person may then be expected to lead or facilitate the group.
However, the presence of a facilitator does undermine the sense of collectivity necessary for analysis.

Third, even though memory work aims to generate insights into the ways in
which selves are formed within sets of social relations, its interpretations are necessarily grounded within the groups that have generated them. Knowledge produced
through memory work is potentially generalizable because the social relations within
which group members produce(d) their memories characterize societies rather than

individuals. However, until many more memory work groups have produced analyses of memories relating to the same or similar topics, our insights must remain limited. Crawford et al. (1992: 42) acknowledge that, 'Confidence in the relevance of the outcome of memory-work to persons other than those taking part in memory-work groups can best be achieved by ensuring heterogeneity of the groups themselves'. Pease's (2000) work with men's groups constitutes a welcome attempt to do just that.

Three epistemological questions

To conclude this chapter on memory work, we need to think about its epistemological stance. We need to be clear about what kind of knowledge claims can be made on the basis of memory work research. As in previous chapters, three epistemological questions will help us to explore this issue.

1 *What kind of knowledge does memory work aim to produce?*
Research using memory work is concerned with the processes involved in the appropriation of the social world by the individual. It works with written memories to gain a clearer understanding of how individuals construct meanings, and thus also themselves, within particular social relations, over time. Memory work is based on the assumption that individuals do not simply model themselves on others or act out prescribed social roles; instead, they are actively creating themselves as they seek meaning and pleasure within a circumscribed social space. Memory work removes the distinction between the 'knower' and the 'known' by letting a collective of researchers study themselves through their own memories. This means that memory work adopts a *hermeneutic* approach to knowledge production. This involves a concern with meaning in context and the claim that interpretation requires knowledge of the context from which actions derive their meanings (see Rennie 1999). Here, the researcher engages theoretically with the experiential; that is, memory work 'does not give priority to either subjective experience or theory; rather it sets them in a reciprocal and mutually critical relationship' (Crawford et al. 1992: 42). As a result, the knowledge produced by memory work is interpretative and reflexive.

2 *What kinds of assumption does memory work make about the world?*
Memory work assumes that the way in which people experience the world is the product of the *social construction* of meaning within a set of social relations. Here, an individual's 'reality' is not directly determined by social and material structures; instead, it is the individual's psychological appropriation of these structures that gives rise to his or her experience of the world. At the same time, however, memory work acknowledges that such constructions of meaning are fundamentally social in nature, which means that experiences and perceptions of the world can be shared, particularly within social or cultural groups. Furthermore, even though social constructions are not fixed reflections of an external reality, they do have continuity and they do exercise a certain amount of control over what we can and cannot experience. Memory work is based on the assumption that we internalize social relations and practices in the process of self-formation. These social relations (e.g. between women and men, between parents and children) are characterized by power and hierarchies,

which suggests that memory work does appeal to a (critical) realist view of the world. Even though memories are always subject to reinterpretation and the process of self-formation is never completed, our sense of individual subjectivity is characterized by continuity and specificity.

3 *How does memory work conceptualize the role of the researcher in the research process?* Memory work produces interpretations of texts (i.e. of written memories) in the hermeneutic sense (see Question 1). The members of a memory work group construct readings of their memories that attempt to account for their production. The aim of the research is not simply to identify the availability of particular discursive constructions (cf. Foucauldian discourse analysis, Chapter 7) but also to trace the ways in which the individual engages with such constructions and (trans)forms him- or herself in the process. Memory work researchers examine their own memories to identify 'traces of the continuing process of the appropriation of the social and the becoming, the constructing, of the self' (Crawford et al. 1992: 39). At the same time, they reflect on their current understandings, which they bring to bear on their readings of the memories. This means that memory work is a highly reflexive exercise. It involves processes of discovery as well as of construction. In memory work, the researcher *authors* the research in that he or she produces an interpretation of the data. However, at the same time, there is also a sense of *discovery* as the researcher works with memories that contain traces of earlier understandings.

Conclusion

In this chapter, I have introduced the basic principles of narrative psychology and, in more detail, the research process associated with memory work. Both methods are concerned with (re)constructions of past events and the role that these play in our experience of the present. Narrative psychology researchers tend to work with other people's accounts of the past while memory work collapses the distinction between researcher and research participants (for a direct comparison between the two approaches, see Stephenson and Kippax 2008: 138). As such, memory work constitutes something of a challenge to the researcher. To be able to carry out memory work, researchers need to be strongly committed to and intensely engaged with the research. It is important to realize that taking part in a memory work group is a personal as well as a research project. The writing of memories and the collective analysis of these memories gives rise to reappraisals and reflections that are likely to impact upon the researcher's sense of self. The method is not suitable for researchers who wish to maintain a separation between themselves and their research. Memory work collapses the distinction between 'researcher' and 'subject matter' and, as such, it constitutes a personal challenge to the researcher. These issues need to be considered when planning to set up a memory work group. Potential members of such a group should always be made aware of what memory work involves. Their decision to join the group must reflect a truly informed choice.

In an attempt to be clear and systematic in my introduction to data collection and analysis in memory work, I may have given the impression that memory work always involves an orderly progression through the three phases of research. However, before closing this chapter, I want to draw attention to the fact that memory work need not, in fact, be linear. Like grounded theory (see Chapter 3), memory work benefits from an openness that allows researchers to move back and forth between phases and to retrace steps. For example, an insight generated through cross-sectional analysis may lead group members to return to individual memories and to expand or even revise their textual analysis of these memories. In addition, new triggers for the same topic may emerge as a result of the group discussion during textual or cross-sectional analysis and prompt the group to return to Step 3 of Phase 1 ('Write memories'). The work of the group continues until the topic has been exhausted, or, to borrow a term from grounded theory, *saturation* has been achieved.

Memory work is a powerful research method that has the potential to change its practitioners. Crawford et al. (1992: 196) conclude their book by acknowledging the effects that memory work has had on them:

> Memory-work has changed our lives. In doing so, it has changed the way we teach, the way we interact with the professional associations of psychologists, the way we do research, and the way we write. In documenting our experiences and our method, we make it possible for others to build upon what we have done.

Interactive exercises

1 Write a memory to the trigger 'feeling relieved' following the guidelines provided in this chapter (step 3). Conduct a textual analysis of your memory. Pay attention to the sequences of actions, role relations, clichés and contradictions invoked in your memory and note absences and gaps. Now reflect on the way in which your memory constructs meaning around the notion of 'feeling relieved'. What may be its implications for experience and practice? Can you think of alternative ways in which 'feeling relieved' may be constructed? How may others experience 'feeling relieved'?

2 Write an account of a significant event that took place in your recent past (e.g. an argument with a friend or partner; a job interview or examination; an accident). Then rewrite the account in a different style and/or voice (e.g. factual as opposed to emotional; from another's perspective as opposed to your own, etc.). Compare the two accounts and reflect on the different ways in which they construct meaning around the 'same' event. What may be their implications for experience and practice? How might they shape our experiences of similar events in the future? Which of the two accounts seems more 'normal' or less unusual? Is one of the accounts privileged within our culture?

Further reading

Crawford, J., Kippax, S., Onyx, J., Gault, U. and Benton, P. (1992) *Emotion and Gender: Constructing Meaning from Memory.* London: Sage.
Gillies, V., Harden, A., Johnson, K., Reavey, P., Strange, V. and Willig, C. (2004) Women's collective constructions of embodied practices through memory work: Cartesian dualism in memories of sweating and pain, *British Journal of Social Psychology*, 43(1): 99–112.

Kippax, S., Crawford, J., Benton, P., Gault, U. and Noesjirwan, J. (1988) Constructing emotions: weaving meaning from memories, *British Journal of Social Psychology*, 27: 19–33.

Koutroulis, G. (1996) Memory-work: process, practice and pitfalls, in D. Colquhoun and A. Kellehear (eds) *Health Research in Practice, Vol. 2 Personal Experiences, Public Issues*. London: Chapman & Hall.

Pease, B. (2000) *Recreating Men: Postmodern Masculinity Politics*. London: Sage.

Stephenson, N. (2003) Rethinking collectivity: practicing memory-work, *International Journal for Critical Psychology*, 9: 160–76.

Stephenson, N. and Kippax, S. (2008) Memory work, in C. Willig and W. Stainton Rogers (eds) *The Sage Handbook of Qualitative Research in Psychology*. London: Sage.

Box 7   How far can memories take us?

Memory work has only recently emerged as a qualitative research method in psychology. Even though the literature on memory work is growing, there are, as yet, no published expressions of disagreement regarding the theory and practice associated with memory work. However, differences of opinion do frequently find expression within memory work groups as they discuss their memories and interpretations. To provide an insight into the nature of such debates, let us look at a short extract of a discussion among the members of a memory work group in which I have taken part (see also Gillies et al. 2004).

The group was interested in embodiment and had, at the time of the discussion, produced and analysed memories of sweating and pain. Some group members felt that the analysis of the memories had been somewhat disappointing in that it had merely confirmed that group members draw on culturally available resources to construct meanings around sweating and pain. The nature of these resources reflected common-sense understandings and ways of thinking, which, some group members felt, could have been anticipated. For example, memories of pain tended to revolve around dualistic conceptualizations of mind/body and were primarily concerned with pain control. Group members went on to discuss the limitations of using memories as data, and began to explore alternative ways of researching embodiment. The following extract illustrates the ensuing debate (group members are referred to as M1, M2 and M3):

M1:   We've just come back to the same problems that we had with methodology and psychology, it's like we always end up showing what we set out to show.

M2:   That's why it would be interesting to look more at exceptions and perhaps memories of where it didn't work that way, to try and work out how it is that we come to or we learn to or where . . . to look for breaks in this, to show that it doesn't have to be this way or maybe try and find out where the things come from rather than just documenting that they're there and focusing on the similarities. Do you know what I mean?

M3:   There were two different things in there then, one is looking for exceptions and one is you said where they come from.

M2:   But the two would go together wouldn't it? If you can find, say . . .

M3:   Where the exceptions come from?

M2:   The exceptions would tell you something about where this mainstream way of looking at it comes from perhaps or where it doesn't work and where it does work and maybe find where it doesn't work. You can find out how we learn it or how it becomes so natural.

M3:   I suppose I'm not absolutely clear about what we're looking for then. We're looking for examples where we're drawing on something other than . . .

M2:   That's what I would find interesting. Rather than just looking for more and more support for a particular construction in the wider culture 'cos we know it's out there.

M3:   I just haven't gone with that because I can't see how we can draw on anything else, in a sense.

M1:   It's like, you know, the suggestion was made that we go back to our childhood memories about pain rather than looking at dualism, whereas I don't see that there's a way of doing that, because that is the way we write about things, so how can we go back . . . [talking together]. Especially if you're particularly conscious of the fact you're supposed to be looking for the role of dualism.

M3:   Unless we actually maybe try and deliberately, I'm sceptical that this could work, but unless we did actually try and think about maybe the pain where we didn't use dualism or . . .

M1:   I think now that we've discussed it and come up with dualism I don't think that we can. We'll have another trigger and then if it comes up, then that's quite interesting but [talking together] . . .

M2:   Perhaps I don't feel quite so, what's the word, structured, completely inherently and consistently by these dominant ways of, I mean not just me personally but I think in everybody there is contradiction and tension when things don't work, like little ruptures or, what do you call them, little gaps, you know.

M1:   Yes, but I don't think that I can actually sit down and look inside myself and say, ah, there's a rupture and there's a gap, I don't think it's possible to actually identify it in my own set of memories whereas certainly, yes, if you were talking to somebody else and they talked about something, you could say, ah there's a rupture but to actually do it on yourself, I don't think it would be possible.

9

Quality in qualitative research

What constitutes 'good' qualitative research? • *Epistemology and evaluation*
• *Evaluation of the methods introduced in this book* • *Some caveats*
• *Opportunities and limitations in qualitative research* • *A word about
technology* • *'What' and 'how'* • *Further reading*

In Chapter 1, I suggested that we think about the research process as a form of
adventure. I proposed that research methods are best thought of as ways of approaching a question and that this involves a creative, rather than mechanical, mode of
working. In addition, I suggested that research methods also constitute ways of justifying our answers to particular research questions. It is this claim that I want to return to
now, in the final chapter of this book.

Qualitative research is concerned with meaning in context. It involves the interpretation of data. The role of the qualitative researcher requires an active engagement
with the data, which presupposes a standpoint or point of departure. This means
that qualitative research acknowledges a subjective element in the research process.
References to creativity and subjectivity can easily invoke romantic notions of artistic
endeavour and intuitive insight, which in turn are often contrasted with notions of
scientific rigour and objectivity. Such a conceptual opposition between 'art' and 'science' does not, in my view, reflect a real division between mutually exclusive ways of
working; qualitative researchers need to address questions about the scientific value
of their work and its contribution to knowledge. The criteria traditionally used to
evaluate the scientific value of quantitative research in psychology (e.g. reliability,
representativeness, validity, generalizability, objectivity) are not, in their current form,
meaningfully applicable to qualitative research (see Chapter 1). As a result, qualitative
researchers have for some time been engaged in discussions about the ways in
which qualitative research ought to be evaluated. The result has been the identification of a number of different sets of criteria and a lively debate around the value of
such criteria.

In the remainder of this chapter, I review some of the evaluation criteria that have been proposed by qualitative researchers. This is followed by a discussion of the relationship between epistemology and evaluation. It is argued that evaluation criteria need to be compatible with the epistemological framework of the research that is being evaluated. This argument is then explored in relation to the methods introduced in this book. The chapter concludes by presenting an overview of the opportunities and limitations associated with qualitative research methods in general.

What constitutes 'good' qualitative research?

Several authors have attempted to identify criteria for judging the quality of qualitative research in psychology. For example, Henwood and Pidgeon (1992) proposed seven attributes that characterize good qualitative research. These are based upon the assumption that the researcher and the researched, the knower and the known, are not independent entities, and that, therefore, 'objectivity' or absence of bias are not meaningful criteria for judging qualitative research. Henwood and Pidgeon's (1992) guidelines for good practice are concerned with ensuring rigour while acknowledging idiosyncrasy and creativity in the research process. They include:

1   *The importance of fit.* Analytic categories generated by the researcher should fit the data well. To demonstrate good fit, the researcher is encouraged to write explicit, clear and comprehensive accounts of why phenomena have been labelled and categorized in particular ways.

2   *Integration of theory.* Relationships between units of analysis should be clearly explicated and their integration at different levels of generality should be readily apparent. The analyst's memos should demonstrate the process of integration and its rationale.

3   *Reflexivity.* Since the research process inevitably shapes the object of inquiry, the role of the researcher needs to be acknowledged in the documentation of the research.

4   *Documentation.* The researcher should provide an inclusive and comprehensive account of what was done and why throughout the research process.

5   *Theoretical sampling and negative case analysis.* The researcher should continuously seek to extend and modify emerging theory. To do this, he or she should explore cases that do not fit as well as those that are likely to generate new insights.

6   *Sensitivity to negotiated realities.* The researcher needs to attend to the ways in which the research is interpreted by the participants who generated the data in the first place. While participant validation is not always a requirement (people may disagree with the researcher's interpretation for all kinds of personal and social reason), the researcher should at least be aware of participants' reactions and attempt to explain differences between his or her own interpretation and those of the participants.

7   *Transferability.* To allow readers to explore the extent to which the study may, or may not, have applicability beyond the specific context within which the data

were generated, the researcher should report the contextual features of the study in full.

More recently, Elliott et al. (1999) have identified their own guidelines for the evaluation of qualitative research reports. They suggest that there are a number of criteria that are applicable to both qualitative and quantitative research (e.g. appropriateness of methods, clarity of presentation, contribution to knowledge) but that the evaluation of qualitative research requires consideration of further attributes that are especially pertinent to qualitative research. These are:

1   *Owning one's perspective.* Qualitative researchers should disclose their own values and assumptions to allow readers to interpret the analysis and to consider possible alternative interpretations (this corresponds broadly to Henwood and Pidgeon's 'reflexivity').

2   *Situating the sample.* Qualitative researchers should describe participants and their life circumstances in some detail to allow the reader to assess the relevance and applicability of the findings (this corresponds broadly to Henwood and Pidgeon's 'transferability').

3   *Grounding in examples.* Qualitative researchers should use examples of the data to demonstrate the analytic procedures used and the understanding they have generated. This also allows the reader to assess the fit between the data and the researcher's interpretations (this corresponds broadly to Henwood and Pidgeon's 'importance of fit').

4   *Providing credibility checks.* Qualitative researchers should check whether their accounts are credible by referring to others' (e.g. colleagues, participants, other researchers) interpretations of the data or by applying other methods of analysis in relation to the same subject matter (e.g. other qualitative perspectives, quantitative data) (some aspects of this are covered in Henwood and Pidgeon's 'sensitivity to negotiated realities').

5   *Coherence.* Qualitative researchers should aim to present analyses that are characterized by coherence and integration (e.g. in the shape of a narrative or story, a 'map', a framework or underlying structure) while preserving nuances in the data (Henwood and Pidgeon are concerned with a similar issue in 'integration of theory').

6   *Accomplishing general versus specific research tasks.* Qualitative researchers need to be clear about their research tasks. If their research seeks to develop a general understanding of a phenomenon, they need to ensure that their study is based upon an appropriate range of instances. If they aim to provide insight into a specific instance or case, they need to ensure that it has been studied systematically and comprehensively. In both cases, limitations of the applicability of the findings beyond their original contexts need to be addressed.

7   *Resonating with readers.* Qualitative researchers should ensure that the material is presented in such a way as to stimulate resonance in the reader. Readers should

feel that the research has clarified or expanded their understanding and appreciation of the subject matter.

We can see that there is some overlap between Henwood and Pidgeon's (1992) criteria and the guidelines of Elliott et al. (1999). According to these authors, 'good practice' in qualitative research requires the systematic and clear presentation of analyses, which are demonstrably grounded in the data and which pay attention to reflexivity issues. In addition, such work is characterized by an awareness of its contextual and theoretical specificity and the limitations that this imposes upon its relevance and applicability. See also Yardley (2000) for a further discussion of principles for assessing the quality of qualitative research.

Similar sets of criteria for the evaluation of qualitative research have been developed within other social scientific disciplines (e.g. Robson 1993; Leininger 1994). While most of these do seem to tap into similar issues (e.g. reflexivity, credibility, transferability), it is clear that authors approach the question of evaluation from the particular standpoint afforded by their own preferred methodological practice(s). For example, Henwood and Pidgeon's (1992) criteria are informed by grounded theory concepts and terminology, whereas Elliott et al. (1999) locate themselves within a phenomenological-hermeneutic tradition. We need to ask ourselves to what extent evaluation criteria generated with a particular qualitative methodology in mind are, in fact, applicable to all types of qualitative research. Some (e.g. Madill et al. 2000; Reicher 2000) have argued that, since there is no such thing as a unified qualitative research paradigm, criteria for evaluating qualitative research need to be tailored to fit the particular method they are meant to evaluate. Qualitative research can be conducted from within different epistemological and ontological frameworks that require different standards of excellence. This is because different methodological approaches are based upon different assumptions about the nature of the world, the meaning of knowledge and the role of the researcher in the research process.

In Chapter 1, I pointed out that, to be able to evaluate research in a meaningful way, we need to know what its objectives were and what kind of knowledge it aimed to produce. In other words, I suggested that, to be able to evaluate a study's contribution to knowledge, we need to have a clear understanding of the epistemological basis of the research method(s) used in the study. To help the reader keep track of the epistemological arguments associated with each of the six research methods detailed in this book, I identified three epistemological questions, which were addressed in relation to each of the six methods.

In the next section, I explore the relationship between epistemology and evaluation in general. This is followed by a discussion of the ways in which we may evaluate research generated by different research methods.

Epistemology and evaluation

Both Reicher (2000) and Madill et al. (2000) argue that qualitative research is characterized by epistemological diversity and that this has implications for evaluation. However, they do not make use of the same classification of approaches in their exploration of this diversity. Reicher (2000) identifies two types of approach to qualitative research (*experiential* and *discursive*), while Madill et al. (2000) trace three epistemological strands (*realist, contextual constructionist* and *radical constructionist*). Reicher (2000) contrasts qualitative research that aims to gain a better understanding of people's experiences, ways of thinking and actions (*experiential*) with qualitative research that is concerned with the role of language in the construction of reality (*discursive*). He argues that experiential qualitative methods (such as grounded theory) are essentially realist because they 'retain[s] the notion that language is a reflection of internal categories of understanding and can therefore be used to "read off" what people really think and experience' (Reicher 2000: 3). By contrast, discursive qualitative methods are social constructionist because they conceptualize language as a form of social action that constructs versions of reality.

Madill and co-workers' (2000) classification does not suggest such sharp contrasts. Instead, the three approaches that they identify are more akin to positions on a continuum with naïve realism on one end and radical relativism on the other. Here, *realist* qualitative research is characterized by a discovery orientation that can take more or less naïve forms. Less naïve forms of realism (e.g. critical realism) have much in common with constructionist approaches because they recognize the subjective element in knowledge production. *Contextual constructionist* research is based upon the assumption that all knowledge is necessarily contextual and standpoint-dependent. This means that different perspectives generate different insights into the same phenomenon. As a result, such research is concerned with completeness rather than accuracy of representations. Finally, *radical constructionism* challenges the notion of representation itself. Here, knowledge is seen as a social construction and the focus of the research is the discursive resources and practices that constitute 'knowledge'. Thus, Reicher's (2000) *experiential* category combines Madill and co-workers' (2000) *realist* and *contextual constructionist* approaches (see Fig. 1).

Both Reicher (2000) and Madill et al. (2000) agree that the differences between the various approaches and their epistemological underpinnings are significant. In Reicher's (2000: 4) words, 'they have different philosophical roots, they have different theoretical assumptions and they ask different types of questions'. As a result, they call for different criteria in their evaluation. According to Madill et al. (2000), studies that are conducted from within a realist epistemology can be evaluated in terms of their *objectivity* and *reliability*. Objectivity here refers to the absence of bias on the part of the researcher. For example, grounded theory researchers would be expected to

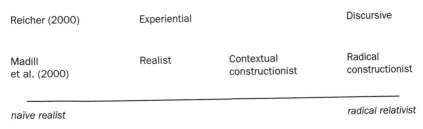

Figure 1 Classification of qualitative epistemologies

ensure that they let categories emerge from the data rather than imposing meanings upon the data. Reliability of the analysis can be demonstrated by using triangulation (of researchers and/or of methods) to show how different perspectives converge and thus confirm one another's observations and interpretations. To demonstrate excellence, studies conducted from within a contextual constructionist epistemology would be expected to show the relationship between accounts and the contexts within which they have been produced. That is, accounts need to be demonstrably grounded in the (e.g. situational, personal, cultural, social, etc.) conditions within which they were produced. This applies to both participants' accounts (e.g. of their experiences, of their thoughts and feelings) and researchers' accounts (i.e. their analyses and inter-pretations of data). Thus, an important criterion for evaluation within this context is *reflexivity*.

Studies conducted from within a radical constructionist epistemology reject the notion that research methods are ways of accessing entities such as experiences, thoughts or feelings owned by participants. As a result, criteria that are concerned with the accuracy or authenticity of accounts are meaningless from a radical con-structionist point of view. Instead, such research needs to be evaluated in its own terms. Madill et al. (2000) propose *internal coherence, deviant case analysis* and *reader evaluation* as appropriate criteria within this context. Internal coherence refers to the extent to which the analysis 'hangs together' and does not contain major contradic-tions. Deviant case analysis constitutes a test of an emerging theoretical formulation and it serves to delimit the context of its applicability. Reader evaluation refers to the extent to which the study is seen to contribute insights and understanding on the part of its readers. In addition, the inclusion of raw data in the form of verbatim quotations or extracts from interview transcripts allows readers to arrive at their own interpretation of the material.

To allow readers to evaluate a qualitative study, researchers need to be clear about what it was they wanted to find out (i.e. the research question) and what kind of knowledge they were trying to generate (i.e. their epistemological position). In add-ition, they have to ensure that the research methods that they use are appropriate to the research question and compatible with their epistemological position. Madill et al. (2000: 17) remind us that, 'qualitative researchers have a responsibility to make their epistemological position clear, conduct their research in a manner consistent with that position, and present their findings in a way that allows them to be evaluated appropriately'.

Evaluation of the methods introduced in this book

At the end of each chapter in this book, three epistemological questions were addres-sed in relation to the methods introduced in each chapter. The questions were: (1) What kind of knowledge does the method produce?, (2) What kinds of assumptions does the method make about the world? and (3) How does the method conceptualize the role of the researcher in the research process? Looking back over Chapters 3–8, we are now able to locate each of the six qualitative research approaches in terms of its epistemological position. On a continuum from naïve realism to radical relativism, they may be positioned as follows (see Fig. 2):

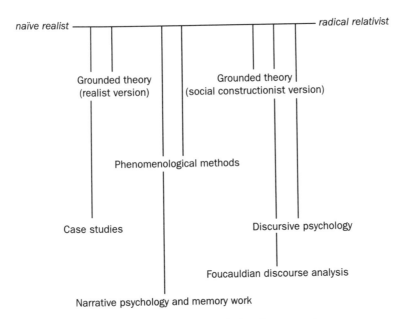

naïve realist ——————————————————— radical relativist

Grounded theory
(realist version)

Grounded theory
(social constructionist version)

Phenomenological methods

Case studies

Discursive psychology

Foucauldian discourse analysis

Narrative psychology and memory work

Figure 2 Epistemological positions associated with the six approaches

Using Madill and co-workers' (2000) classification of epistemologies, case studies and the realist version of grounded theory could be described as 'realist', phenomeno-logical methods, narrative approaches and memory work as well as the social construc-tionist version of grounded theory take a 'contextual constructionist' approach, while discursive psychology could be classified as 'radical constructionist'. Foucauldian discourse analysis can be approached from either a 'contextual constructionist' or from a 'radical constructionist' perspective.

Having classified our six approaches in terms of their epistemological positions, we are now able to identify appropriate evaluation criteria for each of them. Realist versions of grounded theory and case study research may be evaluated with reference to the extent to which they have captured what is really going on (in someone's life, in someone's mind, in a situation). Since their aim is to accurately describe and, where possible, also theorize social and psychological processes, they need to be judged in terms of the *objectivity* and *reliability* of the knowledge that they have generated. This could be done through various forms of triangulation. For example, two researchers could independently code the same section of data to establish the extent to which the categories each of them have identified correspond to one another. Similarly, observa-tions of the same situation could be made by two or more observers to establish the accuracy of the observations made. The purpose of triangulation within this context is to obtain confirmation of findings through convergence of different perspectives. The point at which perspectives converge is seen to represent 'reality'.

Phenomenological methods, narrative approaches and memory work, the social constructionist version of grounded theory and in some cases also Foucauldian discourse analysis may be evaluated by assessing the extent to which they have successfully grounded their observations within the contexts that have generated them. However, it is important to bear in mind that studies using these methods may not aspire to explain the phenomena they describe. Instead, they may be designed to provide a rich and comprehensive description of a phenomenon (e.g. an experience, a way of life, a situation), which communicates to readers a sense of its quality and texture. In this case, the application of evaluative criteria that are concerned with the relationship between the phenomenon and the conditions that may have given rise to it may not be justified. For example, an interpretative phenomenological study would be less likely to be concerned with such a relationship than a critical realist approach to Foucauldian discourse analysis, where the researcher aims to ground discourses in social and institutional practices or even structures (for a discussion of a critical realist approach to discourse analysis, see Willig 1999a, 2000; Sims-Schouten et al. 2007). Nevertheless, a concern with meaning in context and hermeneutic interpretation is shared by these methods, which means that studies using them need to address *reflexivity* issues. That is, they need to acknowledge that, and preferably also demonstrate how, the researcher's perspective and position have shaped the research.

Discursive psychology and Foucauldian discourse analysis are best evaluated by assessing the quality of the accounts they produce. Do they tell a good story? Do they tell a story that is clear, internally coherent and sufficiently differentiated? Does it generate new insights for readers? Is it convincing? As a result of its affiliation with a radical constructionist epistemology, discourse analytic research cannot be evaluated in terms of its correspondence to (as in realist research) or its relationship with (as in contextual constructionist work) external conditions or contexts. Instead, it needs to be evaluated in its own terms – that is, as a discursive construction in its own right, on the basis of its internal coherence, theoretical sophistication and persuasiveness. As Madill et al. (2000: 13) point out, '[T]his does not mean, though, that any interpretation is as good as another'. Evaluation criteria applicable to this type of work are designed to assess the *quality* of the research rather than its *validity*.

Some (e.g. Forshaw 2007) take issue with qualitative psychologists who advocate 'rigour' and 'thoroughness' in qualitative research. They argue that since qualitative research acknowledges that multiple interpretations exist and are equally valid, there is no need to concern ourselves with 'method'. For example, Forshaw (2007: 478) proposes that 'there is a worrying double-standard (. . .): on the one hand we are turning our backs on "truth" but on the other we are working out methods to understand texts and prescribing how we should tackle understanding them'. However, it is important to understand that while offering interpretations is different from making truth claims, method most certainly is implicated in interpretation and understanding. The difference between a methodical interpretation of a text such as an interview transcript, and the researcher's subjective view of it is that the former is based upon a systematic, cyclical process of critical reflection and challenge of the interpreter's own emerging interpretations whereas the latter is the product of the author's unmediated associations and reactions. While both accounts may well be fascinating and insightful, they are the product of different processes. In order for the reader to interpret (and appreciate) the researcher's interpretation, she or he needs to know as much as possible about the process by which it was generated. This is why we need 'methods sections' in research reports.

Some caveats

I have argued that evaluation criteria need to be compatible with the epistemological framework of the research that is being evaluated. I have suggested that before we can evaluate a qualitative study, we need to locate its epistemological position. To help us do that, I identified three epistemological questions that I have addressed in relation to each of the six qualitative research methods introduced in this book. In addition, I have constructed a continuum of epistemological positions ranging from 'naïve realism' to 'radical relativism' (see Figs 1 and 2) on which to place our six methods. This facilitates consideration of methods in relation to one another and it provides a starting point for the selection of appropriate evaluation criteria. However, it is now time to acknowledge that the identification of epistemological positions is not as unproblematic as I have made it appear to be.

The classification of epistemological perspectives into distinct positions necessarily requires a degree of simplification and homogenizing of perspectives. A label such as 'realist' or 'relativist' is unable to capture the true complexities and ambiguities that characterize the various epistemologies. Furthermore, the categorization of any particular method(ology) is itself a matter of judgement. Most approaches combine a number of features that are compatible with more than one epistemological position. In addition, most methods evolve over time and may modify their epistemological assumptions accordingly. Some approaches have evolved into distinct versions that may need to be classified independently from one another. As a result, qualitative researchers do not necessarily agree with one another's classification of methods. For example, while some authors (e.g. Reicher 2000) describe grounded theory as realist in orientation, others (e.g. Rennie 1998) argue that it involves a reconciliation of realism and relativism. Yet others (Madill et al. 2000; Willig, this volume) have suggested that there are distinct versions of grounded theory, some of which are realist and some of which are social constructionist in orientation. A third argument (e.g. Annells 1996) proposes that whereas grounded theory emerged from a post-positivist paradigm, it is now moving towards constructionism. Thus, while the consideration of epistemological issues is an essential part of conducting and evaluating qualitative research, it may not always be possible to identify and subscribe to clear-cut and unambiguous epistemological perspectives. However, the fact that epistemological considerations may give rise to ambiguity, lack of certainty and a certain amount of confusion should not deter us from engaging with them. Thinking, talking and writing about one's own and others' epistemological commitments encourages reflexivity, which in turn helps us to specify the status (and limitations) of our own and others' knowledge claims (for detailed discussions of the relationship between epistemology and psychological research, see Slife and Williams 1995; Bem and Looren de Jong 1997).

Opportunities and limitations in qualitative research

Following our discussion of evaluation criteria for various qualitative methods, I want to consider the opportunities and limitations associated with qualitative research in more general terms. In concluding this book, I want to step back and reflect upon the strengths and weaknesses of qualitative research in order to clarify what it is that such research has to offer researchers in psychology. Such considerations are important for those who are in the process of deciding whether or not qualitative research methods are appropriate for their research purposes. They also help qualitative researchers to develop and maintain realistic expectations about what a qualitative study can, and what it cannot, deliver.

Qualitative research provides the researcher with an opportunity to study meanings. It allows the researcher to tap into the perspectives and interpretations of participants. In this way, it facilitates the generation of genuinely novel insights and new understandings. Qualitative methods of data collection and analysis may be thought of as ways of listening and their strength may be said to lie in their sensitivity to diverse forms of expression. In addition, such methods are able to tolerate and even theorize tensions and contradictions within the data. Unlike much quantitative analysis, which tends to discard 'outliers', qualitative research pays attention to exceptional cases and idiosyncrasies in order to gain a more complete understanding of a phenomenon. Qualitative research tends to be open-ended in the sense that the research process is not predetermined or fixed in advance. As a result, unjustified assumptions, inappropriate research questions, false starts, and so on can be identified, and the direction of the research can be modified accordingly. Kvale (1995: 27) invokes the notion of 'craftsmanship' when he describes the validation process in qualitative research:

> Validation comes to depend on the quality of craftsmanship in an investigation, which includes continually checking, questioning, and theoretically interpreting the findings. In a craftsmanship approach to validation, the emphasis is moved from inspection at the end of the production line to quality control throughout the stages of knowledge production.

However, qualitative research does not provide the researcher with certainty. Qualitative research tends to be concerned with complex social and psychological processes that involve the negotiation of meanings and interpretations among participants, including the researcher. Even those qualitative researchers who work from within a realist paradigm need to address the role of reflexivity in the research process. Although they may attempt to avoid the imposition of meanings through approaching their data without preconceptions or expectations, they recognize that researcher objectivity is an ideal rather than a reality. Alternative interpretations of the data are always possible. Furthermore, qualitative research does not allow the researcher to identify generally applicable laws of cause and effect. Qualitative studies tend to work with small sample sizes in depth, which means that they can generate insights about the dynamics of particular cases. They cannot, however, make claims about trends, regularities or distributions in a population. Similarly, qualitative research is concerned with description and explanation but not with prediction. Since qualitative studies explore phenomena within their natural contexts, they are not able to control some variables so as to focus on others. As a result, qualitative research tends to be holistic and explanatory rather than reductionist and predictive (see also Chapter 5 for a more detailed discussion of generalizability in qualitative research).

Finally, since different qualitative research methods work from different epistemological positions, it is not always possible to compare or integrate their findings even when they are concerned with similar subject matter. Understanding a study's results and evaluating it requires a clear understanding of its epistemological base. Qualitative researchers who are experts in one particular method(ology) are not necessarily good judges of other types of qualitative research. This means that the qualitative research community is characterized by a certain amount of fragmentation and division, which does not facilitate collaboration and communication among its members. It could be argued that the various qualitative research methods should be evaluated purely within their own terms and that a comparison between them should confine itself to outlining their different views and emphases. I have taken a different approach in that I have identified general 'limitations' of each method at the end of each chapter. This means that, on occasion, I have criticized a method for not doing something that it does not claim, or aim, to do. However, in my view, it can be helpful to move beyond immanent critique and identify questions or issues that a particular approach fails to address. This helps us to make informed choices about which methods to use in pursuit of which research questions. For example, grounded theory methodology helps us to map social processes and their consequences for partici- pants; however, it is not designed to help us shed light on the inner workings of an individual participant's psyche. Phenomenological approaches help us to enter the world of our research participants and gain access to (some of its) quality and texture; however, such approaches do not allow us to draw firm conclusions about why their experience is as it is. Case studies allow us to get to know a particular case very well and to begin to understand how and why it came to be what it is. However, case studies are less good at providing a panoramic view of a phenomenon and to identify similarities and patterns across contexts. Discursive psychology is good at revealing the action-oriented nature of language and its achievements within specific con- texts; however, it cannot tell us anything about the individual's inner experience. Foucauldian discourse analysis does offer insights into the relationship between dis- course and subjectivity; however, it does not provide us with the tools to study non-linguistic dimensions of experience. Narrative approaches and memory work help us to understand how participants construct meaning and make connections between the past and the present, and how this may shape their experience of them- selves today; however, such methods cannot tell us what actually happened to our participants and how these events affected them at the time of their occurrence.

There is, of course, no method that does not have its own limitations. An acknow- ledgement of such limitations, however, encourages a reflexive awareness of the boundaries of our own and others' claims to knowledge and understanding.

A word about technology

Qualitative analysis is a time-consuming process that requires a high level of com- mitment from the researcher. Even a small-scale qualitative study is based upon many hours of painstaking exploration of the data (see Appendices 1–3). Larger qualitative studies, such as Ph.D. theses, may involve line-by-line analysis of hundreds of pages of interview transcripts. A frequently asked question concerns the use of computer pro- grams in the analysis of qualitative data. To what extent can the use of computer software speed up the process of qualitative analysis? And would this allow us to analyse larger data sets? As a result, can qualitative research begin to incorporate objectives such as representativeness and generalizability?

There are now a number of computer programs for qualitative analysis available. Flick (1998) puts the figure at around 25; however, new programs continue to be developed. The most well-known software packages are ETHNOGRAPH (http:// www.QualisResearch.com), NUD*IST (http://www.qsr.com.au), ATLAS (http:// www.altlasti.de) (see Seale 2000) and MAXqda (see Silver and Fielding 2008). These programs allow researchers to attach codes to segments of text and to create data files. Researcher memos can also be recorded and filed. Retrieval of data, on the basis of files or features of files, allows the researcher to inspect the data from a variety of perspectives and with different questions in mind. Some programs (e.g. ATLAS) move beyond coding and retrieval of data and offer additional features that facilitate theory development. These include visual displays of the hierarchical relationships between codes and the construction of conceptual diagrams or networks. Computers can certainly speed up the process of data exploration. The easy retrieval of data files and inspection of analytic memos on screen removes the need for physical cutting and pasting, photocopying of extracts, colour coding and manual sorting. In addition, such programs allow the researcher to retrieve files that share certain features based on codes, keywords or descriptive labels in order to identify patterns within the data without having to search through the entire data set. See Silver and Fielding (2008) for a detailed discussion of the various features and functions of computer-assisted qualitative data analysis. However, it is important to remember that the computer can be no more than a tool in the service of the researcher; it has no creative abilities of its own. As Flick (1998: 256) puts it, 'it is of course not the programs which develop the theory – just as it is not the word processor that writes an article'.

The use of computer packages is not appropriate for all types of qualitative research. For example, for discursive analyses concerned with the ways in which meaning is constructed through language and how this varies across contexts, code-and-retrieve operations are unlikely to be particularly helpful. In such analyses, attention is paid to the variability and flexibility of discursive constructions and practices. This means that the same word(s) can mean different things in different contexts, that meanings are socially negotiated and that absences can carry significant meanings. While computers can still be useful in purely practical terms (e.g. for storage of quotations in files, for inserting analytic comments into transcripts, for cutting and pasting extracts into research reports, etc.), it is not advisable to rely on simple codes in the analysis of discourse (but see Silver and Fielding 2008 for a discussion of the use of computer-assisted discourse analysis). This is because codes tend to rely on common-sense meanings, which are themselves the object of deconstruction in discursive analyses. Researchers who use methods that are hermeneutic, reflexive and interpretative (e.g. interpretative phenomenological analysis or memory work) also need to take a cautious approach to the use of computer packages.

It is worth keeping abreast of developments in research-related computer technology. For example, the emergence of software that can store and replay sound recordings is likely to benefit researchers who are interested in discourse and conversation (for a discussion of such programs, see Kvale 1996b; Seale 2000). The use of this technology would make transcription redundant (audio programs such as Adobe

Audition can be used to manage digital data files) and it would allow the researcher to pay more attention to the non-verbal aspects of speech (such as intonation, pitch, volume, etc.). Furthermore, the presentation of a research report in the form of a CD-ROM rather than an article, a book or a thesis would facilitate the inclusion of more text and raw data, thus increasing opportunities for reader evaluation.

It follows that it is of utmost importance that a qualitative researcher's decision to use a computer package is based upon an assessment of the compatibility of the program with the approach to interpretation he or she wishes to take (for a detailed discussion of various packages and their applicability, see Weitzman and Miles 1995).

'What' and 'how'

This book is about the use of qualitative methods in psychology. Even though I have attempted to link methodology with both epistemology and theory, a text devoted to 'methods' can easily appear to privilege the 'how (to do)' over the 'what (to do)'. This attitude has been referred to, and critiqued, as 'methodolatry' (see Chamberlain 2000; Curt 1994; Reicher 2000). I want to endorse Kvale's (1996a: 278) conceptualization of methods as 'the way to the goal' and, in concluding this book, I want to emphasize the importance of choosing our goal. After all, it is our research questions that motivate our research activity and which determine the direction of our research. Research methods are not recipes but ways of approaching questions, and the value of our research depends on the skill with which we manage to match our methods to our questions in the pursuit of knowledge and understanding. The motivation required for sustained research involvement cannot come from an interest in methodology alone. Indeed, it is likely that:

> [T]he best methodologies of qualitative and quantitative research have come from those engaged in active research in which methodology has been subordinated to the ardent desire to know and communicate something significant about human life.
>
> (Orum et al. 1991: 23)

Further reading

Chamberlain, K. (2000) Methodolatry and qualitative health research, *Journal of Health Psychology*, 5(3): 285–96.

Elliott, R., Fischer, C.T. and Rennie, D.L. (1999) Evolving guidelines for publication of qualitative research studies in psychology and related fields, *British Journal for Clinical Psychology*, 38: 215–29.

Henwood, K. and Pidgeon, N.F. (1992) Qualitative research and psychological theorising, *British Journal of Psychology*, 83(1): 97–112.

Madill, A., Jordan, A. and Shirley, C. (2000) Objectivity and reliability in qualitative analysis: realist, contextualist and radical *constructionist* epistemologies, *British Journal of Psychology*, 91: 1–20.

Reicher, S. (2000) Against methodolatry: some comments on Elliott, Fischer and Rennie, *British Journal of Clinical Psychology*, 39: 1–6.

Yardley, L. (2000) Dilemmas in qualitative health research, *Psychology and Health*, 15: 215–28.

Appendix 1

What is understood by 'dominance'? An interpretation through memories

Goran Petronic

Reflexive preface

The idea for the research emerged directly out of the teaching of qualitative methods. One of the first lectures argued for the importance of qualitative research and it emphasized the advantages of this kind of investigation over quantitative research. Nevertheless, it was suggested that quantitative research methods are still the dominant tool in scientific investigations in the social sciences. This issue triggered deeper thoughts about the importance of both types of research. I felt that, to study human behaviour, psychology – if it is to be a scientific discipline – needs to improve its tools and use both methods as one.

First, the topic of study needs to be defined through qualitative research methods and then the investigation can proceed using quantitative research techniques. My thoughts about why such an approach would be difficult to implement returned, again, to the issue of dominance of one research methodology over the other. To demonstrate the importance of using both types of method together, I decided to draw attention to the difficulties in studying dominance as a topic using only quantitative research methods. When I reviewed the research literature into dominance as a topic, it became apparent very quickly that many studies using quantitative methods ended up with contradictory results. For example, studies that were investigating father dominance in relation to homosexuality resulted in ambiguous findings; some suggested that a less dominant father in the family is associated with homosexuality in male offspring while others did not find such an association. The question of what is actually meant by the term 'dominance' is an important issue that these studies did not address. Definitions are important to focus clearly on the subject under investigation, so that later studies can orient towards the same definitions. However, the term 'dominance' is very hard to define and this was confirmed by the findings of my qualitative study into the meaning of dominance.

When I started the study, I thought that I had a clear idea in my mind as to how I was going to proceed. As I learned from previous qualitative studies, it is better to start the study as soon as possible to allow yourself plenty of time in case something goes wrong. This was a good idea because things did not go as smoothly as I had planned. Midway through the study, I wanted to give up because I had already lost myself in this complex topic. The memory work method is not such a difficult method; you simply need to follow the procedure step by step. However, when it comes to the practical side, you realize the amount of work that you have to do to follow the guidelines. The most difficult as well as the most unpleasant part of the research is the transcription of the discussion between participants because it requires very high levels of concentration and it is very time-consuming. All the other parts of the procedure can be easy and good fun.

There are a number of problems that you may encounter while following the method's procedures. For example, I was in trouble when one of the participants who had written a memory did not turn up for the second session. Instead, I had two new participants for the discussion session! The selection of participants and the relations between participants are very important aspects of the research.

For those who do decide to choose this method, please bear in mind that it is time-consuming and that it requires good organizational skills as well as good relations with the members of the memory work group. Most importantly, it requires the group's commitment to the research. Good luck!

Abstract

Dominance is a term that is employed literally everywhere. Within the discipline of psychology, there are many studies using this concept. However, findings remain contradictory; it is suggested that this may be due to the complexity of this phenomenon. In this study, qualitative research was employed to extend our understanding of 'dominance'. Research was conducted using the memory work method, which generates data through reflection and reconstruction of past experience by using written memories as source material. Analysis of the memories suggested that dominance is not a unitary phenomenon. The memories suggest that dominance is perceived and constructed in different ways. The memories reveal various emotions associated with this phenomenon. All the memories were written from a victim position.

Introduction

Dominance is a recurring theme in popular psychology literature. For example, it is being discussed with reference to the increasing convergence of men's and women's roles in Western societies in the past decades. However, when scientists study dominance, they use the same word in many contexts. In neuroscience, for example, dominance is used to refer to the governing hemisphere of the brain. In genetic science, the term 'dominant gene' refers to a parental characteristic that reoccurs in the next generation. Even in social psychology, dominance is used in several contexts (e.g.

with reference to 'dominant parent' or 'dominant partner'). Those who study personality refer to the dominant trait of personality. In ordinary speech, the word embodies a number of different meanings, such as govern, rule, control, master, eclipse, overshadow, influence, manipulate, authority, and so on.

Let us examine closely some of the contexts within which 'dominance' features in social scientific research. Cattell (1965) introduced the 'dominance factor' in his 16 Personality Factors Questionnaire. According to Cattell (1965), a dominant personality is self-assertive, confident, boastful, conceited, aggressive, pugnacious, extrapunitive, vigorous, forceful, wilful and egotistic. Cattell (1965) argued that a dominant individual does not necessarily imply an authoritarian personality. The latter is not a unitary concept and consists of at least four personality factors and possibly as many cultures and still more stereotypes. He suggests that social psychologists studying authoritarian personalities describe a dominant person as one who kicks those beneath and bows to those above, while a dominant person, revealed by his own dominance factor, leads those below and kicks those above him. He bases his argument on a group dynamics experiment by Stice and Cattell (cited in Cattell 1965) in which they found that, if all members of a group have a high dominance score, they establish a more democratic and free society. Cattell suggests that the dominant trait has a fairly strong constitutional component. He claims also that the same pattern is evident in some animal species and in these it is associated with the level of the male hormone in both sexes. Although Cattell produces a strong argument in support of a dominant personality trait, he does not give an explanation as to why social psychologists perceive the same phenomenon differently. In addition, Cattell's questionnaire has been replaced by new and more sophisticated personality questionnaires, such as the 'Big Five', which no longer measure the dominance factor. Does this imply that the dominant personality trait is not recognized any more or simply that Cattell's work could not be replicated?

Another illustration of ambiguity concerning the research on dominance can be seen in family studies. According to some researchers, including Freud (see also West 1959; Snortum et al. 1969), who studied an individual's sexual orientation in relation to a dominant parent, a dominant mother increases the chances of homosexuality in men. However, Bell et al. (1981), Hoeffer (1981, cited in Gross 1992) and Golombok et al. (1983) did not find such a link. The inconsistent findings may be attributed to the use of the term 'dominance'. The term is not used consistently from one study to another. Furthermore, dominance is not necessarily an all-or-nothing matter, because a husband might be dominant in one sphere and a wife in another.

These ambiguous findings confirm that the term 'dominance' is not a simple concept. The meaning of dominance may differ in relation to the relationships that are implicated (e.g. parents, partners, colleagues) and in relation to context (e.g. subject matter, sphere of application).

This study examines the concept of dominance by using qualitative research rather than quantitative research. According to Kirk and Miller (1986), qualitative observation identifies the presence or absence of something, and what defines that thing, in contrast to quantitative research, which involves measuring the extent to which some features are present. In other words, qualitative research has advantages over quantitative research by defining a phenomenon using ordinary people in their own territory using their own language. If we study a situation using people as subjects, then there is a need to study the situation with the same definitions used by these people – that is, we need to 'call things by the right names'.

Here, I use a new and powerful method, memory work, which has emerged from Haug's (1987) theory of socialization, which is similar to Shotter's (1984, 1986, cited in Kippax et al. 1988) theory of the social construction of the person. Although a new method, used so far only in exploring the sexualization of women's bodies and the social construction of emotions, this study will try to use the method for the first time in exploring a concept such as dominance. The method was chosen because it explores social interaction and social construction as well as emotions that are related to the concept. This study will attempt to derive the fundamental meanings of dominance through the analysis of memory.

Method

The study used the memory work method for collection and analysis of data recently introduced by German feminist Frigga Haug (1987). The data for memory work consist of written memories. This has two advantages. First, memories allow for engagement with the past. The memories describe an event or action that was subjectively significant in the past and reflect problematic or unfamiliar episodes. The significance of the memories represents a continuing search for intelligibility caused by unfamiliarity and the lack of resolution. Second, the memories of individuals provide the medium through which their actions are given direction and evaluation (Crawford et al. 1992). As noted by Shotter (1984, cited in Kippax et al. 1988), the process of using one's own past experiences in structuring one's further action is very familiar.

Memory work is a group process; therefore, a group of co-researchers must be formed before it can be done and a group facilitator has to be chosen.

> CW: It is possible to conduct memory work without a clearly identified facilitator. In fact, it could be argued that the presence of a facilitator creates (or reflects) power differentials in the group that are not easily compatible with its aspiration to be a genuinely collective method of research.

Memory work is divided into three phases. The first phase concerns choosing a topic for the memories and writing the memories according to the following rules:

1   Write a memory
2   Of a particular episode, action or event
3   In the third person
4   In as much detail as possible, including even (apparently) inconsequential or trivial detail (it may be helpful to think of a key image, sound, taste, smell, touch)
5   But without importing interpretation, explanation or biography
6   Write one of your earliest memories

CW: Memory work does not necessarily have to be based on childhood memories. Some memory work projects explore adult memories. The choice of memories depends on the subject matter under investigation.

The second phase involves group analysis of the memories:

1 Each memory work group member expresses opinions and ideas about each memory in turn

2 Looks for similarities and differences between the memories and looks for continuous elements among memories whose relation to each other is not immediately apparent. Each member should question in particular those aspects of the events that do not appear amenable to comparison. She or he should not, however, resort to autobiography or biography

3 Each memory work group member identifies clichés, generalizations, contradictions, cultural imperatives, metaphor . . . and

4 Discusses theories, popular conceptions, sayings and images about the topic

5 Finally, each member examines what is not written in the memories (but what might be expected to be included)

There is also a third phase that involves further analysis of memories in relation to a theoretical background from an academic discipline.

CW: These guidelines are taken from Crawford et al. (1992).

Participants

There were eight participants, of whom five were female and three were male. Their names were changed in the transcripts to ensure confidentiality. The age of the participants was 21–50 years. All participants belong to a psychodrama training group. The training runs over one year and involves close relationships because the process includes a practical side that involves sharing past experiences with other members of the group. The participants have different backgrounds, mainly in mental health and education. The group was international; four of them spoke English as a second language. Participants' national origin is highlighted below to allow the reader to consider the extent to which the meaning(s) of the term 'dominance' may, or may not, be culturally specific. Eight participants wrote their memories; however, two of them were not involved in the discussion of the memories. They were replaced by two new members who took part only in the discussion (Ute from Germany and Violeta from Yugoslavia).

Procedure

Prior to the research, ethical approval was obtained from the Ethics Committee at Middlesex University. After discussion with the supervisor of the psychodrama-training group, members of the group were informed about the aims of the research and were asked whether they would like to participate. All members signed a consent form that outlined features of the research and guaranteed anonymity. The research was run over a period of three weeks. In the first week, the participants were asked to write their memories by following the memory work rules printed on the handout that was given to them as a reminder. In the second week, the memories were collected, converted into print and photocopied for each member. Finally, in the third week, the discussion was run, which was recorded on audio-tape by using a Professional Sony Walkman. The discussion was structured and lasted for 45 minutes. Each memory was discussed in turn and also a few further semi-structured questions were discussed.

> CW: It would be helpful to know what these questions were and why they were chosen.

Furthermore, the whole discussion was transcribed from tape[1] into print.

Analysis of memories

First, the memories will be analysed individually. They will then be compared with one another. The analysis will start with Michael's memories.

> CW: At this point, it would be helpful to clarify the extent to which the analysis of memories was the product of the group discussion. Also, it would be a good idea to provide the reader with a clearer sense of what the Analysis section will contain. For example, a reference to the fact that memories will be reproduced verbatim and that the theoretical and methodological implications of the research will be discussed in the Discussion section could be highlighted here.

Michael I (South Africa)

I remember lying in a big bed, I was two years old, the sun streamed into my room, I was very ill. My grandmother brought me bread with Marmite on it. I felt warm and cared for, happy and wanted, even if my parents were far away. I remember the light and the greens of the beautiful garden outside the window. I was happy and away from home.

Michael II

The first time I felt dominated I was sent to my room; I was lying on the floor sliding and crying loudly and laughing on Sunday. My Dad's voice barked 'go to your room'. I was frightened and ran.

Michael did not follow the rules provided in the handout. He wrote his memories in the first person. His first memory is not about dominance; it is one of the first memories that he could remember. In his memory he wrote that he was looked after by his grandmother, who gave him security and a feeling of being loved. He used contrasts: small boy (age 2) in a big bed, sun and illness. He associated his grandmother with a feeling of being cared for (she made him bread with Marmite), happy and wanted while away from home. We can speculate that his relationship with his parents was not very good: 'I was happy and away from home'.

In the second memory, Michael did write about dominance even though he still wrote in the first person. He was dominated by his father. The dominance was expressed by the demand 'go to your room'. Michael reported an emotion of fear in relation to being dominated by his father. A contrast can also be noted: he went suddenly from being happy and laughing to being scared and upset.

Sanja (Yugoslavia)

Sanja was 5 years old. She and her older brother Sacha were sitting at the table in the kitchen. The kitchen was her favourite room in the house, warmest in the winter, coolest in the summer, all in green shades, with pots of flowers on the window ledge and a little balcony. There was a settee. It was warm. Tablecloth was in dark-green checkered pattern. The floor was covered by green carpet. Table and chairs were made of dark wood and very comfortable. She and her brother both hated meal times because their mother would always make them eat something they didn't like. Like soup with too much parsley in it. This evening it was spinach. Sanja and Sacha went quiet. Their mother turned away from the table, facing the sink, washing the dishes. Sanja and her brother exchanged glances and whispered. Sanja didn't dare say anything at first. She started pretending to eat, shoving spinach from one side of the plate to another. Her mother was periodically glancing at them and saying: 'Eat, eat it all up, I don't want to see anything on the plate'. Her brother bent his head down and, as always, started eating obediently. After a few failed attempts, Sanja put her spoon down and said: 'Mama, I can't eat it'. She knew what was coming. If only her dad was here. 'What do you mean you can't eat it?! You must eat it. You will eat this all up!! Look at your brother, he's almost eaten all of it!' She hated her brother at that moment. Her mother took her spoon and filled her mouth with spinach. It was unbearably disgusting. She felt sick and about to throw up. She just couldn't keep it in her mouth any longer, otherwise she would have thrown up. So she spat it all out on the floor. That really angered her mother and she shouted at her: 'What have you done!! I cook for you and you spit it out just like that. Look what mess you've made of the carpet'. She smacked her bottom a couple of times. Sanja started crying. Her mother made her clean up the floor and sent her to bed without dinner, for a punishment.

Sanja's memory is very long and detailed. She is 5 years old and with her brother. She compares her favourite place, the kitchen, with her hatred of having to eat what she does not like, which produces a contrast. Sanja was dominated by her mother and her father was seen as someone who would have protected her: 'if only her dad was here'. Unlike her brother, she is not scared to disobey her mother. Sanja resisted her mother's dominance. Her mother is angry with her, wants to control her but cannot force her to eat, so she physically punishes her and sends her to bed. This account of dominance is concerned with control; a mother is trying to discipline her child and a child is trying to assert her own personality. Emotion is expressed through crying.

Kate (UK)

Kate and Fiona were best friends and played together all the time. On their sixth (?) birthday they were both given baby doll prams. Kate's was made from metal and had shiny purple and white paint. Fiona's was made of red plastic. Both girls were very pleased with their presents. (They were born 2 days apart so always shared birthday parties.) In Kate's back garden there was a narrow path between the wall and the hedge of brambles. Both girls were playing in the garden and wanted to go through the path together. Fiona made Kate push her pram beside the nettles and it got scratched on its shiny new paint. Kate was very upset and angry. Fiona wasn't obviously sorry.

Kate's memory recounts her close friendship with Fiona. It appears that Kate is in a superior position to Fiona: her pram was made from metal and had shiny purple and white paint, whereas Fiona's was made from red plastic. Fiona may have been jealous of Kate's pram. Fiona is the more dominant of the two girls. She gives orders to Kate, tells her what to do ('Fiona made Kate push her pram beside the nettles'). It is interesting that the memory suggests that Kate was superior to Fiona by having a better pram and being in her garden. She also expected Fiona to be sorry because her pram got scratched. It seems that Kate trusted her friend but was intentionally deceived by Fiona so as to damage her pram, so it was a betrayal of trust by her friend. It is suggested that the intention to cause damage was there because Kate expected her friend to be sorry. Kate does not say what happened next. Did they stop playing? Did Kate show any emotion to her friend? Was she scared of her? Did she react? She does not explain how Fiona made her push her pram beside the nettles either.

Julia (South Africa)

(6-year-old, first year of school)

The girl was sitting at the back of the class; everyone was talking, although the teacher had asked them not to. The teacher called Julia up from the back of the class. She walked past the rows of desks, blushing. She looked at Grant's smiling face. The teacher's voice resounded over the class as she shouted at Julia for talking after being told not to. She then told her to bend over and hit her with a bare hand. Julia turned and faced the class as she walked back to her seat. She was biting her lip afraid that she would laugh or cry.

Julia's memory places dominance in the classroom into the teacher–pupil relationship. The teacher is trying to control the children and Julia was picked on even though everyone was talking. Why? The teacher's action appeared unjust to Julia. Julia is embarrassed to go up in front of the whole class but not scared. Dominance is expressed by the teacher shouting at her and physical punishment. Julia reported mixed emotions ('laugh or cry'). She appeared confused, upset by the injustice of the situation, yet maintaining a sense of pride. The memory of Grant's smiling face while Julia blushes is also reported, indicating that Julia might be attracted to Grant.

Goran (Yugoslavia)

Goran was 2–3 years old and had his favourite dummy. The dummy was sky blue with already chewed light yellow rubber at the top that used to be dark yellow when new. It was early spring, still cold and wet. Goran wore a blue hat with a small bobble on the top and cuddly brown winter coat. Goran and his mother went together with Goran's father to a nearby village where his father had to see an old gentleman who kept pigs. His name was Branko and he had grey hair. Branko had in his back garden pig sties where there were many pigs. Goran was fascinated with pigs and the whole scene. It was still muddy and the pigs were dirty and smelt bad. In one moment, Branko turned to Goran and said to him: 'Why is a big boy like you still sucking a dummy?' The next moment he pulled out the dummy from Goran's mouth and made a movement as if throwing the dummy into the pig sty. Goran didn't cry and also never asked for a dummy again.

It appears that Goran was very attached to his dummy, since he provides many details about it. He also gives a good account of his clothing. In the memory, Goran seems quite impressed with the old man and the pigs; the old man represents authority and power. Goran is obedient and listens to him without reacting. There is a contrast between the description of the dummy and his clothes, representing warmth and security, and the muddy sty and pigs that Goran probably sees for the first time.

Dominance is associated with authority and the impression of something not known that Goran learns from the old man, Branko, allowing him to manipulate him with the message 'you've come into the real world' ('Why is a big boy like you still sucking a dummy?'). Even though emotions are not expressed, it appears that they are relevant: 'Goran did not cry and never asked for a dummy again'. It appears that Goran applied the behaviour of an adult by not showing any emotion – that is, 'big boys don't cry'.

Ljubica (Yugoslavia)

It was a sunny afternoon, St. Nicholas Day. A little girl (aged 3 or 4) went with her mother and grandmother to visit her uncle's future wife and her mother. They had a very nice time. The girl liked the atmosphere of the old, pre-revolution atmosphere in the house, icons on the walls, the bell for the servants (now non-existent) hanging from an old-fashioned large chandelier above the dining room table, traditional cakes. On the way back, her mother and grandmother told her that she must not say a word to grandfather about the visit: 'You shall not mention this visit in front of your grandfather. Be a good girl and don't say a word about it'. She was excited to be a part of an intrigue of which even her grandfather did not know. She also wanted to be a good girl, so she agreed. When they arrived at the grandparents' home, grandfather was in his study looking like a scientist from a Hollywood film, with his white hair and blue eyes, wearing navy blue trousers and a white shirt under a burgundy woollen waistcoat and a burgundy bow tie, surrounded by huge books and cigarette smoke. As the little girl came to greet him, he stood up and gave her a present, a pair of beautiful boots, blue with white swans on each ankle, saying, 'This is for you because you are a good girl'. The girl replied, 'Yes, I am and I will not tell you where we have just been'. Silence . . . Over her head she felt the adults exchanging looks. She left the room clutching her new boots and closed the door. Later on, this story became an amusing anecdote about a child's naivety.

It is interesting to note that the memory is written from the perspective of the present by referring to 'child's naivety'. On first reading, it is very difficult to notice the dominance. However, dominance is expressed through the manipulation by the mother and grandmother telling her not to mention the visit. Also, the grandfather manipulates her by saying that she is a good girl and giving her a present. She is confused and tries to satisfy both sides. Domination is expressed by verbal manipulation. There is a similarity between the description of the house she visited with her mother and grandmother, and the description of her grandfather as something fascinating, very authoritative and powerful. Dominance by the grandfather is expressed by impressing the girl with a surprise (i.e. beautiful boots) and by calling her a 'good girl'. Confused and fascinated by the gift, she tries not to disappoint either side by making a diplomatic compromise.

Radovan I (Yugoslavia)

Radovan is a 2-year-old boy, he cannot speak completely. She is a big 40-year-old woman in boots. The boy is desperately waiting for his good, tender mother. Afraid of Anica he watches through the window to see if his mother is coming. He removes the small curtain. Anica says 'No' and smashes him over the hands. Radovan is scared and tearful.

Radovan II

With Anica on the street, raining, muddy, crowded. Anica shouts, 'Stay here and don't move'. Radovan stays alone in the crowd, scared of Anica, scared of the crowd.

Radovan has two very short but very emotional memories connected to home. The boy is helpless in that he cannot express himself and is dominated by a '40-year-old woman in boots'. The boy waits to be saved from the woman by his tender mother. He is very afraid of Anica. Dominance is expressed in terms of the fear of Anica's punishment. He reports emotions of fear and acts scared and tearful. In the second memory, he is dominated by the same woman but this time it happens on a crowded street in bad weather. This time dominance is represented by control. He reported being scared of Anica and of the crowd.

Sara (Ethiopia)

(Age 5)

The playground culture is rough, and survival of the fittest is in play. It can be a cruel place for a child who is different and can't adhere to the playground rules or converse in its language. Sara was the new kid at school and couldn't speak much English. Her accent was different; the other children found this funny and would often mimic her when she spoke. For Sara, play times were a dreaded punishment, especially the long lunch-hour breaks. On most days she took comfort knowing that Mrs Mortimer was on playground duties. Mrs Mortimer was the favourite dinner lady at school. Sara would spend most dinner breaks accompanying Mrs Mortimer around the playground, often holding her hand. Mrs Mortimer was much loved by most of the children, who would periodically come up to her to give her a hug or smile. One lunch break, Sara took her trusted place by Mrs Mortimer's side, but Patrick spotted her. Patrick was a big West Indian boy who was always getting into trouble in class. Sara had often heard the teacher tell Patrick to wait after class, or told him to report to the headmaster. Patrick casually made his way up to Sara and he insisted that Mrs Mortimer give him some attention. While Mrs Mortimer was busy, Patrick turned around to Sara and told her to leave Mrs Mortimer alone or he'd beat her up. She was his dinner lady and only he was allowed to hold her hand. He then informed Sara that if she were to tell anyone on him, he'd beat her up. She was now in a predicament and felt like her whole life was about to crumble around her. She could feel the tears in her eyes starting to swell and her nose become runny. The rest of the noises in the playground now seemed to fade away into insignificance. She could not face play times alone, and she could not bear the thought of having the other kids point and call her funny names. Sara felt overcome by emotion and quickly ran as fast as she could in the direction of the classroom. She tried to ensure no-one was watching her and went to sit by her desk. She felt lonely and afraid, and took comfort in knowing that lunchtime was nearly over. You see, children are not allowed in the classroom at break times. Sara felt bitter towards Patrick and came up with all kinds of scheming ideas to make him pay for the way he'd made her feel. But deep inside her she knew that she would not be able to do anything to Patrick, as he was much bigger than she was.

Sara's memory of dominance is associated with a school playground. She was dominated by Patrick, a physically stronger boy. It is interesting to note that Sara perceives the school playground as a tough and cruel place and dreads punishment. Mrs Mortimer represents a safe place, providing security to Sara. Patrick is a scary and naughty boy. He dominates Sara by threatening her with physical punishment if she does not obey the rules that he makes. She reports that she was scared and tearful, her eyes starting to swell, her nose becoming runny and also she is afraid of being called funny names. It seems that she is angry with Patrick for showing her up in front of the other children who may call her funny names. She feels lonely and afraid but also bitter towards Patrick and tries to make him pay for it, but she also knows that she is not the kind of person to do that.

Comparison of memories

When all the memories had been analysed, a difference between male and female participants was evident in terms of the length of the memories; the female participants tended to write longer and more descriptive memories than the males. There is also a difference between male and female participants in terms of the age at which events were remembered to have taken place; males tended to recount earlier memories of dominance than females. Dominance is associated with a fear of physical punishment in most memories (e.g. Sara, Michael, Julia, Sanja and Radovan) and also with verbal manipulation, in terms of authority and discipline (e.g. Goran, Ljubica and Kate) (see Table 1 for a summary of the contents of the memories).

> CW: At this point, the reader should be provided with a brief but clear verbal account of the contents of the table. Concepts and symbols used in the table should be explained before an interpretation of the findings is presented.

Table 1 Summary of memories

Memories	Michael II	Sanja	Kate	Julia	Goran	Ljubica	Radovan I	Radovan II	Sara
Age	2	5	6	6	2–3	3–4	2	2	5
D/e* Physical	no	yes	no	yes	yes	no	yes	no	no
Verbal	yes	yes	no	yes	yes	yes	yes	yes	yes
Other	no	no	yes	no	no	no	no	no	no
Behaviour	Run away	Crying/cleaning	Pushed pram	Biting lip	Confused	Agreeing	Tearful	Stay alone	Run to classroom
Emotion	Fear	?	Upset, angry	Afraid to laugh/cry	?	Excited	Scared	Scared	Lonely, afraid, bitter
Place	Home	Kitchen	Garden	Classroom	Garden	Home	Home	Street	Playground
Dominant	no	no	no	no	no	no	no	no	no
Dominated	yes	yes	yes	yes	yes	yes	yes	yes	yes
D/b* Peers	no	no	yes	no	no	no	no	no	no
Sibling	no	no	no	no	no	no	no	no	no
Mother	no	yes	no	no	no	no	no	no	no
Father	yes	no	no	no	no	no	no	no	no
Others	no	no	no	Teacher	Adult	Grandfather	Babysitter	Babysitter	
Compliant to dominance	yes	no	yes	yes	yes	yes	yes	yes	yes
Justify	yes	yes	?	no	yes	yes	yes	no	yes

Notes
* D/e: dominance expressed.
* D/b: dominated by.

It appears from Table 1 that dominance is also connected with injustice and a feeling of helplessness or even anger, as in the cases of Michael, Sanja, Radovan, Sara and Julia. In both Goran's and Ljubica's accounts, the type of dominance appears to be similar. They were manipulated by referral to them as 'big boy' or 'good girl' and, therefore, they try to behave in such a way. Kate's memory is exceptional in that she was dominated by her friend but it is not clear how exactly she was made to behave in a certain way. It is also evident from the table that Sanja is the only person who is not compliant with attempts to dominate her. Nevertheless, dominance is not necessarily related to negative experiences. In the case of Goran, for example, we can see how dominance can be used to exercise discipline to bring about desirable behaviour change. It is interesting that all the memories represented the writers as victims of dominance; nobody wrote about being in a dominant position over someone. The memories were similar in that the protagonists tended to be dominated by 'bigger' people (older, stronger, people with authority). Furthermore, some of the memories were interpreted from a perspective of the present; for example, Ljubica's account shows this, and also Sara's memory when she states 'playground culture is rough, and survival of the fittest is in play'.

Discussion

The memories suggest that dominance is not a single phenomenon. It is evident that dominance is interpreted in different ways in the memories and defined in various ways in the recorded discussion.

CW: It should be pointed out here that an analysis of the group discussion could not be presented in this paper, due to limitations of space.

The context is ambiguous in that it can be both positive (e.g. in teaching discipline) and negative (e.g. when it involves manipulation). The emotions predominantly associated with dominance are fear and anger. It appears that there are a variety of ways in which dominance can be expressed. The most widely used form was verbal followed by physical punishment. The act of domination is more likely to happen at home and there is a variety of characters that are dominant in the memories; they are always described as bigger and stronger than the person who is being dominated. The data also show that males reported earlier memories of dominance than females; however, this observation requires further investigation. The final and most striking finding is that all participants wrote their memories from a victim position.

The result that dominance is not a single phenomenon and, therefore, difficult to measure is in line with the concerns outlined in the Introduction. It can be seen from the memories, and later from the group discussion, that the group members had access to different meanings of the term. This is particularly evident in Ljubica's and Kate's memories, where the dominance is subtle and hardly recognizable. It is also apparent from the memories that the dominant person in the memories is akin to the characterization provided by social psychologists, namely as one who 'kicks those under him and tries to please those above him'. This is evident from the hierarchical order of dominance stated in Sanja's (i.e. father's presence would save Sanja from mother's dominance), Radovan's (i.e. presence of Radovan's mother will change the situation) and Sara's (i.e. the fact that the boy is concerned that Sara will report the incident to the teacher) memories.

The most interesting finding is that all memories were written from a victim position even though this was not specified in the instructions given to participants. The discussion produced speculation that dominance is a learned process, in which we learn to dominate by being dominated first by someone else. The other reason for this finding could be that people present themselves in a victim position because it is more socially acceptable. It would be interesting to test both speculations, for example by using the same method but giving a different, potentially socially unacceptable 'trigger' for the memories. For instance, 'Write your earliest memory of an experience of aggression'. It would be interesting to see if the pattern of victim position is repeated.

The concept of dominance is associated predominantly with emotions of fear and anger. Therefore, the method is a useful tool in the investigation of emotions, as suggested by Kippax et al. (1988) and Crawford et al. (1992). The method is also in keeping with Haug's (1987) suggestion that memory work is a useful tool in the investigation of the construction of self, because it enables an engagement with the past as well as contemporary interpretations of the past, which is evident in Ljubica's (i.e. 'an anecdote of a child's naivety') and Sara's (i.e. 'playground as survival of the fittest') memories. However, the memory work method can be questioned: Are the memories our own account of an event from the past or are they simply narrative stories that someone told us about ourselves which we cannot remember? This could easily be the case, especially with our earliest memories.

Memory work is a useful method for exploring the construction of the self as stated by Haug (1987) and the construction of emotions as noted by Kippax et al. (1988) and Crawford et al. (1992). It is also a good method for defining phenomena. However, the memory work method is time-consuming[2] and depends largely on group work.[3] It is important to have reliable co-workers who share the same interests in memory work and contribute equally towards exploring the phenomena that interest them. It is also important to limit the number of co-researchers, as too many can raise difficulties when transcribing the discussion.

References

Bell, A.P., Weinberg, M.S. and Hamersmith, S.K. (1981) *Sexual Preference: Its Development in Men and Women*. Bloomington, IN: Indiana University Press.

Cattell, R.B. (1965) *The Scientific Analysis of Personality*. Harmondsworth: Penguin.

Crawford, J., Kippax, S., Onyx, J., Gault, U. and Benton, P. (1992) *Emotion and Gender*. London: Sage.

Haug, F. (1987) *Female Sexualization*. London: Verso Press.

Golombok, S., Spencer, A. and Rutter, M. (1983) Children in lesbian and single-parent households: psychosexual and psychiatric appraisal, *Journal of Child Psychology and Psychiatry*, 24: 551–72.

Gross, R.D. (1992) *Psychology: Science of Mind and Behaviour*, 2nd edn. London: Hodder & Stoughton.

Kippax, S., Crawford, J., Benton, P. and Gault, U. (1988) Constructing emotions: weaving meaning from memories, *British Journal of Social Psychology*, 27: 19–33.

Kirk, J. and Miller, M.L. (1986) *Reliability and Validity in Qualitative Research.* London: Sage.

Snortum, J.R., Marshall, J.E. and Gillespie, J.F. (1969) Family dynamics and homosexuality, *Psychological Reports*, 24: 763–70.

West, D.J. (1959) Parental relationships in male homosexuality, *International Journal of Social Psychiatry*, 5: 85–97.

Notes

1   This part was very difficult because eight members took part in the discussion. There were moments when three or four members were talking at the same time. It is very difficult to transcribe a group discussion and it took seven days to transcribe the whole discussion. Concentration has to be very high to pick up all contributions, especially as some of the participants were second-language English speakers.

2   Unfortunately, after two months of working on this essay, it amounted to double the specified length (the memories alone account for 2000 words). It is very difficult to do justice to such a topic in a mere 5000 words and cutting it short has resulted in an inadequate account.

3   It is important to report an incident that occurred concerning the group members. Sanja, who had attended some psychodrama training sessions in the past, was not a regular group member. The day on which the discussion was to be run, Sanja attended the session. She understood that the discussion would take place before the drama session. However, this was not the case and Sanja openly told the group about the misunderstanding between us and that she was not willing to attend the psychodrama session first. Some of the group members were disappointed and asked her to leave the group. The researcher felt responsible for this misunderstanding and for causing distress. So I insisted on resolving the problem, which resulted in splitting the group into those who supported Sanja's decision to be open about her feelings and those who perceived Sanja's openness as rudeness. After settling the problem, Sanja decided not to stay for the discussion of memories. In addition to Sanja, Sara also missed the discussion. However, the discussion was performed and two new members took part, Ute and Violeta.

Appendix 2

A qualitative study of the occurrence of abuse in one heterosexual and in one lesbian relationship

Kris dew Valour

Reflexive preface • Abstract • Introduction • Method • Reflexivity • Results • Discussion • References • Appendix

Reflexive preface

The study constituted an effort to explore and bring to light some of the complex and difficult issues that face individuals involved with domestic violence in an intimate relationship. It emerged from discussion with others and my own internal dialectic and thoughts. When hearing others condemn those who stay with an abusive partner and the frivolity of statements such as 'it takes two to tango' and 'I'd be out of that door if they ever laid a finger on me!' (of course, unconsenting physical violence is not the only type of abuse), I wondered whether these were statements of ignorance or naïvety. Inspired by the experiences of others and my own, the project was conceived. For those who may criticize the study for detracting from the issue of male violence and see this as the only true source of violation, I draw attention to issues of gender, power and agency (among others). It is much more difficult to challenge that which remains unacknowledged, denied or hidden. Classification of biological sex is not the issue.

I hope the study succeeds in showing how qualitative research can be conducted, within the boundaries of an undergraduate project. The research did not seek to bring about emancipatory change, as in action research, but to act as a 'stepping stone' to further our understanding of the issue and to generate further discussions and a focus for future research.

As an undergraduate student trained predominantly in statistical and quantitative techniques, the position from which I worked – new to the use of grounded theory – was daunting, but gave me a sense of liberation and expression in relation to the kind of psychological research I wanted to engage in. Qualitative research is concerned with the meaning and interpretation of human experience, and how this has come about. With an interest in conducting phenomenological research (exploring and categorizing subjective accounts of experience), I felt semi-structured interviews as a method of data collection and the use of grounded theory analysis were particularly suited to my focus of research.

At times, the research process can be frustrating and demoralizing. A participant may withdraw, the transcription work does not seem to end, there never seems to be enough time, and how can you be confident that it really is 'all coming together'? Despite the difficulties, do not give up! Meeting people and talking and listening to them can be a great way to collect your data. Whether it be in their home or relaxing somewhere (appropriate) with a glass of wine. Interviews give people an opportunity to talk about their life experiences. In this study, I believe that this was mutually rewarding to myself and those involved in the research. Most of all, I thank Essme and Louise for their participation and their willingness to share their stories with others. At times, my involvement in the analysis was difficult and uncomfortable, and I give a special thanks to those who continued to encourage and support me.

In conclusion, I would like to say that, whatever your motivation, doing research need not be an arduous task. It can be a lot of fun! Go off the trodden path, and get your hands dirty . . . you never know where it could lead or what you may find.

Abstract

This study examines the experiences of two women who were involved with an abusive partner. Semi-structured interviews were conducted with the women, one of whom identified as lesbian and the other as heterosexual. Questions centred around descriptions of their sexuality, the best and worst experiences with their partner while in the relationship, medical treatment for injuries sustained through the abuse, termination of the abuse, disclosure to others and their views in relation to media coverage of the topic. Grounded theory analysis found that both physical and psychological abuse were experienced regardless of the partner's gender. Sexual abuse by a woman perpetrator was also identified. Accessibility of support services was shown to be problematic. Further analysis identified 11 potential contributors to the risk of staying with an abusive partner: social support, respect shown by abusive partner, respect shown towards the abusive partner, hope/denial/acceptance, trust in the abusive partner, commitment, loss of reality, self-esteem, a non-violent philosophy, responsibility (self-blame) and 'emotional captivity' (fear and emotional attachment). The study contributes to highlighting the complexity of issues involved in examining domestic violence.

Introduction

In examining the problem of domestic violence, both quantitative and qualitative research methods have been implemented. Many researchers regard such violence as a problem for both sexes and they agree that domestic violence is gender-neutral in definition and in reality (Dwyer et al. 1996). There has been an increasing amount of literature examining male violence in heterosexual relationships, but there still remains scope for further exploration. Some researchers in the USA have suggested that the area of women-battering is gaining recognition as a major social and public health problem (Roberts 1996). In light of the available literature, gay male abuse is only recently being highlighted (Letellier 1994) and there remains a poor examination of women perpetrators (Kelly 1992, cited in Chandler and Taylor 1995). This is the case in particular in relation to women's abusive behaviour towards other women, although there is evidence of an increase in awareness of the issue in both the USA (e.g. Lobel 1986; Lie and Gentlewarrier 1991; Renzetti 1992) and in Britain (Chandler and Taylor 1995).

There remains a need to clarify the definition of domestic violence and what constitutes abusive behaviour. Dwyer et al. (1996) point out that conventional definitions tend to focus on some form of observable, physical injury. Both a medical and a legal context limit definitions of battering to physical acts (Petretic-Jackson and Jackson 1996), while marginalizing emotional and psychological aspects. Dwyer and colleagues (1996) remind us that the determination of what constitutes a violent act is culturally determined and thus reflects societal biases. This has serious implications for social, economic and legal policy development. Indeed, there is wide recognition that domestic abuse extends beyond the boundaries of a medical definition. Zubretsky and Digirolamo (1996) point out that domestic violence is now recognized to involve behaviour that is directed towards establishing and maintaining power and control over an intimate partner. Such behaviours include physical, sexual, economic, emotional and psychological forms of abuse. A range of abusive behaviours has been explored by several researchers (e.g. Renzetti 1992; Mooney 1993, 1994; Chandler and Taylor 1995; Dwyer et al. 1996; Hester et al. 1997).

There are several theories exploring causal explanations of domestic violence. Psychological research has examined individual differences, such as self-control and self-esteem, mental health, internalized blame, substance abuse, and so on (see Dwyer et al. 1996). Others have suggested that psychopathology in batterers or in those battered (see Hamberger and Hastings 1991, cited in Hamberger 1994) and head injury (Rosenbaum and Hoge 1989, cited in Hamberger 1994) may contribute to domestic violence. Research suggests that women who have experienced abuse often express self-blame and feelings of being responsible for the incident (Dobash and Dobash 1979, cited in Dwyer et al. 1996; Langhinrichsen-Rohling et al. 1995).

Gondolf and Fisher (1988, cited in Dwyer et al. 1996) have focused on the cognitive-behavioural process of 'learned helplessness', arguing that the battered partner continues to remain in the relationship through a 'state of submissive passivity': 'The abuse lessens the woman's sense of control, and she may internalize blame or simply stop struggling to extricate herself from the abuse. Either of these behaviours enables the situation to perpetuate'. Walker (1993, cited in Roberts 1996) applied the concept of 'learned helplessness' in an attempt to explain why women do not leave their abuser. In her conceptualization of 'battered women's syndrome', Walker argues that people who suffer from learned helplessness tend to select behavioural options that will generate predictable effects. This means that they would avoid responses that involve an unfamilar or unknown situation, including escape.

Such work has contributed to the understanding of why an individual may not seek to escape from their abuser. In severe circumstances, this can lead to what can be considered a last resort to terminate the abuse, namely killing their partner. While this may be appropriate in explaining how some individuals deal with a violent partner, there are other dimensions involved in staying with an abusive partner that go beyond self-blame and acceptance. These also need to be taken into account when examining this area. For example, Foreman and Dallos (1995) examined how discourse contributes to oppression. In addition, Dutton (1988, cited in Dwyer et al. 1996) advocated 'traumatic bonding theory', which focuses upon the development of strong emotional ties between two persons where one of them intermittently abuses the other. Dutton and Painter (1993, cited in Dwyer et al. 1996) suggest that this theory is useful in examining domestic violence because it highlights the role of power imbalance within the relationship. Here, the abused individual's need for support and affection grows as a result of the abuse itself. The abuser's apologies and promises are, therefore, accepted and the couple may become, once again, loving until the next violent incident.

However, the social context of domestic violence should not be ignored either. The impact of social tolerance and the legal system are important issues that should not be overlooked. Initial domestic violence often intensifies as it becomes an effective way for the perpetrator to control their partner. Social tolerance and lack of retribution lead the perpetrator to believe that their behaviour is acceptable (Zubretsky and Digirolamo 1996). Kitzinger (1995, cited in Hester et al. 1997) argues that the campaign of 'zero tolerance' to domestic violence has helped to identify domestic violence as a crime and an issue to be taken seriously.

Much of theory development has been the result of research into male violence in heterosexual partnerships. The lack of research into abusive behaviour within same-sex couples is striking. As Hamberger (1994) indicates, strictly gender-based theories of partner abuse require re-evaluation in relation to gay and lesbian domestic violence. In her exploration of partner abuse within lesbian couples, Renzetti (1992) found that intense dependency on their partner on the part of the perpetrator was a major factor within such relationships. She argues that the extent and severity of the abuse reflects the degree of dependency of the abusive partner. Through the abuse, the perpetrator succeeds in cutting her partner off from other people and interests. However, success in controlling the partner in turn increases the perpetrator's dependency upon her partner. Renzetti also explores how substance abuse can facilitate abuse. She suggests that batterers may use violence as a means of gaining power and control to compensate for feeling powerless in other ways.

Chandler and Taylor (1995) acknowledge the difficulty in recognizing partner abuse in lesbian relationships because its existence constitutes a challenge to the idea of a safe lifestyle among women. Within lesbian communities there remains a silence surrounding the issue of abuse. It has been argued that the lesbian and gay press has provided 'superficial' and 'unhelpful' coverage of the topic (Chandler and Taylor 1995). Partner abuse can occur in relationships regardless of cultural or ethnic background (Walker 1984, cited in Bonilla-Santiago 1996). Regardless of social and economic background, age, sexual preference, level of education, physical ability or lifestyle, abuse may occur.

Available literature suggests difficulties in accessing support and help when women find themselves involved in domestic violence. Women who are involved with a female perpetrator are less likely to be economically trapped or refer to children as reasons for staying with their partner (Chandler and Taylor 1995). Yet they face other obstacles, including homophobia and a lack of legal and civil rights. Those who practise sadomasochism are often denied recognition of their needs. Such discrimination, prejudice and lack of recognition, even within lesbian communities, contributes to further suffering and isolation. As Creith (1996) argues, issues such as rape, assault or abuse remain taboo within such communities. Accessibility of information and support are a major area of concern for all sufferers of abuse.

The study presented here aims to examine the accounts of individuals who have experienced abuse by a partner. It focuses upon the extent of the abuse and the availability of support. It is noted that the focus of the research is open to revision as the study seeks to explore the data using grounded theory procedures.

CW: Either at this point or within the Method section, the author should provide a rationale for the use of grounded theory in general and the abbreviated version in particular. It should become clear why grounded theory, as opposed to other types of qualitative methodology, was used and what kind of knowledge the author was hoping to produce on the basis of the study. It should also be made clear that the author is aware that the study does not constitute gounded theory in the full sense.

Method

Semi-structured interviews with two individuals were carried out. Participants were female and consisted of one full-time undergraduate student and one part-time further education student. They were aged 23 years and 32 years, respectively. Their ethnic backgrounds were European in one case and Afro-Caribbean in the other. At the time of the interview, participants were not involved in a committed or steady relationship. Written consent to take part in the study was obtained from both participants. In addition, participants were made aware of their right to withdraw at any time during the interview and they were assured of the confidential nature of the interview. Participants were interviewed at a place of their choice, the interviews lasting 40 and 75 minutes, respectively. The interview schedule was based on the topic area of 'abusive behaviour' within an intimate relationship. This included questions on sexuality, the best and worst experiences with their partner while in the relationship, medical treatment required, elimination of abuse, disclosure to others and media coverage (see Appendix on page 198 for a list of questions).

CW: Even though the issues covered by the interview schedule resonate with issues raised in the Introduction/Literature review, it would be helpful to provide a more explicit account of how the interview questions were conceived. Also, some of the categories identified later in the analysis reflect those used in some of the questions. The relationship between the interview agenda and the categories identified in the analysis should be addressed at some point within the report.

All interviews were audio-taped and transcribed. A pseudonym was agreed with each participant prior to the interview to ensure confidentiality and anonymity. Participants were given the opportunity to discuss any questions or concerns about the study itself or the topic area, listen to the tape-recording afterwards in the presence of the interviewer, and request a copy of the transcript or final copy of the research report. Participants were provided with further information or sources of contact in relation to their experience of abuse, if required. Transcription notation was based on the notation devised by Jefferson (1984, cited in Potter and Wetherell 1987).

Analysis of the data was based on grounded theory procedures (Strauss and Corbin 1990). Transcripts were read and analysed by coding each sentence, where possible, through conceptual labels. These were either written onto a copy of the transcript or onto a piece of paper, together with relevant extracts from the transcript. Using Strauss and Corbin's (1990) guidelines, concepts were labelled ('open coding') and examined for connections. Strauss and Corbin suggest 'axial coding' procedures to highlight links. Although a useful technique, this was used flexibly to avoid limitations in analytic focus. Finally, categories were integrated to facilitate theory generation. This involved primarily 'selective coding', although 'process' procedures can also be useful (see also Charmaz 1995).

> CW: It is better not to use specialist terms such as 'selective coding', 'process procedures' and 'axial coding' without specifying what is meant by them. This is because not all readers will necessarily know what these terms refer to, and even grounded theory researchers themselves may have different interpretations of what kinds of activities these terms refer to.

Analysis was carried out on each interview transcript in turn. Throughout the analysis, and especially during the initial stages of coding, the analysis remained close to the data. Transcripts were read and reread repeatedly during the process of analysis to provide further evidence to support or challenge emerging categories.

Reflexivity

Despite the severe emotional pain and other obstacles in their lives, these women have shown great courage and determination in their struggle to rebuild their lives. The experience is often lonely and painful. It is often at times of tragedy and suffering that we become stronger. Experience can be of positive value if viewed from a positive angle. It is not that individuals should be denied their right to anger. Anger can motivate political action. Anger can aid the healing process but ultimately 'moving on' stems from 'letting go'. The strength shown by these women, and others in similar circumstances, is a comfort and inspiration to other survivors. The continual lack of social acknowledgement of domestic violence is unacceptable. Blaming the individual, social silence surrounding the issue, lack of political or governmental commitment to recognize the problem, the practical difficulties often involved in gaining support, as well as social intolerance are a reflection of the continued injustice suffered by many victims of abuse. It is a problem that affects both straight and gay society.

The use of grounded theory allows the development of theory that is grounded in reality. Grounded theory procedures take into account the importance of the active role of persons in shaping the worlds they live in and the need to get out into the field if one wants to understand what is going on (Strauss and Corbin 1990). The change of focus within this study (from availability of social support to risk factors involved in the maintenance of an abusive relationship) is a reflection of the flexibility of the method and its ability to interact with the data. However, the findings in this study reflect a particular way of constructing the data. It is open to reinterpretation, since the construction of categories inevitably reflects the researcher's own interpretations and labelling. Alternative explorations of the data could have included discourse analysis and an examination of how various discourses may have contributed to the oppression and silencing of individuals in their suffering. The issue of domestic violence is a very sensitive one. The interview provides the researcher with a method of data collection that allows for him or her to interact with the interviewee in a manner that is appropriate to the subject matter. However, interviews are subject to self-report bias and it is important to acknowledge that aspects of the researcher's identity may have influenced participants' responses.

Results

Several core categories emerged from the analysis of the data. Some categories did not emerge within both sets of data. Therefore, core categories are illustrated and described for each participant in turn.

> CW: The term 'core category' needs to be defined before the Results are presented.

Identity

Figure A1 provides a summary of the core category 'identity' and its subcategories for Essme. For Essme, IDENTITY involved sexuality, self-esteem, self-perception and self-preservation (see Fig. A1). For Louise, IDENTITY was composed of sexuality, self-esteem, self-image, patience and self-preservation (see Fig. A2).

Identity of partner

Figure A3 provides a summary of the core category 'identity of partner' and its subcategories for Essme. IDENTITY OF PARTNER in Essme's account involves partner's image and state of physical health (Fig. A3). Very similar subcategories constitute this core category for Louise (see Fig. A4). For example, Louise invokes

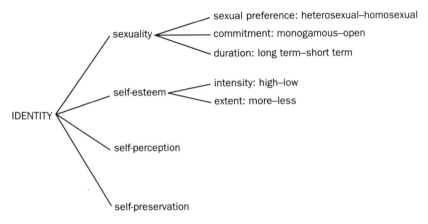

Figure A1 'Identity' in Essme's account

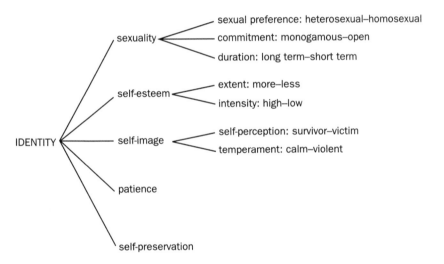

Figure A2 'Identity' in Louise's account

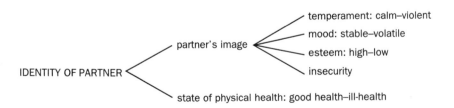

Figure A3 'Identity of partner' in Essme's account

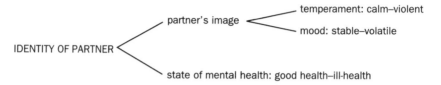

Figure A4 'Identity of partner' in Louise's account

her partner's mood and temperament when she says, 'He just suddenly looked at me and called me a piece of shit and pushed me over onto my back'.

> *CW: The use of quotations to illustrate categories and relations between categories is common practice in grounded theory reports. However, it is important to be clear about why particular quotations have been selected and what they contribute to the reader's understanding of the analysis. The quotations included in this report do illustrate categories; however, it is not always clear why particular categories are illustrated through quotations and others are not.*

Respect

RESPECT emerged as a core category for both Essme and Louise in the same way. It involved both feelings of respect towards the partner, as well as respect shown by the partner towards the self (Fig. A5).

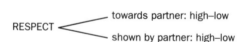

Figure A5 'Respect' in Essme's and Louise's accounts

Psychological abuse

For Essme, 'psychological abuse' involved emotional abuse through the induction of guilt and fear (see Fig. A6). For Louise, 'psychological abuse' was brought about

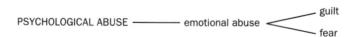

Figure A6 'Psychological abuse' in Essme's account

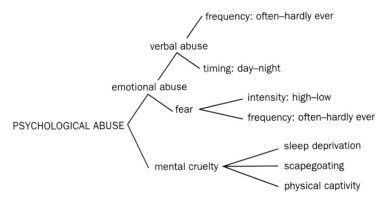

Figure A7 'Psychological abuse' in Louise's account

through both emotional abuse and mental cruelty (see Fig. A7). In both cases, fear constituted part of the emotional abuse.

> CW: It is not clear on what grounds the core category 'psychological abuse' was constructed. Since it is made up of only one subcategory (emotional abuse), it is not clear to what extent or in what ways 'psychological abuse' goes beyond or involves more than 'emotional abuse' in Essme's account.

For example, Essme describes an experience of emotional abuse when she says: 'She said that I was selfish and that I was worthless and that I was I should be thankful that she was staying with me 'cos nobody else would want anything to do with me'.

Physical abuse

For both Essme and Louise, the core category PHYSICAL ABUSE involved various dimensions of violence (see Figs A8 and A9). For example, Essme describes an

Figure A8 'Physical abuse' in Essme's account

Figure A9 'Physical abuse' in Louise's account

incidence of intense physical abuse thus: 'It's like she had turned into someone else and um she punched me in the face and the next thing I knew she had me up against the wall you know with her hands around my throat'.

> *CW: Again, it is not clear on what grounds this core category was constructed. Since it is made up of only one subcategory (violence), it is not clear to what extent or in what ways 'physical abuse' goes beyond or involves more than 'violence'.*

Sexual abuse

Only one of the participants, Essme, invoked SEXUAL ABUSE; this category involved both physical and emotional pain in relation to sexual feelings and practices (see Fig. A10).

Figure A10 'Sexual abuse' in Essme's account

> *CW: Given that the last three core categories revolve around notions of abuse, it would have made sense to integrate these categories further and to create an overarching category (ABUSE), which could then be further subdivided into the various types of abuse specified by the participants.*

Pain

Both Essme and Louise invoked PAIN. Pain could be inflicted, accepted and, in Louise's case, also avoided. The experience of PAIN was also quantified (e.g. more–less, strong–weak) (see Figs A11 and A12). For example, Essme refers to the intensity of the emotional pain she experienced: 'I think at the time what hurt most was the things she used to say to me'.

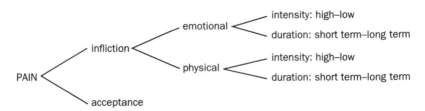

Figure A11 'Pain' in Essme's account

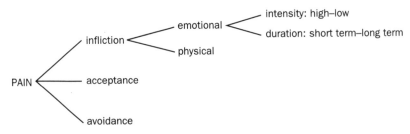

Figure A12 'Pain' in Louise's account

Romantic love

A core category of ROMANTIC LOVE was mobilized by both participants; however, while ROMANTIC LOVE involved emotional attachment, commitment, image, loss of reality, and trust for Essme, Louise also referred to compatibility. She did not, however, invoke image as an aspect of ROMANTIC LOVE (see Figs A13 and A14).

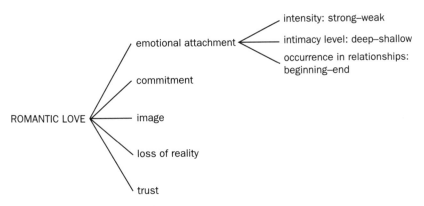

Figure A13 'Romantic love' in Essme's account

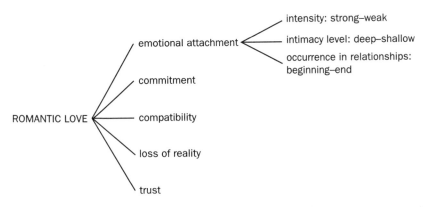

Figure A14 'Romantic love' in Louise's account

CW: Some of the category labels are not self-explanatory and would benefit from further elaboration and explanation. For example, 'image' within the context of ROMANTIC LOVE needs to be unpacked.

Louise acknowledges the importance of love when she says, 'It's not just because of practical issues, it's emotional . . . You've got a lot of strong ties there, for that person'.

Social support

Both Essme and Louise invoked SOCIAL SUPPORT; however, while Essme referred to SOCIAL SUPPORT in general terms (e.g. types of support), Louise's account included a detailed description and evaluation of specific support services and networks (see Figs A15 and A16). For example, Essme identifies the limitations in her access to personal support networks when she says, "Cos you could feel quite isolated as a black lesbian'. Louise identifies some of the difficulties in accessing sources of support when she says, 'It's very hard to, at the moment to find a poster when you're looking for one you know'.

CW: Figure A16 ('Social support' in Louise's account) introduces subcategories to subcategories. In all other visual displays so far (see Figs 1–15), core categories (e.g. PAIN) were broken down into a number of subcategories (e.g. 'infliction' and 'acceptance'), some of which were in turn dimensionalized (e.g. intensity: high–low). In Fig. 16, however, subcategories (e.g. women's refuge) are themselves further broken down into subcategories (e.g. safety, support of staff, reliability, etc.). While this is entirely compatible with grounded theory methodology, it does constitute a departure from an established pattern within this report and should, therefore, be commented upon by the author.

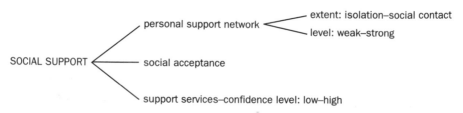

Figure A15 'Social support' in Essme's account

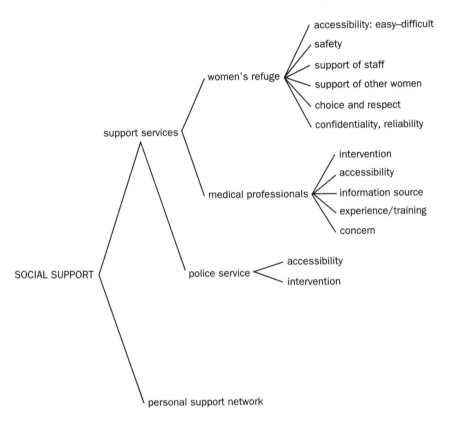

Figure A16 'Social support' in Louise's account

Gay image

Essme's account of her experience of abuse included references to a GAY IMAGE. These revolved around both ideology and coming out/disclosure of sexuality (see Fig. A17).

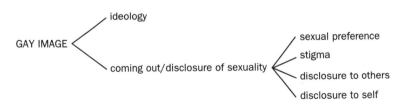

Figure A17 'Gay image' in Essme's account

Non-violent philosophy

Both Essme and Louise subscribed to a philosophy of non-violence. However, for Essme a NON-VIOLENT PHILOSOPHY involved both guilt and politics, whereas for Louise it was about calmness and pain avoidance (see Figs A18 and A19).

Figure A18 'Non-violent philosophy' in Essme's account

Figure A19 'Non-violent philosophy' in Louise's account

Coping/survival strategies

Both Essme's and Louise's accounts identified a range of strategies that they used to cope with or survive their experiences of abuse. Essme referred to three such strategies (see Fig. A20), whereas Louise invoked five (see Fig. A21).

Figure A20 'Coping/survival strategies' in Essme's account

Figure A21 'Coping/survival strategies' in Louise's account

Responsibility

Both participants invoked RESPONSIBILITY, both in relation to themselves (self-blame) and their partners (blaming partner) (see Fig. A22).

Figure A22 'Responsibility' in Essme's and Louise's accounts

Drug/substance use

Both Essme and Louise referred to the use of drugs; however, Essme invoked three types of drug (alcohol, medication and marijuana), whereas Louise only talked about alcohol and its various uses (see Figs A23 and A24).

Figure A23 'Drug/substance use' in Essme's account

Figure A24 'Drug/substance use' in Louise's account

CW: With the exception of 'environment', it appears as though the subcategories of 'alcohol consumption' are dimensions that may be conceptualized in terms of the extent to which they are, or are not, present. However, there is no indication that they can, in fact, be dimensionalized. This needs to be clarified.

Aspects of vulnerability

Further integration of categories across the two participants led to the identification of ASPECTS OF VULNERABILITY. Vulnerability to abuse emerged as a potential link between many of the core categories identified in the analysis. These categories constitute potential risk factors for abuse, since they contributed to an individual's decision to remain within the abusive relationship. Levels of social support, respect, hope/denial/acceptance, trust in and commitment to the partner, loss of reality, a non-violent philosophy, self-blame and what may be termed 'emotional captivity' (through fear and emotional attachment) appeared to enhance the risk of staying with an abusive partner (see Fig. A25).

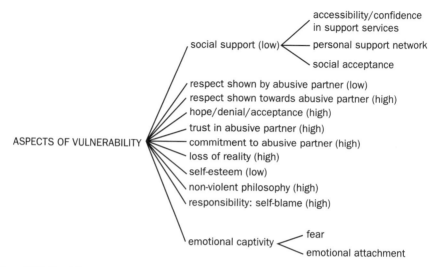

Figure A25 Contributors to increased risk of staying with an abusive partner

Discussion

Grounded theory analysis of two interviews with a heterosexual and a lesbian woman, respectively, on the topic of abusive relationships identified several core categories. In relation to the original focus of the research (occurrence of abuse and availability of social support), the core categories of psychological abuse, physical abuse and pain featured in both participants' experiences, and sexual abuse was also evident in the lesbian woman's relationship. Both participants spoke about the impact of the emotional abuse they suffered and the long-term effects of their emotional pain. The results suggest that psychological, physical and sexual abuse can occur regardless of sexual orientation. Access to support appeared to occur on two levels – personal networks and dedicated support services. Accessibility of such services was not guaranteed. Confidence in support services was an important feature in accessing such services. For the gay individual, social acceptance was also an issue, which influenced accessibility. To explore these areas in depth, further data collection would be required.

Further analysis of the data led to a revision of the research focus. Core categories appeared to revolve around issues involved in staying within abusive relationships. This led to the identification of aspects of vulnerability that potentially increase an individual's risk of staying with an abusive partner. These included social support (accessibility/confidence in support services, personal support networks and social acceptance), respect (shown by the abusive partner), respect (shown towards the abusive partner), hope/denial/acceptance, trust in the abusive partner, commitment, loss of reality, self-esteem, nonviolent philosophy, responsibility (self-blame) and 'emotional captivity' (fear and emotional attachment).

Social support reflects accessibility of, and confidence in, support services, the existence of a personal support network and the presence of social acceptance. A low level of social support may increase the likelihood of staying with an abusive partner. Low levels of respect shown by the abusive partner, together with high levels of respect shown towards the abusive partner, may also increase the risk of staying with an abusive partner, as do high levels of hope/denial/acceptance. A high level of trust in an abusive partner, commitment and a sense of loss of reality that often accompanies 'falling in love', together with a high level of self-blame may also contribute to the maintenance of an abusive relationship. A low level of self-esteem and non-violent philosophy appear to contribute to staying with an abusive partner. The relationship between the experience of persistent emotional abuse and low levels of self-esteem requires further exploration. A commitment to non-violence means that the abused partner is unlikely to retaliate. A high level of fear of, and emotional attachment to, an abusive partner can lead to feelings of 'emotional captivity'. Interconnections between all of these aspects of vulnerability appeared to contribute to the decision to stay with an abusive partner.

The study has several limitations. Further exploration of the extent to which each aspect of vulnerability influences an individual's experience is needed. The potential contributors identified within this study require extensive clarification. Additional data collection is recommended to facilitate theory development and revision of analysis, if necessary. Other areas for exploration include the relationship between self-esteem and trust, and the relationship between emotional attachment, trust, commitment and hope. In addition, the role of trust and respect in communication breakdown, and the role of concepts such as 'unconditional love' and 'loyalty', require further exploration if we are to understand the dynamics involved in the struggle to break free from an abusive partner.

The study used a non-random sample of only two participants and no generalizations can be made on the basis of the study.

CW: At this point, it would be helpful to differentiate between theoretical and statistical generalizability (see Chapter 5). Also, the notion of theoretical sampling could be introduced within this context.

In addition, it is important to be aware that any conclusions drawn are based upon participants' self-reports.

In response to some people's view of the battered partner as colluding with the abuse, the identification of aspects of vulnerability can help us understand why an individual may not leave an abusive partner. The study highlights the complexity of issues involved when an individual finds him- or herself involved in an abusive relationship. There are also practical and economic aspects to such an involvement that have not been highlighted within the context of this study. Individuals may feel pressure to stay in the relationship, for example 'to save face' if relatives and friends did not approve of the relationship from the beginning. Individuals may fear loneliness. The role of sex within the relationship and the meanings that individuals attach to sex did not feature in this study. The study's findings are bounded by the limitations of the data, the method of analysis and the research focus. As a result, it can only reflect a small piece of a complex jigsaw.

Although the theory of learned helplessness can explain how some people deal with a violent partner (see Introduction), it does not provide an adequate explanation as to why some stay with a violent partner even though they may not have an extensive fear of the unknown. Foreman and Dallos (1995) argue that women's helplessness and powerlessness tends to be conceptualized as the cause, rather than the consequence, of abuse. However, it has been argued that battered women are resourceful and courageous, and that their experiences of abuse constitute a temporary 'descent into hell' from which they can, and do, emerge as a result of an active struggle. Some may ask why abused partners do not leave sooner. To such a naïve question the answers are complex. The individuals who have shared their experiences in this study are testimony to this. The women in this study referred to their love and desire for their partner as a crucial factor in staying with them for as long as they did. Smail (1993) suggests that the close relationship between love and power is generally overlooked. Smail argues that relations between self and others are constructed through perceived power. Smail is critical of a psychological focus that has little interest in pursuing the origins of the immediately apparent circumstances into the further reaches of the social network. This study is open to Smail's criticism of studies that do not explore the field of power beyond the immediate relations between individuals. The relationship between love and power requires further exploration.

Accessibility of social support is also an area for further examination. The results of this study suggest difficulties in access to support services. There is a need to examine issues that prevent access to appropriate information and support concerning domestic violence across the wide spectrum of relationships. Confidence in support services was apprehensive. This was complicated further by a fear of homophobia and an awareness of the lack of legal recognition associated with same-sex relationships.

The implementation of law within the area of domestic violence remains a cause for concern. Often perpetrators are not punished as a result of prosecution. Often there is a lack of visual or forensic evidence, and there is a fear of not being believed in one's accusations of abuse. In addition, victims are often made to feel responsible for the abuse. There remains the difficult problem of establishing boundaries between consent and abuse. This is especially relevant in the area of sexual abuse. Some may argue that by staying with an abusive partner, individuals are consenting to be part of the abusive situation. This study helps to reaffirm exisiting research findings in this area, which suggest that staying within an abusive relationship is a complex issue that involves multiple causes, including those that go beyond the individual's actions and choices.

The mass media can trivialize and sensationalize the issue (Mooney 1994). Often the seriousness of domestic violence becomes a lost message in a cloud of frivolous headlines that make for tabloid entertainment. The gay media seek to maintain a censored view, continuing to promote an image of unity and solidarity. While unity is important in the ongoing fight against discrimination and for equal rights in a homophobic society, failing to address an issue as serious as domestic violence continues to aid oppression and fuels acceptance of abusive behaviour within same-sex relationships.

It is only through acknowledgement and openness that we can break the silence and break down the barriers that continue to protect perpetrators. Silence serves to legitimize abusive behaviour. Those experiencing abuse need to be given access to a supportive network. They need to know that they will not face social exclusion for 'rocking the boat' while their abusers gain recognition for 'keeping their spouse in check'. Is abuse part of a utopia? Exerting power over another to meet one's own needs, without regard for one's partner, is nothing but blatant exploitation – no such abuse is 'love'.

On a cynical note, people wake up and smell the coffee – the image may be wonderful, but what does it really taste like? Sometimes it does not taste that good.

References

Bonilla-Santiago, G. (1996) Latino battered women: barriers to service delivery and cultural considerations, in A.R. Roberts (ed.) *Helping Battered Women: New Perspectives and Remedies*. Oxford: Oxford University Press.

Chandler, T. and Taylor, J. (1995) *Lesbians Talk: Violent Relationships*. London: Scarlett Press.

Charmaz, K. (1995) Grounded theory, in J.A. Smith, R. Harré and L. Van Langenhove (eds) *Rethinking Methods in Psychology*. London: Sage.

Creith, E. (1996) *Undressing Lesbian Sex: Popular Images, Private Acts and Public Consequences*. London: Cassell.

Dwyer, D.C., Smokowski, P.R., Bricut, J.C. and Wodarski, J.S. (1996) Domestic violence and women battering: theory and practice implications, in A.R. Roberts (ed.) *Helping Battered Women: New Perspectives and Remedies*. Oxford: Oxford University Press.

Foreman, S. and Dallos, R. (1995) Domestic violence, in R. Dallos and E. McLaughlin (eds) *Social Problems and the Family*. London: Sage.

Hamberger, L.K. (1994) Domestic partner abuse: expanding paradigms for understanding and intervention, *Violence and Victims*, 9(2): 91–4.

Hester, M., Pearson, C. and Radford, L. (1997) *Domestic Violence: A National Survey of Court Welfare and Voluntary Sector Mediation Practice*. Bristol: The Policy Press.

Langhinrichsen-Rohling, J., Neidig, P. and Thorn, G. (1995) Violent marriages: gender differences in levels of current violence and past abuse, *Journal of Family Violence*, 10(2): 159–76.

Letellier, P. (1994) Gay and bisexual male domestic violence victimization: challenges to feminist theory and responses to violence, *Violence and Victims*, 9(2): 95–106.

Lie, G. and Gentlewarrier, S. (1991) Intimate violence in lesbian relationships: discussion of survey findings and practice implications, *Journal of Social Service Research*, 15(1–2): 41–59.

Lobel, K. (1986) *Naming the Violence: Speaking Out about Lesbian Battering*. Seattle, WA: Seal Press.

Mooney, J. (1993) *The Hidden Figure: Domestic Violence in North London*. London: Middlesex University Press.

Mooney, J. (1994) *The Prevalence and Social Distribution of Domestic Violence: An Analysis of Theory and Method*. London: Middlesex University Press.

Petretic-Jackson, P. and Jackson, T. (1996) Mental health interventions with battered women, in A.R. Roberts (ed.) *Helping Battered Women: New Perspectives and Remedies*. Oxford: Oxford University Press.

Potter, J. and Wetherell, M. (1987) *Discourse and Social Psychology*. London: Sage.

Renzetti, C.M. (1992) *Violent Betrayal: Partner Abuse in Lesbian Relationships*. London: Sage.

Roberts, A.R. (1996) A comparative analysis of incarcerated battered women and a community sample of battered women, in A.R. Roberts (ed.) *Helping Battered Women: New Perspectives and Remedies*. Oxford: Oxford University Press.

Smail, D. (1993) When I was little – the experience of power, in D. Smail (ed.) *The Origins of Unhappiness*. London: HarperCollins.

Strauss, A. and Corbin, J. (1990) *Basics of Qualitative Research*. London: Sage.

Zubretsky, T.M. and Digirolamo, K.M. (1996) The false connection between adult domestic violence and alcohol, in A.R. Roberts (ed.) *Helping Battered Women: New Perspectives and Remedies*. Oxford: Oxford University Press.

Appendix

Interview Schedule (guide)
Hi [name] thank you for being here/allowing me to be here
How do you feel at the moment? (Just relax. Please answer as honestly as you can)
I may make some notes, just for my reference. Is that okay with you?
Could I ask your age? Your gender? Your ethnic background?
How long have you lived in [name of place]?
Have you always lived in England?
Are you a student?
What activities are you interested in?
How would you describe yourself as a person?
How would you describe your sexuality?
Some people find themselves in situations with an abusive partner. Is this relevant to you?
What was their gender?
Were you involved in a 'monogamous' or 'open' relationship at the time?
Were you living with your partner?
What was the best experience for you, with your partner, while you were in that relationship?
What was the worst experience for you, with your partner, while you were in that relationship?
Did you at any time require medical treatment as a result of your partner's behaviour?
Did you inform anyone else of the incident(s)?
How long were you in the relationship? How did the abuse stop?
What do you consider were the reasons for your partner's behaviour?
How would you describe the (gay) media coverage concerning the area of abuse in relationships?
[Thank participant]

Appendix 3

The emotional experience of looking at art: an observation in the National Gallery

Karolina Mörnsjö

Reflexive preface • *Abstract* • *Introduction* • *Method* • *Setting* • *Participants* • *Ethical consideration* • *The paintings* • *Practical considerations* • *Analysis* • *Discussion* • *References*

Reflexive preface

I chose to study qualitative research methods in my final year. I was interested in this module because its content seemed fundamentally different from that of the (compulsory) quantitative methods modules that I had previously taken. What appealed to me was the more holistic approach to psychological research, whereby the individual was not merely considered in terms of his or her response time on a computerized test, but as a human being with the ability to feel as well as think. Most scientists do, of course, acknowledge that people have emotions, but finding ways of obtaining valid measures of these can be difficult. I was therefore happy to learn that there are several methods that can be used to study people from the alternative viewpoint of qualitative methods. I wanted to take advantage of the new freedom that I felt qualitative methods could offer, both in terms of topic and location. As you do not require a scientific laboratory, qualitative research can be carried out practically anywhere. Also, it is recognized that the topic is closely linked to the researcher. I love art and beautiful pictures and I think that they can affect your emotions in a way similar to music and poetry, perhaps because the artist, like the poet or musician, is expressing something personal. As for the location, I wanted to get away from the academic environment! That is how I ended up in the National Gallery. Using qualitative methods made me feel like an independent, capable field researcher and empowered me to trust in myself and my ability to produce a study of my own. Watching people was good fun and I enjoyed my position as a secret observer. I would also have been interested in hearing people talk about their art experience, but that would have entailed a study of its own (so there's an idea for your final year project!).

Abstract

This observational study was carried out in the National Gallery in London. Several individuals who visited the gallery were unobtrusively observed as they stopped to look at two different pieces of art work. The researcher did not interact with the participants at any time. The aim of the study was to identify behaviours that would typically occur when visitors view art. However, the major finding was that the paintings seemed to provoke strong emotional responses in the viewer. Although this finding was unexpected, there is a link between this study and existing theories of the dynamic nature of art appreciation. Implications of the findings are discussed.

Introduction

Visiting an art gallery is a popular form of recreation for many people. Although people may visit galleries for many different reasons, a gallery is an artistic environment that is likely to invite certain types of behaviour and reactions in the viewer. The aim of the present study was to take a look at the different behaviours that people may display in art galleries. One might expect an array of different behaviours that could occur in such a context and this may reveal something about the ways in which visual art is experienced by viewers. For example, people may adopt different body postures when looking, depending on the degree to which a painting captures their interest. When looking at pictures in pairs or small groups, people may engage in behaviours such as pointing. They may or may not discuss their visual experience of the picture with one another. There may be gender differences in such behaviours. For example, it was suggested to me that men may be inclined to point more and attempt to explain what is happening in the picture, whereas women may absorb the whole picture visually without pointing to specific details. `

The observational method seemed to lend itself to discrete watching and the famous National Gallery with its wide variety of art work was chosen because it attracts so many visitors of different age groups and nationalities. In this way, I hoped that my sample would be as heterogeneous as possible. No previous studies on this particular subject were found prior to obervation. It was therefore not possible to outline any further specific expectations about what was going to be found or to identify aspects of the situation that deserve particular attention. However, there was an expectation that something new and interesting would be found about art gallery visitors.

Method

This study was carried out using the observational method, which is concerned with 'the accurate watching and noting of phenomena as they occur in nature' (Banister et al. 1994: 18). The essence of qualitative observation is that it deals with naturally occurring behaviours. The method was chosen because it was suitable for the purposes of the present study; namely, to explore people's behaviour in an art gallery.

It was also chosen because I felt comfortable with a non-interactive approach to qualitative research.

CW: At this point, it would have been a good idea to provide more information about the actual procedure of observation and note-taking. For example, what types of notes did the researcher produce? Did they include reflexive and analytical material or were they purely descriptive? Also, how were the notes analysed and integrated to produce a coherent account? What was left out and what was included in the account, and why?

Setting

The data were gathered at the National Gallery near Trafalgar Square in London, on Saturday, 20 February 1999. The observation was structured in so far as one painting had been chosen as the focus for observation beforehand. On the day of the observation, a second painting was chosen to obtain two sets of data that could be compared and contrasted.

CW: It would be helpful to be told, at this point, what caused the researcher to decide to take a comparative approach on the day of the observation.

However, during data collection, a broad focus was maintained, and I tried to be open to whatever behaviours would occur. The intention was to observe viewers' behaviour in relation to two different pictures.

Participants

A considerable number of people visited the National Gallery on the day of observation. Most of these were adults of various age groups. A small number of teenagers and children could also be seen. However, there were relatively few children, perhaps 10 to 15 in all, who seemed to be around 7–10 years of age. The people who viewed the two chosen paintings appeared alone, in pairs or in small groups. A large group (around 20 people) led by a guide appeared once. No explanations or debriefing were given to the participants, who were unaware that the observation took place.

Ethical consideration

It seems safe to assume that ethical considerations are not an issue within this context, since the data were gathered in a public place and all participants remained anonymous. Furthermore, I observed naturally occurring behaviour and no manipulation was involved.

The paintings

The first painting was 'Whistlejacket', painted in 1762 by George Stubbs (1724–1806) (see Fig. A26). The information note next to the picture in the gallery states that the racehorse 'Whistlejacket', painted in near life-size for its owner, is considered to be Stubbs' masterpiece. Furthermore, it is described as 'perhaps one of the most original portraits of a horse in British history'. As for technical information, the note reads: 'The plain background acts as a foil to the strikingly lifelike depiction of the horse, creating an impression of monumentality that transcends any specific time or place'. Indeed, the reason for choosing the horse as a focal point for the observation was the way in which I was initially touched as I strolled about the gallery on an earlier

Figure A26 'Whistlejacket' by George Stubbs, 1724–1806

Note: Reproduced with permission of the National Gallery, London.

occasion, so as to see what would attract my interest. Thus, my assumption and starting point for the research was that a picture that captured me would have a similar effect on other viewers.

CW: It is important to acknowledge that the way in which the picture was chosen means that the observation is going to be about how viewers look at a certain kind of picture; namely, one that has the ability to attract interest and touch its viewer.

Although only one picture had been chosen before the day of observation, I decided to choose another one in order to compare and contrast people's behaviour in front of two rather different pictures. A walk around the gallery before the collection of the first set of data, however, did not give me any further idea about which picture to choose. I therefore started out observing the viewers of 'Whistle-jacket'. As the data were being collected, I noticed that a picture to my right attracted a great deal of interest. I therefore decided to use that picture to generate the second set of data. The picture was 'An Experiment on a Bird in the Air Pump', painted in 1768 by Joseph Wright of Derby (1734–1797) (see Fig. A27). The note next to this painting explains the context of the picture, which shows a lecturer

Figure A27 'An experiment on a Bird in the Air Pump' by Joseph Wright of Derby, 1734–1797

Note: Reproduced with permission of the National Gallery, London.

demonstrating to a family audience the creation of a vacuum. A white cockatoo is imprisoned in a glass flask from which the air is extracted until the bird can no longer breathe.

Practical considerations

It was important to be able to observe the participants unobtrusively. 'Whistlejacket' hung in the middle of the wall in a large rectangular room, which had seats placed in the middle. This position lent itself to discrete watching and note-taking. The physical location of 'Whistlejacket' contributed to my choice of this painting. The data for 'Whistlejacket' were collected during a 45-minute session between 1.30 and 2.15 p.m. Subsequently, the people looking at the picture of the experiment with the bird were observed from 2.15 to 3 p.m.

Analysis

The observation resulted in a set of notes describing the most frequently occurring behaviours that the participants displayed in relation to each painting.

> CW: It is not clear why the author has decided to focus on the most frequently occurring behaviours. Qualitative research does not assume that the most frequent occurrences are necessarily the most interesting or the most significant.

The most prevalent features of the data are described below.

Painting 1: 'Whistlejacket'

Results

Many people stopped in front of the picture and looked at it before they walked up to the wall to read the information note. They then stepped back so that they could see the horse properly again. As this painting was a large one, most people watched it from a distance of five or six metres. However, some looked at it from a distance of as much as 15 metres. Since I had expected some interaction between the viewers who looked at the picture in pairs or in small groups, I was initially surprised by the lack of such behaviour. However, it soon became evident that this absence of communication was probably a significant part of the experience of looking at the horse. The most striking finding was that a softened expression appeared on the participants' faces when looking at 'Whistlejacket'. This softened expression almost invariably developed into a smile. Where people arrived in pairs, they stood next to each other, smiling, with their gaze fixed upon the horse. If they commented on the painting, they tended to do so without taking their eyes off the horse to face each other. However, a few people first looked at the picture and then turned towards each other and smiled. Many people also tilted their heads while looking at the painting. A great number held one hand in front of their mouths or kept their arms crossed while looking. This behaviour pattern of softened facial expression, smiling and displaying either of the hand/arm movements occurred regardless of whether people were looking at the picture alone or with others. It was also similar among both men and women and among people from different ethnic backgrounds.

Another interesting finding was that the participants changed their position from which they looked at the painting. For example, after having looked from some distance, some viewers went on to look at the picture very closely. In particular, the horse's hooves received close scrutiny. In fact, because of the size of the painting, the horse's back hooves were at eye level for most people. Unlike, for example, impressionistic work, which looks detailed and exact from a distance but diffuse at close-up, Whistlejacket's hooves do look very real even at close-up, and this seemed to fascinate people. However, more importantly, people moved around in front of the picture as if attempting to view the horse from different angles.

Finally, it should be noted that not everybody stopped to pay close attention to 'Whistlejacket'. There may be various reasons for this. For example, these people may have looked at the picture earlier during their visit and were on their way out or they may not have found it interesting. Also, small children were not impressed. Despite efforts from accompanying adults and many pointing gestures, the children turned their backs to the picture and ignored it.

Interpretation

During the observation it was noted that the picture of the horse affected the viewers in different ways. There are two aspects to this. First, it seemed that the painting evoked certain feelings in the viewers. Behaviours such as a softened expression on people's faces and tilting of the head indicated positive feelings, such as affection and tenderness. This emotional response was probably enhanced by the fact that the horse was depicted in a way that made it appear to be looking at the viewer and by the fact that it was near life-size. These characteristics can probably also account for the second aspect; namely, that in the looking process the horse seemed to be transformed from a two dimensional picture into a 'real' horse. In other words, people regarded it as a three-dimensional animate object. Although this may seem far-fetched, it could explain that most viewers seemed to look at the horse from different angles. For example, many observed the horse from a right angle as if attempting to see it not from the side (as it is depicted) but from the front. Even a close look at the back hooves did not make the horse appear less life-like. To sum up, it could be said that 'Whistlejacket' created a very real image of a horse in people's minds and that this evoked a positive emotional response.

Painting 2: 'An Experiment on a Bird in the Air Pump'

Results and interpretation

The way in which the second painting influenced its viewers was very different from the first. The initial spontaneous response to this picture involved frowning. People looked worried and disturbed, as if asking themselves, 'What is happening here?' As this picture was smaller than the previous one, people stood closer to it and also went to read the information note on the wall immediately, as if they felt a pressing need to find out what was going on. They then invariably looked rather offended, presumably on behalf of the bird. What was striking was that people turned around to look at each other, without necessarily communicating verbally. This may be seen as a sign of needing reassurance. In addition, people interacted more with one another in front of this picture. Many pointed towards the different characters in the picture and talked a great deal to each other. Small children also pointed.

On one occasion, a group of Americans viewed the picture accompanied by their group leader who acted as their guide. This was interesting because, although the initial response of these people was similar to that of those described above, the group started to behave differently when the picture was explained to them by the guide. There were two main aspects to this. First, the guide talked about the different characters in the painting and how it was typical for women to show more emotion and distress while the men showed interest in the proceedings. The reaction of the women in the group to this claim was one of uneasy laughter and fidgeting. Their body language seemed to suggest that they were not comfortable with such a sexist generalization. However, when the guide continued to say that this was typical of women of the time when the picture was painted, the group seemed to settle down again. Second, the guide explained how the artist had used light and darkness to create a very dramatic effect. This was remarkable because of the impact it had on the viewers. The expression on their faces suddenly changed as if they were realizing that they had been subject to deception; after all, they seemed to be thinking, this painting is just a picture and not necessarily a portrayal of a real event. Thus it seemed that they experienced a sense of relief as they realized that perhaps no real suffering had been inflicted on the bird after all.

Discussion

In the present study, people's behaviour in an art gallery was investigated using the observational method. The initial aim of the research was to explore different ways in which viewers relate to paintings and how they interact with one another when looking at the paintings. The results showed that, although people engaged in various behaviours, the most striking finding was the emotional response that the paintings evoked in the viewers. This somewhat surprising finding was obtained through maintaining a broad focus throughout data collection, thus remaining open to the unexpected. I was pleased to find that, when people were captured by a painting, they seemed to experience various emotions, to the point that the boundaries between reality and the world created by the artist became blurred.

It has been widely documented that artists express emotion through their work. For example, it has been suggested that Rembrandt's use of light and darkness in his self-portraits reflected his mood at the time of painting, especially during periods of depression (Postma 1993). However, as far as the emotional experience of the viewers is concerned, considerations seem to have been largely theoretical. Different theoretical approaches emphasize different aspects of the aesthetic experience. For example, from a psychoanalytical perspective, the emotionally expressive power of art work is explained in terms of a system of tension and release between the picture and the viewer (Rose 1991). However, this viewpoint has been criticized for being too limited. It has been argued that art experience is a process of transformation in which both imagination and aesthetic emotion play a role (Guimaraes-Lima 1995).

CW: These are interesting ideas. It would be helpful to find out more about them, and to read a more explicit discussion of their relevance in relation to the present study.

Observational studies of people's emotional responses to art seem to have been rare. The present piece of research was probably novel in that it was carried out within a natural setting and therefore succeeded in capturing the spontaneous reactions of the participants. Although I was not aware that emotion would play a major role in the findings, the results of my study link well with psychological theories of art appreciation. For example, Funch (1997) discussed the relationship between art and viewer, and suggested that there are various ways in which visual art can affect the viewer. First, according to Funch, there is a spontaneous preference for a certain picture. I believe that this was experienced by myself when I chose the horse painting and by the participants who stopped to look at it. Conversely, the idea of spontaneous preference explains why some people, including small children, were not captured by the horse. According to Funch, art appreciation can also be something like a blissful experience of transcendence. This phenomenon, which is seen as a characteristic of a personal encounter with a work of art, could be observed in the softened facial expressions and smiles of many people who looked at the horse. According to Funch, aesthetic experience also provides emotion with its distinct focus. Perhaps this can explain why most people who looked at the picture of the bird experiment seemed to experience the same type of emotion; the setting combined with the light/dark effects created a dramatic impact on the viewers, which was clearly observable. Nevertheless, the viewers were able to distance themselves from the first captivating encounter with the painting and look at it more objectively once the guide highlighted its specific features. This implies that art can be experienced in two ways. The personal aesthetic experience is likely to invoke emotions, whereas exploring an artist's techniques and motives requires a more detached, analytical approach.

For future research, the present study could be extended in a number of ways. For example, if data were collected on more than one occasion, the data sets could be compared to assess the extent to which the same, or similar, observations would be made. Using an open-ended questionnaire or interviews, one could investigate the spontaneous preferences of art gallery visitors for particular paintings. People could be asked to describe how the picture affected them, what kinds of thoughts and feelings it provoked, and so on. This would provide an insight into the ways in which different paintings appeal to people. It would also be possible to see whether the same painting evoked similar emotional responses in all viewers.

It should be noted that different findings may have been obtained in a different cultural environment or with different participants such as young children. However, for the purposes of this piece of research, it is unlikely that the emotional responses of the participants were misinterpreted. My confidence in the findings is increased because I was not, in fact, looking for emotional responses in the viewers to begin with.

Reflexivity

Personal dimension

I intended to carry out some kind of observational research within an environment that appealed to me. I have a personal interest in art, both looking at it and creating my own pieces of art. I therefore liked the idea of being able to spend time in an art gallery and to study some of the aspects of other people's art experience, and doing my course assignment at the same time!

I was very pleased to see how people reacted emotionally to the first painting, 'Whistlejacket', which I had chosen for the research. I could see that people are in a sense bound together in their ability to feel a kind of absorbed involvement when encountering art work. This proved to me that there is so much more to human beings' capacity for imagination than many cognitive psychologists would often have us believe. In seeing that this was the case, I realized that people have a creative and emotional potential that is frequently ignored in 'scientific' psychological studies, especially those using quantitative methods.

Similarly, when I saw people gathering in front of the second painting (the experiment with a bird) and looked to see what was happening in the picture, my own reaction resembled that of the other viewers. When I went up to the picture to read the information note, I found another lone viewer who looked at me for reassurance with a frown that told me that he was upset on behalf of the poor bird. This reassured me that humans are instantly capable of feeling empathy.

Being a rather perceptive and emotional person, it is likely that this facilitated my ability to pick up and interpret the reactions of the participants in the way that I did. The main way in which the study changed me was to restore my faith in people's capacity to let themselves be emotionally touched by paintings and the way in which paintings seemed to 'come alive' for viewers.

Epistemological dimension

As I set out to observe overt behaviour such as pointing, the only method that could have been used was observation. However, this method limited the findings, since the way people felt could only be inferred from their behaviour. They were not actually asked how they felt. An alternative approach, such as the use of open-ended question-naires or semi-structured interviews, would perhaps have yielded richer data and more detailed information. Still, I believe that an alternative interpretation would have been unlikely to have emerged.

References

Banister, P., Burman, E., Parker, I., Taylor, M. and Tindall, C. (1994) *Qualitative Methods in Psychology: A Research Guide*. Buckingham: Open University Press.

Funch, B.S. (1997) *The Psychology of Art Appreciation*. Copenhagen: Museum Tusculanum Press.

Guimaraes-Lima, M. (1995) From aesthetics to psychology: notes on Vygotsky's psychology of art, *Anthropology and Education Quarterly*, 26(4): 410–24.

Postma, J.U. (1993) Did Rembrandt suffer from depressive periods? A photo-analytic study of his self-portraits, *European Journal of Psychiatry*, 7(3): 180–84.

Rose, G. (1991) Abstract art and emotion: expressive form and the sense of wholeness, *Journal of the American Psychoanalytic Association*, 39(1): 131–56.

References

Alasuutari, P. (1995) *Researching Culture: Qualitative Method and Cultural Studies.* London: Sage.

Anfara, V.A. and Mertz, N.T. (2006) *Theoretical Frameworks in Qualitative Research.* London: Sage.

Annells, M. (1996) Grounded theory method: philosophical perspectives, paradigm of inquiry, and postmodernism, *Qualitative Health Research,* 6(3): 379–93.

Antaki, C., Billig, M., Edwards, D. and Potter, J. (2003) Discourse analysis means doing analysis: a critique of six analytical shortcomings, *Discourse Analysis Online,* 1, available from http://www.shu.ac.uk/daol/previous/v1/n1/index.htm.

Arribas-Ayllon, M. and Walkerdine, V. (2008) Foucauldian discourse analysis, in C. Willig and W. Stainton Rogers (eds) *The Sage Handbook of Qualitative Research in Psychology.* London: Sage.

Ashworth, P. (2003) An approach to phenomenological psychology: the contingencies of the lifeworld, *Journal of Phenomenological Psychology,* 34(2): 145–56.

Atkinson, J.M. and Heritage, J.C. (eds) (1984) *Structures of Social Action: Studies in Conversation Analysis.* Cambridge: Cambridge University Press.

Banister, P., Burman, E., Parker, I., Taylor, M. and Tindall, C. (1994) *Qualitative Methods in Psychology: A Research Guide.* Buckingham: Open University Press.

Bannister, D. and Fransella, F. (1986) *Inquiring Man: The Psychology of Personal Constructs,* 3rd edn. London: Croom Helm.

Bem, S. and Looren de Jong, H. (1997) *Theoretical Issues in Psychology: An Introduction.* London: Sage.

Billig, M. (1991) *Ideology and Opinions: Studies in Rhetorical Psychology.* London: Sage.

Billig, M. (1997) Rhetorical and discursive analysis: how families talk about the royal family, in N. Hayes (ed.) *Doing Qualitative Analysis in Psychology.* Hove: Psychology Press.

Billig, M., Condor, S., Edwards, D. et al. (1988) *Ideological Dilemmas: A Social Psychology of Everyday Thinking.* London: Sage.

Brinkmann, S. and Kvale, S. (2008) Ethics in qualitative psychological research, in C. Willig and W. Stainton Rogers (eds) *The Sage Handbook of Qualitative Research in Psychology.* London: Sage.

Brocki, J.M. and Wearden, A.J. (2006) A critical evaluation of the use of interpretative phenomenological analysis (IPA) in health psychology, *Psychology and Health,* 21(1): 87–108.

Bromley, D.B. (1986) *The Case Study Method in Psychology and Related Disciplines*. Chichester: John Wiley.

Burr, V. (1995) *An Introduction to Social Constructionism*. London: Routledge.

Burr, V. (2002) *The Person in Social Psychology*. Hove: Psychology Press.

Burr, V. (2003) *Social Constructionism*, 2nd edn. London: Routledge.

Butt, T. and Langdridge, D. (2003) The construction of self: the public reach into the private sphere, *Sociology*, 37(3): 477–94.

Calle, S. (2007) *Take Care of Yourself*. Arles: Acts Sud.

Carabine, J. (2000) Unmarried motherhood 1830–1990: a genealogical analysis, in M. Wetherell, S. Taylor and S.J. Yates (eds) *Discourse as Data: A Guide for Analysis*. London: Open University Press.

Chalmers, A.F. (1999) *What is this Thing Called Science?*, 3rd edn. Buckingham: Open University Press.

Chamberlain, K. (2000) Methodolatry and qualitative health research, *Journal of Health Psychology*, 5(3): 285–96.

Chamberlain, K., Camic, P. and Yardley, L. (2004) Qualitative analysis of experience: grounded theory and case studies, in D.F. Marks and L. Yardley (eds) *Research Methods for Clinical and Health Psychology*. London: Sage.

Charmaz, K. (1990) 'Discovering' chronic illness: using grounded theory, *Social Science and Medicine*, 30(11): 1161–72.

Charmaz, K. (1995) Grounded theory, in J.A. Smith, R. Harré and L. Van Langenhove (eds) *Rethinking Methods in Psychology*. London: Sage.

Charmaz, C. (2000) Constructivist and objectivist grounded theory, in N.K. Denzin and Y. Lincoln (eds) *Handbook of Qualitative Research*, 2nd edn. Thousand Oaks, CA: Sage.

Charmaz, C. (2002) Grounded theory analysis, in J.F. Gubrium and J.A. Holstein (eds) *Handbook of Interview Research*. Thousand Oaks, CA: Sage.

Charmaz, C. (2003) Grounded theory, in J.A. Smith (ed) *Qualitative Psychology: A Practical Guide to Research Methods*. London: Sage.

Charmaz, C. (2006) *Constructing Grounded Theory: A Practical Guide Through Qualitative Research*. London: Sage.

Charmaz, C. and Henwood, K. (2008) Grounded theory, in C. Willig and W. Stainton Rogers (eds) *The Sage Handbook of Qualitative Research in Psychology*. London: Sage.

Clarke, A.E. (2003) Situational analyses: grounded theory mapping after the postmodern turn, *Symbolic Interaction*, 26: 553–76.

Clarke, A.E. (2005) *Situational Analyses: Grounded Theory After the Postmodern Turn*. Thousand Oaks, CA: Sage.

Clarke, A.E. (2006) Feminism, grounded theory, and situational analysis, in S. Hess-Biber and D. Leckenby (eds) *Handbook of Feminist Research Methods*. Thousand Oaks, CA: Sage.

Colaizzi, P. (1978) Psychological research as the phenomenologist views it, in R. Valle and M. King (eds) *Existential-phenomenological Alternatives for Psychology*. New York: Oxford University Press.

Crawford, J., Kippax, S., Onyx, J., Gault, U. and Benton, P. (1992) *Emotion and Gender: Constructing Meaning from Memory*. London: Sage.

Crawford, J., Kippax, S. and Waldby, C. (1994) Women's sex talk and men's sex talk: different worlds, *Feminism and Psychology*, 4(4): 571–87.

Crossley, M.L. (2000) *Introducing Narrative Psychology: Self, Trauma and the Construction of Meaning*. Buckingham: Open University Press.

Curt, B.C. (1994) *Textuality and tectonics: troubling social and psychological science*. Buckingham: Open University Press.

Davies, B. and Harré, R. (1999) Positioning and personhood, in R. Harré and L. Van Langenhove (eds) *Positioning Theory*. Oxford: Blackwell.

Deutscher, I. (1978) Asking questions cross-culturally, in N.K. Denzin (ed.) *Sociological Methods: A Sourcebook*. London: McGraw-Hill.

Dey, I. (1999) *Grounding Grounded Theory: Guidelines for Qualitative Inquiry*. London: Academic Press.

Dey, I. (2004) Grounded theory, in C. Seale, G. Gobo, J.F. Gubrium and D. Silverman (eds) *Qualitative Research Practice*. London: Sage.

Drew, P. (1995) Conversation analysis, in J.A. Smith, R. Harré and L. Van Langenhove (eds) *Rethinking Methods in Psychology*. London: Sage.

Duncombe, J. and Jessop, J. (2002) 'Doing rapport' and the ethics of 'faking friendship', in M. Mauthner, M. Birch, J. Jessop and T. Miller (eds) *Ethics in Qualitative Research*. London: Sage.

Eatough, V. and Smith, J.A. (2008) Interpretative phenomenological analysis, in C. Willig and W. Stainton Rogers (eds) *The Sage Handbook of Qualitative Research in Psychology*. London: Sage.

Edley, N. and Wetherell, M. (2001) Jekyll and Hyde: men's constructions of feminism and feminists, *Feminism and Psychology*, 11(4): 439–57.

Edwards, D. (2004) Discursive psychology, in K. Fitch and R. Sanders (eds) *Handbook of Language and Social Interaction*. Mahwah, NJ: Lawrence Erlbaum.

Edwards, D., Ashmore, M. and Potter, J. (1995) Death and furniture: the rhetoric, politics and theology of bottom line arguments against relativism, *History of the Human Sciences*, 8(2): 25–49.

Edwards, D. and Potter, J. (1992) *Discursive Psychology*. London: Sage.

Elliott, R., Fischer, C.T. and Rennie, D.L. (1999) Evolving guidelines for publication of qualitative research studies in psychology and related fields, *British Journal of Clinical Psychology*, 38: 215–29.

Elmes, D.G., Kantowitz, Z.H. and Roediger, H.L. (1995) *Research Methods in Psychology*, 5th edn. St Paul: West Publications Company.

Elsbree, L. (1982) *The Rituals of Life: Patterns in Narrative*. Port Washington, NY: Kennikat Press.

Ess, C. and the AoIR Ethics Working Committee (2002) Ethical decision-making and Internet-research: recommendations from the AoIR Ethics Working Committee, approved by Association of Internet Researchers, 27 November 2002, available from http://www.aoir.org/reports/ethics.pdf.

Evans, A., Elford, J. and Wiggins, D. (2008) Using the internet for qualitative research, in C. Willig and W. Stainton Rogers (eds) *The Sage Handbook of Qualitative Research in Psychology*. London: Sage.

Fairclough, N. (1995) *Critical Discourse Analysis: The Critical Study of Language*. London: Longman.

Fischer, C. and Wertz, F. (1979) Empirical phenomenological analysis of being criminally victimised, in A. Giorgi, R. Knowles and D.L. Smith (eds) *Duquesne Studies in Phenomenological Psychology*, Vol. 3. Pittsburgh, PA: Duquesne University Press.

Flick, U. (1998) *An Introduction to Qualitative Research*. London: Sage.

Flowers, P., Smith, J.A., Sheeran, P. and Beail, N. (1997) Health and romance: understanding unprotected sex in relationships between gay men, *British Journal of Health Psychology*, 2: 73–86.

Flowers, P., Smith, J.A., Sheeran, P. and Beail, N. (1998) 'Coming out' and sexual debut: understanding the social context of HIV risk-related behaviour, *Journal of Community and Applied Social Psychology*, 8: 409–21.

Forshaw, M.J. (2007) Free qualitative research from the shackles of method, *The Psychologist*, 20(8): 478–79.

Foucault, M. (1982) 'The subject and power': an afterword, in H. Dreyfus and P. Rabinow, *Michel Foucault: Beyond Structuralism and Hermeneutics*. Chicago, IL: University of Chicago Press.

Foucault, M. (1990) *The History of Sexuality*. Translated from the French by Robert Hurley. London: Penguin.

Frank, A.W. (1995) *The Wounded Storyteller: Body, Illness, and Ethics*. London: The University of Chicago Press Ltd.

Frosh, S., Phoenix, A. and Pattman, R. (2003) Taking a stand: using psychoanalysis to explore the positioning of subjects in discourse, *British Journal of Social Psychology*, 42: 39–53.

Frosh, S. and Saville Young, L. (2008) Psychoanalytic approaches to qualitative psychology, in C. Willig and W. Stainton Rogers (eds) *The Sage Handbook of Qualitative Research in Psychology*. London: Sage.

Gergen, K.J. (1973) Social psychology as history, *Journal of Personality and Social Psychology*, 26(2): 309–20.

Gergen, K.J. (1989) Social psychology and the wrong revolution, *European Journal of Social Psychology*, 19: 463–84.

Gergen, K.J. and Gergen, M. (1986) Narrative form and the construction of psychological science, in T. Sarbin (ed.) *Narrative Psychology: The Storied Nature of Human Conduct*. New York: Praeger.

Giddens, A. (1984) *The Constitution of Society*. Berkeley, CA: University of California Press.

Gillies, V., Harden, A., Johnson, K., Reavey, P., Strange, V. and Willig, C. (2004) Women's collective constructions of embodied practices through memory work: Cartesian dualism in memories of sweating and pain, *British Journal of Social Psychology*, 43(1); 99–112.

Gilligan, C. (1982) *In a Different Voice*. Cambridge, MA: Harvard University Press.

Giorgi, A. (1970) *Psychology as a Human Science*. New York: Harper & Row.

Giorgi, A. (1975) An application of phenomenological method in psychology, in A. Giorgi, C. Fischer and E. Murray (eds) *Duquesne Studies in Phenomenological Psychology*, Vol. 2. Pittsburgh, PA: Duquesne University Press.

Giorgi, A. (1985) The phenomenological psychology of learning and the verbal learning tradition, in A. Giorgi (ed.) *Phenomenology and Psychological Research*. Pittsburgh, PA: Duquesne University Press.

Giorgi, A. (1994) A phenomenological perspective on certain qualitative research methods, *Journal of Phenomenological Psychology*, 25: 190–220.

Giorgi, A. (in press) Types of phenomenological methods being practiced in psychology, *Journal of Phenomenological Psychology*.

Giorgi, A., Fischer, C. and Murray, E. (eds) (1975) *Duquesne Studies in Phenomenological Psychology*, Vol. 2. Pittsburgh, PA: Duquesne University Press.

Giorgi, A. and Giorgi, B. (2003a) The descriptive phenomenological psychological method, in P.M. Camic, J.E. Rhodes and L. Yardley (eds) *Qualitative Research in Psychology: Expanding Perspectives in Methodology and Design*. Washington, DC: American Psychological Association.

Giorgi, A. and Giorgi, B. (2003b) Phenomenology, in J.A. Smith (ed.) *Qualitative Psychology: A Practical Guide to Research Methods*. London: Sage.

Giorgi, A. and Giorgi, B. (2008) Phenomenological psychology, in C. Willig and W. Stainton Rogers (eds) *The Sage Handbook of Qualitative Research in Psychology*. London: Sage.

Glaser, B.G. (1978) *Theoretical Sensitivity*. Mill Valley, CA: Sociology Press.

Glaser, B.G. (1992) *Emergence vs Forcing: Basics of Grounded Theory Analysis*. Mill Valley, CA: Sociology Press.

Glaser, B.G. (1999) The future of grounded theory. Keynote address from the Fourth Annual Qualitative Health Research Conference, *Qualitative Health Research*, 9(6): 836–45.

Glaser, B.G. and Strauss, A.L. (1967) *The Discovery of Grounded Theory: Strategies for Qualitative Research*. New York: Aldine.

Gordon, C. (1968) Self-conceptions: configurations of content, in C. Gordon and K.J. Gergen (eds) *The Self in Social Interaction*. New York: John Wiley.

Hamel, J. (1993) *Case Study Methods*. London: Sage.

Hammersley, M. (1992) *What's Wrong with Ethnography? Methodological Explorations*. London: Routledge.

Haraway, D.J. (1988) Situated knowledges: the science question in feminism and the privilege of partial perspective, *Feminist Studies*, 14(3): 575–97.

Haraway, D.J. (1991) *Simians, Cyborgs, and Women: The Reinvention of Nature*. London: Free Association Press.

Harden, A. and Willig, C. (1998) An exploration of the discursive constructions used in young adults' memories and accounts of contraception, *Journal of Health Psychology*, 3(3): 429–45.

Harding, S. (1991) *Whose Science? Whose Knowledge? Thinking from Women's Lives*. Buckingham: Open University Press.

Harré, R. (1986) *The Social Construction of Emotion*. Oxford: Blackwell.

Harré, R. (1997) An outline of the main methods for social psychology, in N. Hayes (ed.) *Doing Qualitative Analysis in Psychology*. Hove: Psychology Press.

Harré, R. and Gillett, G. (1994) *The Discursive Mind*. London: Sage.

Harré, R. and Van Langenhove, L. (eds) (1999) *Positioning Theory*. Oxford: Blackwell.

Hart, E. and Bond, M. (1995) *Action Research for Health and Social Care: A Guide to Practice*. Buckingham: Open University Press.

Haug, F. (ed.) (1987) *Female Sexualisation*. London: Verso.

Have, P.T. (1999) *Doing Conversation Analysis*. London: Sage.

Hayes, N. (ed.) (1997) *Doing Qualitative Analysis in Psychology*. Hove: Psychology Press.

Henriques, J., Hollway, W., Urwin, C., Venn, C. and Walkerdine, V. (1984) *Changing the Subject: Psychology, Social Regulation and Subjectivity*. London: Methuen.

Henwood, K.L. and Pidgeon, N.F. (1992) Qualitative research and psychological theorising, *British Journal of Psychology*, 83(1): 97–112.

Henwood, K.L. and Pidgeon, N.F. (1995) Grounded theory and psychological research, *The Psychologist*, 8(3): 115–18.

Henwood, K.L. and Pidgeon, N.F. (2006) Grounded theory, in G. Breakwell, S. Hammond, C. Fife-Shaw and J. Smith (eds) *Research Methods in Psychology*. 3rd edn. London: Sage.

Hepburn, A. and Potter, J. (2003) Discourse analytic practice, in C. Seale, D. Silverman, J.F. Gubrium and G. Gobo (eds) *Qualitative Research Practice*. London: Sage.

Hepburn, A. and Wiggins, S. (2005) Developments in discursive psychology, *Discourse & Society*, 16: 595–602.

Hepburn, A. and Wiggins, S. (eds) (2007) *Discursive Research in Practice: New Approaches to Psychology and Everyday Interaction*. Cambridge: Cambridge University Press.

Heritage, J. (1997) Conversation analysis and institutional talk: analysing data, in D. Silverman (ed.) *Qualitative Research: Theory, Method and Practice*. London: Sage.

Hewitt, J.P. and Stokes, R. (1975) Disclaimers, *American Sociological Review*, 40: 1–11.

Hiles, D. and Čermák, I. (2008) Narrative psychology, in C. Willig and W. Stainton Rogers (eds) *The Sage Handbook of Qualitative Research in Psychology*. London: Sage.

Hollway, W. (1989) *Subjectivity and Method in Psychology: Gender, Meaning and Science*. London: Sage.

Hollway, W. and Jefferson, T. (2000) *Doing Qualitative Research Differently: Free Association, Narrative and the Interview Method.* London: Sage.

Holzkamp, K. (1983) 'Aktualisierung' oder Aktualität des Marxismus? Oder: Die Vorgeschichte des Marxismus ist noch nicht zuende, *Aktualisierung Marx: Argument-Sonderband.* AS 100. Berlin: Argument Verlag.

Husserl, E. (1931) *Ideas.* Translated by W.R. Boyce Gibson. London: George Allen & Unwin.

Jarman, M., Smith, J.A. and Walsh, S. (1997) The psychological battle for control: a qualitative study of healthcare professionals' understandings of the treatment of anorexia nervosa, *Journal of Community and Applied Social Psychology,* 7: 137–52.

Karson, M. (2006) *Using Early Memories in Psychotherapy: Roadmaps to Presenting Problems and Treatment and Impasses.* Oxford: Rowman & Littlefield.

Kelly, G.A. (1955) *The Psychology of Personal Constructs,* Vols 1 and 2. New York: Norton.

Kendall, G. and Wickham, G. (1999) *Using Foucault's Methods.* London: Sage.

Kidd, P.S. and Parshall, M.B. (2000) Getting the focus and the group: enhancing analytical rigor in focus group research, *Qualitative Health Research,* 10(3): 293–308.

Kidder, L.H. and Fine, M. (1987) Qualitative and quantitative methods: when stories converge, in M.M. Mark and L. Shotland (eds) *New Directions in Program Evaluation.* San Francisco, CA: Jossey-Bass.

Kippax, S., Crawford, J., Benton, P., Gault, U. and Noesjirwan, J. (1988) Constructing emotions: weaving meaning from memories, *British Journal of Social Psychology,* 27: 19–33.

Kippax, S., Crawford, J., Waldby, C. and Benton, P. (1990) Women negotiating heterosex: implications for AIDS prevention, *Women's Studies International Forum,* 13(6): 533–42.

Kirk, J. and Miller, M. (1986) *Reliability and Validity in Qualitative Research.* London: Sage.

Kohlberg, L. (1976) Moral stages and moralization: the cognitive developmental approach, in T. Lickona (ed.) *Moral Development and Behaviour.* New York: Holt, Rinehart & Winston.

Koutroulis, G. (1996) Memory-work: process, practice and pitfalls, in D. Colquhoun and A. Kellehear (eds) *Health Research in Practice, Vol. 2 Personal Experiences, Public Issues.* London: Chapman & Hall.

Koutroulis, G. (2001) Soiled identity: memory-work narratives of menstruation, *Health,* 5(2): 187–205.

Kugelmann, R. (1997) The psychology and management of pain: gate control as theory and symbol, *Theory and Psychology,* 7(1): 43–65.

Kuhn, T. ([1962] 1970) *The Structure of Scientific Revolutions.* Chicago, IL: University of Chicago Press.

Kvale, S. (1995) The social construction of validity, *Qualitative Inquiry,* 1(1): 19–40.

Kvale, S. (1996a) The 1000-page question, *Qualitative Inquiry,* 2(3): 275–84.

Kvale, S. (1996b) *InterViews: An Introduction to Qualitative Research Interviewing.* London: Sage.

Langdridge, D. (2004) *Research Methods and Data Analysis in Psychology.* London: Pearson Prentice Hall.

Langdridge, D. (2007) *Phenomenological Psychology: Theory, Research and Method.* London: Pearson Prentice Hall.

Larkin, M., Watts, S. and Clifton, E. (2006) Giving voice and making sense in interpretative phenomenological analysis, *Qualitative Research in Psychology,* 3: 102–20.

Leininger, M. (1994) Evaluation criteria and critique of qualitative research studies, in J.M. Morse (ed.) *Critical Issues in Qualitative Research Methods.* London: Sage.

Lemon, N. and Taylor, H. (1997) Caring in casualty: the phenomenology of nursing care, in N. Hayes (ed.) *Doing Qualitative Analysis in Psychology.* Hove: Psychology Press.

Lorion, R.P. (1990) Evaluating HIV risk reduction efforts: ten lessons from psychotherapy and prevention outcome strategies, *Journal of Community Psychology,* 18: 325–36.

MacMartin, C. and LeBaron, C. (2006) Multiple involvements within group interaction:

a video-based study of sex offender therapy, *Research on Language and Social Interaction*, 39: 41–80.

MacNaghten, P. (1993) Discourses of nature: argumentation and power, in E. Burman and I. Parker (eds) *Discourse Analytic Research*. London: Routledge.

Madill, A. and Doherty, K. (1994) 'So you did what you wanted then': discourse analysis, personal agency and psychotherapy, *Journal of Community and Applied Social Psychology*, 4: 261–73.

Madill, A., Jordan, A. and Shirley, C. (2000) Objectivity and reliability in qualitative analysis: realist, contextualist and radical constructionist epistemologies, *British Journal of Psychology*, 91: 1–20.

Mann, C. and Stewart, F. (2000) *Internet Communication and Qualitative Research: A Handbook for Researching Online*. London: Sage.

Marsh, P., Rosser, E. and Harre, R. (1978) *The Rules of Disorder*. London: Routledge.

Melia, K.M. (1996) Rediscovering Glaser, *Qualitative Health Research* (Special Issue: Advances in Grounded Theory), 6(3): 368–78.

Middleton, D. and Brown, S. (2005) *The Social Psychology of Experience: Studies in Remembering and Forgetting*. London: Sage.

Moran, D. (2000) *Introduction to Phenomenology*. London: Routledge.

Morse, J.M. (ed.) (1992a) *Qualitative Health Research*. London: Sage.

Morse, J.M. (1992b) Negotiating commitment and involvement in the nurse–patient relationship, in J.M. Morse (ed.) *Qualitative Health Research*. London: Sage.

Moustakas, C. (1994) *Phenomenological Research Methods*. London: Sage.

Murray, M. (2003) Narrative psychology, in J.A. Smith (ed.) *Qualitative Psychology: A Practical Guide to Research Methods*. London: Sage.

Murray, M. and Chamberlain, K. (eds) (1999) *Qualitative Health Psychology: Theories and Methods*. London: Sage.

Neisser, U. (1981) John Dean's memory: a case study, *Cognition*, 9: 1–22.

Nightingale, D. and Cromby, J. (1999) *Social Constructionist Psychology: A Critical Analysis of Theory and Practice*. Buckingham: Open University Press.

O'Connell, D.C. and Kowal, S. (1995) Basic principles of transcription, in J.A. Smith, R. Harré and L. Van Langenhove (eds) *Rethinking Methods in Psychology*. London: Sage.

O'Connor, K. and Hallam, R.S. (2000) Sorcery of the self: the magic of you, *Theory and Psychology*, 10(2): 238–64.

Ogden, J. (1995) Changing the subject of health psychology, *Psychology and Health*, 10: 257–65.

Orum, A.M., Feagin, J.R. and Sjoberg, G. (1991) Introduction: the nature of the case study, in J.R. Feagin, A.M. Orum and G. Sjoberg (eds) *A Case for the Case Study*. London: University of North Carolina Press.

Osborn, M. and Smith, J.A. (1998) The personal experience of chronic benign lower back pain: an interpretative phenomenological analysis, *British Journal of Health Psychology*, 3: 65–83.

Packer, M. and Addison, R. (eds) (1989) *Entering the Circle: Hermeneutic Investigation in Psychology*. Albany, NY: State University of New York Press.

Parker, I. (1992) *Discourse Dynamics: Critical Analysis for Social and Individual Psychology*. London: Routledge.

Parker, I. (1994) Reflexive research and the grounding of analysis: social psychology and the psy-complex, *Journal of Community and Applied Social Psychology*, 4(4): 239–52.

Parker, I. (1997) Discursive psychology, in D. Fox and I. Prilleltensky (eds) *Critical Psychology: An Introduction*. London: Sage.

Parker, I. (ed.) (1998) *Social Constructionism, Discourse and Realism*. London: Sage.

Parker, I. and the Bolton Discourse Network (1999) *Critical Textwork: An Introduction to Varieties of Discourse and Analysis*. Buckingham: Open University Press.

Parker, I., Georgaca, E., Harper, D., McLaughlin, T. and Stowell-Smith, M. (1995) *Deconstructing Psychopathology*. London: Sage.

Pease, B. (2000) *Recreating Men: Postmodern Masculinity Politics*. London: Sage.

Pidgeon, N. and Henwood, K. (1997) Using grounded theory in psychological research, in N. Hayes (ed.) *Doing Qualitative Analysis in Psychology*. Hove: Psychology Press.

Pidgeon, N.F. and Henwood, K.L. (2004) Grounded theory, in M. Hardy and A. Bryman (eds) *Handbook of Data Analysis*. London: Sage.

Pomerantz, A. (1986) Extreme case formulations: a new way of legitimating claims, in G. Button, P. Drew and J. Heritage (eds) *Human Studies* (Special Issue: Interaction and Language Use), 9: 219–30.

Popper, K.R. (1969) *Conjectures and Refutations*. London: Routledge & Kegan Paul.

Potter, J. (1992) Constructing realism: seven moves (plus or minus a couple), *Theory and Psychology*, 2: 167–73.

Potter, J. (1996) *Representing Reality: Discourse, Rhetoric and Social Construction*. London: Sage.

Potter, J. (1997) Discourse analysis as a way of analysing naturally occurring talk, in D. Silverman (ed.) *Qualitative Research: Theory, Method and Practice*. London: Sage.

Potter, J. (1998) Fragments in the realization of relativism, in I. Parker (ed.) *Social Constructionism, Discourse and Realism*. London: Sage.

Potter, J. and Hepburn, A. (2005) Qualitative interviews in psychology: problems and possibilities, *Qualitative Research in Pychology*, 2: 38–55.

Potter, J. and Wetherell, M. (1987) *Discourse and Social Psychology: Beyond Attitudes and Behaviour*. London: Sage.

Potter, J. and Wetherell, M. (1994) Analysing discourse, in A. Bryman and R.G. Burgess (eds) *Analysing Qualitative Data*. London: Routledge.

Potter, J. and Wetherell, M. (1995) Discourse analysis, in J.A. Smith, R. Harré and L. Van Langenhove (eds) *Rethinking Methods in Psychology*. London: Sage.

Puchta, C. and Potter, J. (2004) *Focus Group Practice*. London: Sage.

Qualitative Research in Psychology (2005) Special Section on Interviewing, 281–325.

Radley, A. and Chamberlain, K. (2001) Health psychology and the study of the case: from method to analytic concern, *Social Science and Medicine*, 53: 321–32.

Reicher, S. (2000) Against methodolatry: some comments on Elliott, Fischer, and Rennie, *British Journal of Clinical Psychology*, 39: 1–6.

Reid, K., Flowers, P. and Larkin, M. (2005) Exploring lived experience, *The Psychologist*, 18(1): 20–23.

Rennie, D.L. (1998) Grounded theory methodology: the pressing need for a coherent logic of justification, *Theory and Psychology*, 8(1): 101–19.

Rennie, D.L. (1999) Qualitative research: a matter of hermeneutics and the sociology of knowledge, in M. Kopala and L.A. Suzuki (eds) *Using Qualitative Methods in Psychology*. London: Sage.

Robinson, K.M. (2001) Unsolicited narratives from the internet: a rich souce of qualitative data, *Qualitative Health Research*, 11(5): 706–14.

Robson, C. (1993) *Real World Research: A Resource for Social Scientists and Practitioner-researchers*. Oxford: Blackwell.

Rose, N. (1999) *Governing the Soul: The Shaping of the Private Self*, 2nd edn. London: Free Association Books.

Rosenblatt, P.C. (1995) Ethics of qualitative interviewing with grieving families, *Death Studies*, 19: 139–55.

Schegloff, E.A. (1997) 'Whose text? Whose context?', *Discourse and Society*, 8(2): 165–88.

Schleiermacher, F. (1998) *Hermeneutics and Criticism and Other Writings*, Andrew Bowie (ed.), Cambridge: Cambridge University Press.

Schmidt, L.K. (2006) *Understanding Hermeneutics*. Stocksfield: Acumen Publishing Limited.

Seale, C. (2000) Using computers to analyse qualitative data, in D. Silverman (ed.) *Doing Qualitative Research: A Practical Handbook*. London: Sage.

Silver, C. and Fielding, N. (2008) Using computer packages in qualitative research, in C. Willig and W. Stainton Rogers (eds) *The Sage Handbook of Qualitative Research in Psychology*. London: Sage.

Silverman, D. (1993) *Interpreting Qualitative Data: Methods for Analysing Talk, Text and Interaction*. London: Sage.

Silverman, D. (ed.) (2000) *Doing Qualitative Research: A Practical Handbook*. London: Sage.

Sims-Schouten, W., Riley, S. and Willig, C. (2007) Critical realism in discourse analysis: a presentation of a systematic method of analysis using women's talk of motherhood, childcare and female employment as an example, *Theory & Psychology*, 17(1): 127–50.

Sistrunk, F. and McDavid, J.W. (1971) Sex variable in conforming behaviour, *Journal of Personality and Social Psychology*, 17: 200–07.

Slife, B.D. and Williams, R.N. (1995) *What's Behind the Research? Discovering Hidden Assumptions in the Behavioural Sciences*. London: Sage.

Smith, J.A. (1991) Conceiving selves: a case study of changing identities during the transition to motherhood, *Journal of Language and Social Psychology*, 10: 225–43.

Smith, J.A. (1993) The case study, in R. Bayne and P. Nicolson (eds) *Counselling and Psychology for Health Professionals*. London: Chapman & Hall.

Smith, J.A. (1995a) Repertory grids: an interactive case-study perspective, in J.A. Smith, R. Harré and L. Van Langenhove (eds) *Rethinking Methods in Psychology*. London: Sage.

Smith, J.A. (1995b) Semi-structured interviewing and qualitative analysis, in J.A. Smith, R. Harré and L. Van Langenhove (eds) *Rethinking Methods in Psychology*. London: Sage.

Smith, J.A. (1996) Beyond the divide between cognition and discourse: using interpretative phenomenological analysis in health psychology, *Psychology and Health*, 11: 261–71.

Smith, J.A. (1997) Developing theory from case studies: self-reconstruction and the transition to motherhood, in N. Hayes (ed.) *Doing Qualitative Analysis in Psychology*. Hove: Psychology Press.

Smith, J.A. (1999) Towards a relational self: social engagement during pregnancy and psychological preparation for motherhood, *British Journal of Social Psychology*, 38: 409–26.

Smith, J.A. (2004) Reflecting on the development of interpretative phenomenological analysis and its contribution to qualitative research in psychology, *Qualitative Research in Psychology*, 1: 39–54.

Smith, J.A., Harré, R. and Van Langenhove, L. (1995) Idiography and the case study, in J.A. Smith, R. Harré and L. Van Langenhove (eds) *Rethinking Psychology*. London: Sage.

Smith, J.A., Jarman, M. and Osborn, M. (1999) Doing interpretative phenomenological analysis, in M. Murray and K. Chamberlain (eds) *Qualitative Health Psychology: Theories and Methods*. London: Sage.

Smith, J.A. and Eatough, V. (2006) Interpretative phenomenological analysis, in G. Breakwell, S. Hammond, C. Fife-Schaw and J.A. Smith (eds) *Research Methods in Psychology*. 2nd edn. London: Sage.

Speer, S.A. (2007) On recruiting conversation analysis for critical realist purposes (comment), *Theory & Psychology*, 17(1): 151–61.

Spinelli, E. (1989) *The Interpreted World: An Introduction to Phenomenological Psychology*. London: Sage.

Spradley, J.P. (1979) *The Ethnographic Interview*. New York: Holt, Rinehart & Winston.

Stake, R.E. (1994) Case studies, in N.K. Denzin and Y.S. Lincoln (eds) *Handbook of Qualitative Research*. London: Sage.

Stake, R.E. (1995) *The Art of Case Study Research*. London: Sage.

Stanley, L. and Wise, S. (1983) *Breaking Out: Feminist Consciousness and Feminist Research*. London: Routledge.

Stephenson, N. (2003) Rethinking collectivity: practicing memory-work, *International Journal for Critical Psychology*, 9: 160–76.

Stephenson, N. and Kippax, S. (2008) Memory work, in C. Willig and W. Stainton Rogers (2007) *The Sage Handbook of Qualitative Research in Psychology*. London: Sage.

Stevick, E.L. (1971) An empirical investigation of the experience of anger, in A. Giorgi, W. Fisher and R. Von Eckartsberg (eds) *Duquesne Studies in Phenomenological Psychology*, Vol. 1. Pittsburgh, PA: Duquesne University Press.

Strauss, A.L. (1987) *Qualitative Analysis for Social Scientists*. Cambridge: Cambridge University Press.

Strauss, A.L. and Corbin, J. (1990) *Basics of Qualitative Research: Grounded Theory Procedures and Techniques*. London: Sage.

Strauss, A.L. and Corbin, J. (1998) *Basics of Qualitative Research: Grounded Theory Procedures and Techniques*, 2nd edn. London: Sage.

Urwin, C. (1984) Power relations and the emergence of language, in J. Henriques, W. Hollway, C. Urwin, C. Venn and V. Walkerdine, *Changing the Subject: Psychology, Social Regulation and Subjectivity*. London: Methuen.

Van Dijk, T. (1987) *Communicating Racism*. Newbury Park, CA: Sage.

Van Kaam, A. (1959) Phenomenal analysis: exemplified by a study of the experience of 'really feeling understood', *Journal of Individual Psychology*, 15(1): 66–72.

Van Manen, M. (1990) *Researching Lived Experience: Human Science for an Action Sensitive Pedagogy*. Albany, NY: SUNY Press.

Vingoe, L. (2008) *The Construction of Personality Disorder: A Discourse Analysis of Contemporary Professional, Cultural and Political Texts*, unpublished DPsych dissertaton, City University, London.

Weitzman, E. and Miles, M.B. (1995) *Computer Programs for Qualitative Data Analysis: A Software Sourcebook*. London: Sage.

Wetherell, M. (1998) Positioning and interpretative repertoires: conversation analysis and post-structuralism in dialogue, *Discourse and Society*, 9(3): 387–413.

Wetherell, M. (2001) Debates in discourse research, in M. Wetherell, S. Taylor and S.J. Yates (eds) *Discourse Theory and Practice: A Reader*. London: Sage.

Wetherell, M., Taylor, S. and Yates, S.J. (2001) *Discourse as Data: A Guide for Analysis*. London: Sage.

Wetherell, M. and Potter, J. (1992) *Mapping the Language of Racism: Discourse and the Legitimation of Exploitation*. Hemel Hempstead: Harvester Wheatsheaf.

Wiggins, S. and Potter, J. (2008) Discursive psychology, in C. Willig and W. Stainton Rogers (eds) *The Sage Handbook of Qualitative Research in Psychology*. London: Sage.

Wilkinson, S. (1998) Focus groups in health research: exploring the meanings of health and illness, *Journal of Health Psychology*, 3(3): 329–48.

Willig, C. (1995) 'I wouldn't have married the guy if I'd have to do that' – heterosexual adults' accounts of condom use and their implications for sexual practice, *Journal of Community and Applied Social Psychology*, 5: 75–87.

Willig, C. (1997) The limitations of trust in intimate relationships: constructions of trust and sexual risk-taking, *British Journal of Social Psychology*, 36: 211–21.

Willig, C. (1998) Constructions of sexual activity and their implications for sexual practice: lessons for sex education, *Journal of Health Psychology*, 3(3): 383–92.

Willig, C. (1999a) Beyond appearances: a critical realist approach to social constructionist work in psychology, in D. Nightingale and J. Cromby (eds) *Psychology and Social Constructionism: A Critical Analysis of Theory and Practice*. Buckingham: Open University Press.

Willig, C. (ed.) (1999b) *Applied Discourse Analysis: Social and Psychological Interventions*. Buckingham: Open University Press.

Willig, C. (2000) A discourse-dynamic approach to the study of subjectivity in health psychology, *Theory and Psychology*, 10(4): 547–70.

Willig, C. (2004) Discourse analysis and health psychology, in M. Murray (ed.) *Critical Health Psychology*. NY: Palgrave Macmillan.

Willig, C. (2008) Discourse analysis, in J.A. Smith (ed.) *Qualitative Psychology: A Practical Guide to Research Methods*. 2nd edn. London: Sage.

Willig, C. (2007) Reflections on the use of the phenomenological method, *Qualitative Research in Psychology*, 4: 1–17.

Willig, C. and dew Valour, K. (1999) Love and the work ethic: constructions of intimate relationships as achievement. Paper presented to the *Annual Conference of the British Psychological Society*, London, 20–21 December.

Willig, C. and dew Valour, K. (2000) 'Changed circumstances', 'a way out' or 'to the bitter end'? A narrative analysis of 16 relationship break-ups. Paper presented to the *Annual Conference of the Social Psychology Section of the British Psychological Society*, Nottingham, 6–8 September.

Willig, C. and Stainton Rogers, W. (eds) (2008) *The SAGE Handbook of Qualitative Research in Psychology*. London: Sage.

Wodak, R. (1996) *Disorders of Discourse*. Harlow: Addison Wesley Longman.

Wooffitt, R. (2005) *Conversation Analysis and Discourse Analysis: A Comparative and Critical Introduction*. London: Sage.

Yardley, L. (ed.) (1997) *Material Discourses of Health and Illness*. London: Routledge.

Yardley, L. (2000) Dilemmas in qualitative health research, *Psychology and Health*, 15: 215–28.

Yardley, L. and Bishop, F. (2008) Mixing qualitative and quantitative methods: a pragmatic approach, in C. Willig and W. Stainton Rogers (eds) *The Sage Handbook of Qualitative Research in Psychology*. London: Sage.

Yin, R.K. (1993) *Applications of Case Study Research*. London: Sage.

Yin, R.K. (1994) *Case Study Research: Design and Methods*. London: Sage.

Index